ORACLE®

Oracle Press™

Oracle R Enterprise: Harnessing the Power of R in Oracle Database

About the Author

Brendan Tierney, Oracle ACE Director, is an independent consultant (Oralytics) and lectures on data science, databases, and Big Data at the Dublin Institute of Technology/Dublin Technological University. He has 24+ years of experience working in the areas of data mining, data science, Big Data, and data warehousing. Brendan is a recognized data science and Big Data expert and has worked on projects in Ireland, the UK, Belgium, Holland, Norway, Spain, Canada, and the U.S. Brendan is active in the Oracle User Group community, where he is one of the leaders for the OUG in Ireland. Brendan has also been editor of the *UKOUG Oracle Scene* magazine and is a regular speaker at conferences around the world. He is an active blogger and also writes articles for OTN, *Oracle Scene, IOUG SELECT Journal, ODTUG Technical Journal,* and ToadWorld. He is also on the board of directors for DAMA in Ireland. Brendan has published two other books with Oracle Press (*Predictive Analytics Using Oracle Data Miner* and *Real World SQL and PL/SQL: Advice from the Experts*).

Web and blog: www.oralytics.com
Twitter: @brendantierney

About the Technical Editor

Mark Hornick is a director of Oracle Advanced Analytics Product Management, currently focusing on Oracle's R technologies. He works with internal and external customers in the application of R for scalable advanced analytics in Oracle Database, Oracle Exadata, and Oracle Big Data Appliance—both on-premises and in the cloud. Mark is coauthor of *Using R to Unlock the Value of Big Data, Oracle Big Data Handbook,* and *Java Data Mining: Strategy, Standard, and Practice,* and he blogs at blogs.oracle.com/R. Mark joined Oracle's Data Mining Technologies group in 1999 through the acquisition of Thinking Machines Corp., and he transitioned to R technologies in 2010. Prior to that, Mark contributed to research and development in the areas of distributed object management, extended transaction models, workflow management systems, and telecommunications network monitoring and control object models at GTE Laboratories (now Verizon). Mark is a founding member of and Oracle Advisor to the IOUG Business Intelligence Warehousing and Analytics (BIWA) SIG, serving as Content Selection Committee Chair for BIWA Summit events. He is also the Oracle representative to the R Consortium. Mark holds a bachelor's degree from Rutgers University and a master's degree from Brown University, both in computer science.

Oracle Press™

Oracle R Enterprise: Harnessing the Power of R in Oracle Database

Brendan Tierney

New York   Chicago   San Francisco
Athens   London   Madrid   Mexico City
Milan   New Delhi   Singapore   Sydney   Toronto

Cataloging-in-Publication Data is on file with the Library of Congress

McGraw-Hill Education books are available at special quantity discounts to use as premiums and sales promotions, or for use in corporate training programs. To contact a representative, please visit the Contact Us pages at www.mhprofessional.com.

Oracle R Enterprise: Harnessing the Power of R in Oracle Database

1 2 3 4 5 6 7 8 9 DOC 21 20 19 18 17 16

ISBN   978-1-25-958516-6
MHID   1-25-958516-6

Sponsoring Editor	**Technical Editor**	**Production Supervisor**
Wendy Rinaldi	Mark Hornick	Lynn M. Messina
Editorial Supervisor	**Copy Editor**	**Composition**
Jody McKenzie	Barton Reed	Cenveo® Publishing Services
Project Editor	**Proofreader**	**Illustration**
Rachel Gunn	Lisa McCoy	Cenveo Publishing Services
Acquisitions Coordinator	**Indexer**	**Art Director, Cover**
Claire Yee	Jack Lewis	Jeff Weeks

Contents at a Glance

Contents

Acknowledgments

Thank you Grace, Daniel, and Eleanor for your constant support and encouragement while I was working on this book and another book at the same time. Yes, it wasn't easy working on two books at the same time, and they wouldn't be possible without your support.

Many thanks to Mark Hornick for taking on the role of technical editor for the book. He provided detailed comments and suggestions on almost every line written for the book, as well as on the examples given in each of the chapters.

A few other people deserve a mention for their support and help with some of the sections in the book. First, I would like to thank Roel Hartman for his help with APEX. Also, thanks to Charlie Berger, Mark Kelly, and Pedro Rata of the Oracle Data Mining team as well as Sherry LaMonica of the Oracle R Enterprise team.

Many thanks go to Wendy, Brandi, Claire, and Rachel from McGraw-Hill Professional, who worked with me on this project from its conception. Also, thanks to Bart Reed for copyediting the book.

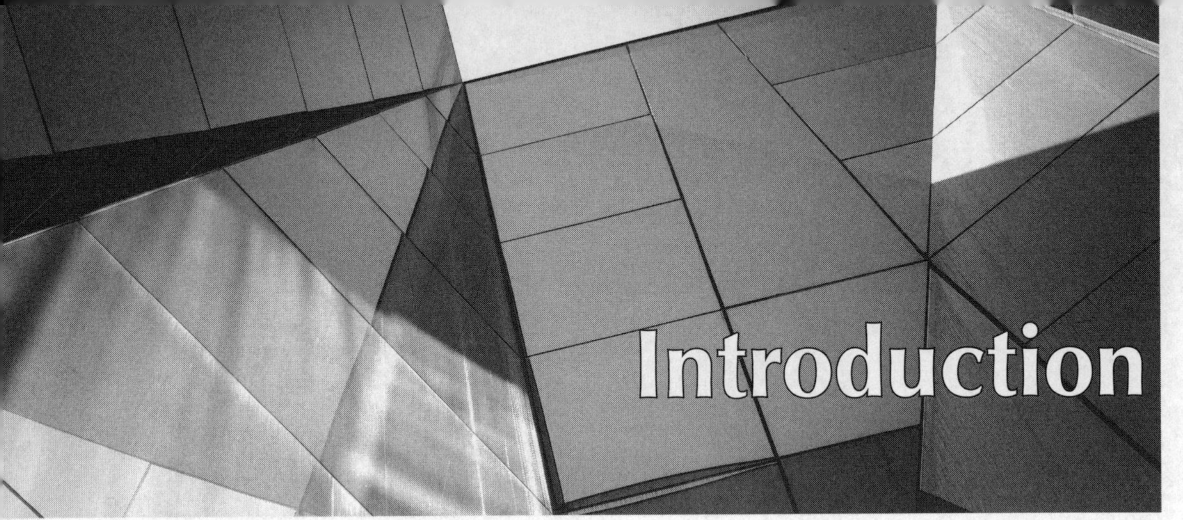

The world of advanced analytics and Big Data is constantly evolving—evolving with new products to help us manage our data, in all its various forms and volumes. A constant challenge that companies have always faced is the ability to process their ever-growing volumes of data and to be able to extract meaningful and useful information.

The R language is an open source language that has been around for 20+ years. We have seen the widespread adoption of the R language across the globe and in almost every industry, with many thousands of graduates coming into the marketplace every year. This has allowed organizations to create data analysts and set them to work on analyzing their data. Although the R language has many advantages, it also has a number of limitations. The limitations are mainly centered around the ability of the language to scale to work with the typical data volumes most organizations today are faced with.

With Oracle R Enterprise, Oracle has overcome the limitations of the R language. Oracle has taken the R language and integrated it into the Oracle Database. By doing this, it has overcome any scalability and performance issues. Oracle R Enterprise enables parallel execution of R scripts, and using the database server as a compute engine allows for significantly larger volumes of data to be processed at a given time. Having the R language integrated in with the Oracle Database, you can now use SQL and PL/SQL, the main programming languages of the database, to execute R scripts and process the results. With this integration with the SQL language, you can now very easily include R analytics and R graphing into your production environment or front-end applications. Any programming language that can call and process SQL can now run R scripts and process the results.

This book is aimed at three groups of users. The first group consists of data scientists who use the R language for their analytics and advanced analytics work. As their data sets grow, they will use Oracle R Enterprise to interface with the Oracle Database and the database server. This book will help them understand how they can use Oracle R Enterprise and how they can use Oracle R Enterprise with other products. The second group includes SQL and Oracle Business Intelligence developers. There is an increasing need for these users to use and integrate analytics produced using R with their applications and analytic dashboards. These developers can use the SQL API functions that come with Oracle R Enterprise to easily integrate user-defined R scripts with their workflows, applications, and dashboards. The third group includes users who have a hybrid role that crosses the use of analytics, Big Data, and advanced analytics. These users work with Oracle Database, Hadoop, the R language, SQL, PL/SQL, APEX, and a variety of advanced analytic tools. This book contains details on how Oracle R Enterprise can be used by users in each of these three groups.

With this book, you will learn and understand:

- How to install Oracle R Enterprise

- How to set up and configure Oracle Database schemas for use with Oracle R Enterprise

- What the transparency layer is and how you can use it to seamlessly use the data in your database

- How to access, work with, transform, and sample, your data using data in the Oracle Database

- The various components of Oracle R Enterprise and the additional advanced analytic algorithms that come with this product

- How to use the in-database Oracle Data Mining algorithms using R

- How to use Oracle R Advanced Analytics on Hadoop to perform analytics and how to use the Spark-enabled algorithms

- How to use Oracle R Enterprise and user-defined R scripts with the Oracle Data Miner GUI tool

- How to include user-defined R scripts in your applications, such as Oracle APEX and OBIEE

- What tasks the database administrator will need to perform to support Oracle R Enterprise

Code Available for Download

Most of the chapters in this book come with extensive examples. To save you the time of having to retype these (along with fixing all the typing errors you might make), I have created a set of code files. For the chapters where there is code, all the code is available in a separate file. This will allow you to quickly try out the examples shown in each of the chapters.

You can download the ZIP file from the McGraw-Hill Professional website at www.mhprofessional.com. Simply enter this book's title or ISBN (1259585166) in the search box and then click the Downloads & Resources tab on the book's home page.

CHAPTER 1

Introduction to Oracle R Enterprise

The world of advanced analytics and Big Data is constantly evolving. The Big Data world is evolving with new products to help us manage our data, in all its various forms and volumes. A constant challenge that companies have always faced is the ability to process their ever-growing volumes of data and extract meaningful and useful information. There are many tools and vendors in the marketplace that offer solutions that make this ability to extract meaningful information easier. One of the primary data management tools available to us is the database, including relational databases, NoSQL databases, databases on Hadoop, and more. The database is traditionally used to capture, store, and analyze the various forms of data in an organization. But in more recent times we have seen a number of alternative data management solutions that help us manage our data in specific scenarios. This is particularly evident in the Big Data world, where we have seen a significant uptake in the use of Hadoop and NoSQL databases. Similarly for the analytics tool environment, we have seen the development of languages and tools to make it easier to process and extract meaningful information from data. One of the most commonly used languages for data analytics is R.

Figure 1-1 illustrates the different categories of analytics. Typically, most organizations will be focused on their descriptive analytics because it focuses on the here and now of how the organization is performing, what is currently

Prescriptive Analytics	Internet of Things (IoT)	Automation for IoT.
	Decision making under uncertainty	Determining best outcomes given variability.
	Ensemble decision making	Multiple predictive models and other techniques involved in decision making.
	Self-optimizing	Continuously evolving; looking to get the best outcome.
Automatic Analytics	Back-end applications	Batch processing, decision making, alerting, etc.
	Front-end applications	Decision making, scoring, alerting, etc.
	Real-time	Real-time predictions as data is processed.
	Automatic updating	Rebuilding of models is automated.
	Embedded analytics	Advanced analytics is part of...
	What-if analysis	What happens if the data is changed?
Predictive Analytics	Predictive modeling	What will happen next?
	Forecasting	What if these trends continue?
	Simulation	What could happen if...?
	Alerts	An action is needed.
Descriptive Analytics	Statistical analysis	Advanced statistical techniques, correlations, etc.
	Query/drill down	What exactly is the problem?
	Ad hoc reporting	How many, how often, where?
	Standard reporting	What happened?

FIGURE 1-1. *Different categories of analytics*

happening, and why something has happened. As an organization matures (or sometimes due to competitive reasons), it will move into the predictive analytics area. This area is focused on understanding the patterns that may exist in the data and how the organization can use these patterns to predict things that might happen. Some examples include predicting customer revenue, predicting when sensors or equipment might fail, managing staff and identifying who is likely to leave the organization, and so on. It is this category of predictive analytics that has been attracting the most attention in recent times. The technology and the machine learning techniques used for predictive analytics have been around for several decades, but what we are seeing is that these techniques are now being applied to a wider range of industries and problems than ever before.

The R language is an open source language that has been around for 20-plus years. We have seen the widespread adoption of the R language across the globe and in almost every industry, with many thousands of graduates coming onto the marketplace every year with experience using R for analytics. This has allowed organizations to create data science teams to work on analyzing their data. The R language allows you to include various R packages that have been developed by specialists around the world. These packages build upon the functionality in the base R language, and they provide a vast array of statistical and machine learning techniques. Some R packages are specifically built for certain types of problems or for specific problems that are faced by certain industries.

Although the R language has many advantages, it also has a number of limitations. The limitations are mainly focused around the ability of the language to scale to work with the typical data volumes that most organizations work with today. What Oracle has done with the R language is to enable it to work in an integrated way with the Oracle Database and the database server. The aim for doing this is to overcome the three main limitations of the R language:

- **Scalability**   The R language has been built to use only the CPU on your computer. It doesn't matter how many CPUs your computer has, your data processing is going to be limited. As your data volumes and analytics complexity grow, you will quickly reach the limits of your machine. There are a number of R packages available to allow you to overcome this problem, but they involve multithreaded programming, which can be beyond the programming capabilities of most programmers, never mind data analysts.

- **Memory management**   The R language is constrained by the amount of available RAM on your machine. Because most of the analytics is being performed on data analysts' laptops and desktops, all of the available RAM can be quickly consumed when working with organizational data.

A common example of this limitation is when you try to open a large Excel spreadsheet, it doesn't open and you get an error message. Parallelism of the processing of your data can be a challenge. Again, there are R packages available to help you to overcome this challenge, but these packages are limited and require significant programming expertise.

- **Production deployment**   Most of the development work with the R language by the data analysts and data scientists will be on their local machines or on small servers. The challenge here is how to take all these analytics and predictive models out of the analytics lab environment and add them into a production architecture at the back end for batch processing or into a front-end application. The ability to integrate the R language with other languages is severely limited, and in a lot of cases requires you to redevelop your analytics and predictive models using other languages such as C, Java, SQL and so on.

Most organizations are faced with having to deal with these limitations when they look to move their advanced analytics work out of the lab environment and into an enterprise architecture and their various operational and business delivery solutions.

With Oracle R Enterprise, Oracle has overcome these limitations of the R language. Oracle has taken the R language and integrated it into the Oracle Database. By doing this, Oracle has overcome the scalability and performance issues just described. Oracle R Enterprise enables parallel execution of R scripts, and using the database server as a compute engine allows for significantly larger volumes of data to be processed at a given time. Because the R language is integrated with the Oracle Database, you can now use SQL and PL/SQL, the main programming languages of the database, to execute R scripts and process the results. With this integration with the SQL language, you can now easily include any analytics or R graphing into your production environment or front-end applications. Any programming language that can call and process SQL can now run R scripts and process the results.

Aim of This Book

It is important to set the aim of this book at this point so that you understand the type of material covered throughout this book and what you will be able to do upon completing all the chapters and examples. This book will not teach you how to write R code and therefore is not an introductory book for novices. This book is aimed at people who have experience working with and using the R language, as well as working with data in an Oracle Database. Each of the chapters in this book work through the main topics and areas that R developers will need to know and use when working with the Oracle Database. Some of the chapters are aimed at the SQL developer who has some exposure to the R language or has been tasked with including R scripts, stored in the Oracle Database, in their various analytical dashboards, reporting environments, business applications, back-end processes, and so on. Each chapter provides examples to illustrate how to use the various features of Oracle R Enterprise, including the suite of R API functions and the ORE SQL API functions. These examples have been kept simple so that you can easily follow them and replicate them within your own test environment. As your experience with using these functions grows, you will find that you can build more complex examples yourself.

Oracle Advanced Analytics Option

The Oracle Advanced Analytics option has two components: Oracle Data Mining and Oracle R Enterprise. The Oracle Advanced Analytics option is available as an extra license cost option with the Oracle Database Enterprise Edition. By combining the powerful in-database advanced data mining algorithms and the power and flexibility of R, Oracle has provided a set of tools that allows everyone, from the data scientist to the Oracle developer and the DBA, to perform advanced analytics on their data to gain deeper insight and have an advantage over their competitors.

The focus of this book is the various features of Oracle R Enterprise and how you can use them.

Oracle Data Mining contains a suite of advanced data mining algorithms that are embedded in the Oracle Database and allow you to perform advanced analytics on your data. The data mining algorithms are integrated into the Oracle database kernel and operate natively on the data stored in the tables in the database, or on any data that is accessible by the database—for example, data stored in files on the operating system (via external tables), data stored in other databases (via database links), and data stored in Hadoop (via Oracle Big Data SQL). This removes the need for extraction or transfer of data into stand-alone mining/analytic servers, as is typical with most data mining and data science applications. This can significantly reduce the timeframe for your data science projects by having near-zero data movement.

In addition to the suite of data mining algorithms listed in Table 1-1 for the Oracle 12c Database, Oracle has a variety of interfaces for using these algorithms. These interfaces include PL/SQL packages that allow you to build and apply models to new data, a variety of SQL functions for real-time scoring of data, and the Oracle

Data Mining Technique	Data Mining Algorithms
Anomaly Detection	One-class Support Vector Machine
Association Rule Analysis	Apriori
Attribute Importance	Minimum Description Length
Classification	Decision Tree
	Generalized Linear Model
	Naïve Bayes
	Support Vector Machine
Clustering	Expectation Maximization
	k-Means
	Orthogonal Partitioning Clustering
Feature Extraction	Non-Negative Matrix Factorization
	Singular Value Decomposition
	Principal Component Analysis
Regression	Generalized Linear Model
	Support Vector Machine

TABLE 1-1. *Oracle Data Mining Algorithms Available in the Oracle Database*

Data Miner tool (part of SQL Developer), which provides a graphical workflow interface for creating your data mining projects.

In addition to the Advanced Analytics option, all versions of the Oracle Database come with a comprehensive collection of statistical functions built into the database. These statistical functions come standard with the Oracle Database and do not require any additional licenses. There are 110+ SQL and PL/SQL statistical functions in the database, and these can be grouped under a variety of headings given in Table 1-2.

Some advanced statistical functions were introduced in more recent versions of the Oracle Database that allow you to perform various statistics using windowing or moving window calculations, pivot, rankings, lead/lag, model clause, MATCH_RECONGNIZE, and so on. These are particularly useful in data warehousing and advanced analytics projects.

Ranking Functions

Rank, dense_rank, cume_dist, percent_rank, ntile.

Window Aggregate Functions

(moving and cumulative)

Avg, sum, min, max, count, variance, stddev, first_value, last_value.

LAG/LEAD Functions

Direct interrow reference using offsets.

Reporting Aggregate Functions

Sum, avg, min, max, variance, stddev, count, ratio_to_report.

Statistical Aggregates

Correlation, linear regression family, covariance.

Linear Regression

Fitting of an ordinary-least-squares regression line to a set of number pairs.

Frequently combined with the COVAR_POP, COVAR_SAMP, and CORR functions.

Descriptive Statistics

DBMS_STAT_FUNCS: summarizes numerical columns of a table and returns count, min, max, range, mean, median, stats_mode, variance, standard deviation, quantile values, +/− n sigma values, top/bottom 5 values.

Correlations

Pearson's correlation coefficients, Spearman's, and Kendall's (both nonparametric).

Cross Tabs

Enhanced with % statistics: chi squared, phi coefficient, Cramer's V, contingency coefficient, Cohen's kappa.

Hypothesis Testing

Student t-test, F-test, Binomial test, Wilcoxon Signed Ranks test, Chi-square, Mann Whitney test, Kolmogorov- Smirnov test, One-way ANOVA

Distribution Fitting

Kolmogorov-Smirnov Test, Anderson-Darling Test, Chi-squared Test, Normal, Uniform, Weibull, Exponential.

TABLE 1-2.   *Summary of the Free Statistical Functions in Oracle*

Oracle R Enterprise

When working with R in a traditional environment, you typically have to extract data from the database to your local machine. All your analytics are then performed in the R environment on your local machine before transferring results back to the database. In addition to the limitations of the R language described earlier, we have issues around having to extract data from the Oracle Database, particularly with the time involved in extracting the data as you work with larger and larger data sets.

With Oracle R Enterprise, you will have an installation of the R engine on the Oracle Database server, which is then accessible by the Oracle Database.

Oracle R Enterprise provides a suite of R packages and Oracle Database features that allow data scientists, using the R language, to work with their data while it is still in an Oracle Database. By working with the data in the Oracle Database, you no longer have to extract data to a local machine. This can save you a significant amount of time on your data analytics projects. Oracle R Enterprise also allows you to utilize the performance and scalability features of the Oracle Database and the database server machine. Additionally, R scripts can be stored in the Oracle Database, which allows for one or more embedded R engines to be spawned on the database server.

With Oracle R Enterprise, you have a set of R packages that transparently work with the Oracle Database. This allows data scientists, who are familiar with working with the R language, to quickly and easily start using the in-database capabilities of Oracle R Enterprise. In addition to these R functions, Oracle R Enterprise comes with a SQL interface that allows you to access and run R scripts stored in the database. Figure 1-2 illustrates the typical architecture of Oracle R Enterprise.

When Oracle R Enterprise is installed, you will have a number of R packages that provide the transparency layer. These R packages contain functions that are overloaded versions of most of the common R functions; these include the functions in the base, stat, and graphics packages. The transparency layer seamlessly converts an R function into a SQL function, runs the SQL function in the database, and then returns the results. The transparency layer manages this processing, without the data scientist, working with the R language, needing to know or understand what is happening in the transparency layer.

The Oracle Database comes with a large range of statistical and analytic functions. Additionally, the Oracle Database has the in-database data mining functions that are part of Oracle Data Mining. The Oracle Data Mining algorithms have been exposed to Oracle R Enterprise, and data scientists can automatically take advantage of these features, as well as use the database as a high-performance and scalable compute engine. Oracle R Enterprise also comes with some additional data mining algorithms, such as random forests. These capabilities allow the data scientists to work with larger and larger data sets, while allowing the data to reside in the Oracle Database and ensuring data security.

Oracle R Enterprise comes with a core set of R packages, but these can be supplemented with functionality that is contained in many of the R packages available. Oracle R Enterprise allows you to install a new R package and to instantly start using the analytic functionality contained in this package in your analytics.

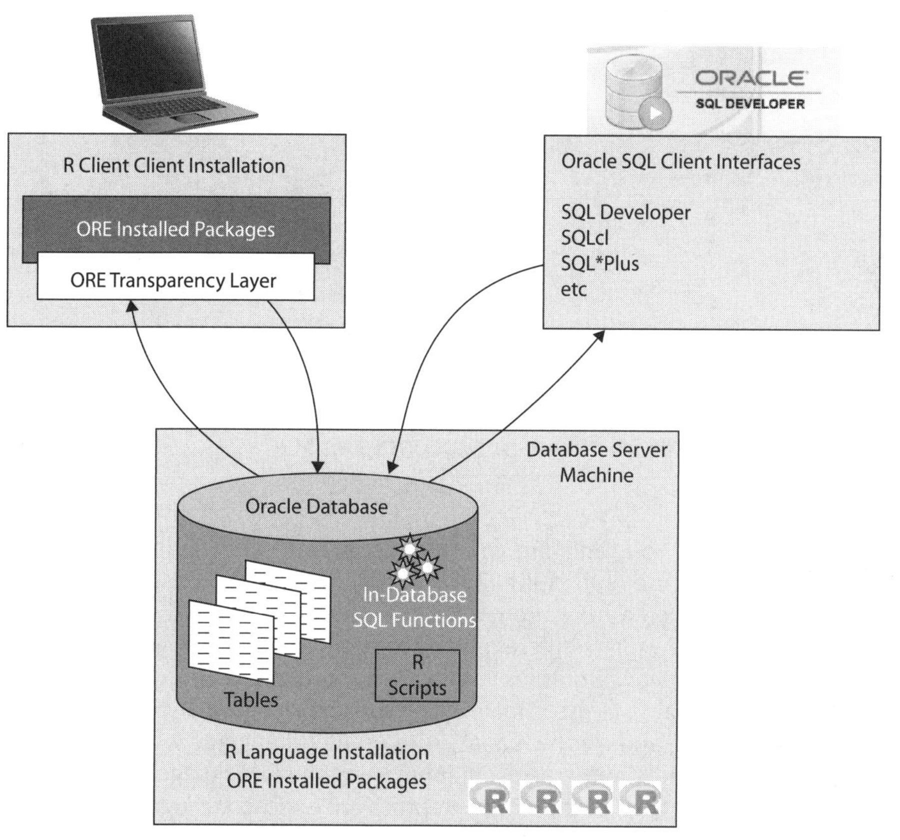

FIGURE 1-2.   *Overview of the Oracle R Enterprise architecture*

Deploying R Is Easy with Oracle R Enterprise

Oracle R Enterprise comes with a number of SQL API functions that allow you to run an R script, stored in the database, and return the results using a SQL SELECT statement. This means that any application or language that can run a SQL statement on data in the database can now run an R script and present the results in the application. With traditional R, you are limited as to the type of interactions your applications can have with your R code. To overcome this difficulty when deploying your R analytics, you would have to recode your analytics in another language that can be used in your production environment. With Oracle R Enterprise, deploying

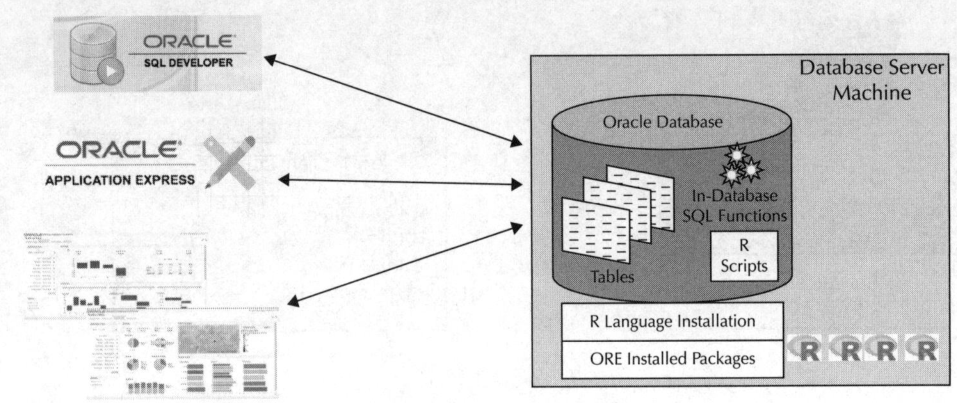

FIGURE 1-3. *You can run ORE from your applications using SQL.*

your R analytics is easy. You can store your R code in an R script in the Oracle Database and then use one of the ORE SQL API functions to call this R script. The results will be returned as rows from a SELECT statement. This allows for your R scripts to be included in many different types of applications (see Figure 1-3) and made available to a wide range of roles within your organization.

In addition to being able to use Oracle R Enterprise for your analytics, you can use the vast charting and graphic capabilities of the R language within Oracle R Enterprise. You can define and create a graphic using the R language and have that graphic appear in your applications. These graphics are exposed using the ORE SQL API functions, with the R graphics being returned as part of the query result set.

The Advantages of Using Oracle R Enterprise

Oracle R Enterprise allows data scientists, data analysts, and application developers to quickly and efficiently analyze their data in an Oracle Database. There are many advantages of using Oracle R Enterprise over using traditional R, including the following:

- **Near-zero data movement**   With the Oracle R Enterprise transparency layer, you no longer need to extract data from the database and move it to your local R environment for additional processing. The data can remain in the database, and your R functions will be performed on the data in the database. This can significantly reduce the amount of time it takes to process data and also makes your analytics scalable as your data volumes grow.

- **Use R to prepare data and build models**   With very few changes to your R code, you can now use the same code to run against data and R objects that are resident in the Oracle Database. You can also create new R objects that are resident in the Oracle Database. Oracle R Enterprise gives an R user the impression of working with local R objects and data, but instead these are located in the Oracle Database.

- **Use R to analyze your data**   Traditionally when working with a database, an R user would have to switch between using R and SQL to perform certain functions. With Oracle R Enterprise, the R user can work with the data to perform a wide range of analytics using just the R language.

- **Use the power of the database server machine**   Typically, the database server will be a much more powerful server than what is used for analytics. By using the database server, you can work with significantly greater volumes of data than you could typically when working with data on a local machine. In addition to working with a larger volume of data, the computing engine of the database server allows you to process this data quicker, reducing the time to analyze and process your data from hours to seconds.

- **Improve data security**   Keeping your data in the Oracle Database allows you to keep the data secure. This reduces the spread of data around your organization, consisting of various subsets of the data in your database. All the typical data security features of the Oracle Database can be utilized to ensure that your data is protected in a consistent manner for all people who are accessing your data. Similarly, any new data your analytics will be producing will also come under the security policies enabled in the Oracle Database.

- **Work with all your data**   As your data volumes grow over time, you may find yourself working with subsets of the data in a local R environment. When using Oracle R Enterprise, you can use the performance and scalability features of the database server to work with all your data. No longer will you have to create different subsets or perform sampling of your data. You can now work with all your data, up to and beyond billions of records.

- **Store R objects in the database**   As your analytics environment grows, you will be creating various data sets and R objects. In a traditional R environment, it can be difficult to share these objects with other members of your team. Oracle R Enterprise allows you to store these objects in the Oracle Database using the Oracle R Enterprise datastore and then share these with other members of your analytics team.

- **Create R charts and graphics**   The R language has a vast array of charting and graphing features and packages. With the ability to supplement Oracle R Enterprise with new R packages, you can expand the analytic, charting, and graphing capabilities available to you. Additionally, these can be exposed to end users in their applications such as OBIEE, BICS, and APEX because Oracle R Enterprise comes with a set of SQL APIs. These can be used to display R-produced charts and graphics in your applications.

- **Build predictive models and score your data**   You can build advanced analytics and predictive models using the various R packages and the in-database data-mining algorithms on data that is resident in the database. These same models can be stored in the Oracle Database and used to score or label new data in batches or in real time.

- **Embedded R execution**   Embedded R execution allows you to store and run R scripts in the Oracle Database in the Oracle R Enterprise datastore. When these R scripts are run, the Oracle Database manages the creation of R processes, and for some of the embedded R execution functions, these processes can run in parallel on the database server, on different partitions of the data, thereby taking advantage of the performance and scalability of the database server.

- **Easy integration with your technical architecture**   Oracle R Enterprise easily integrates into your technical environment. It can be integrated with many of your back-end and front-end applications to allow R analytics to be performed on the data where it resides. With the ORE SQL API functions, you can easily run R scripts to generate and process your analytics and return any results to the user or the calling application using SQL. Similarly, you can now integrate charts and graphics produced by R within your applications.

- **Easily expand your analytics using R packages**   The R ecosystem is very active, and new algorithms and analytics are being released as new or updated R packages. You can expand the analytic capabilities of the Oracle Database and Oracle R Enterprise by including (installing) R packages on the database server. These then become available to you to use in your analytics and applications using embedded R execution.

- **Easily deploy and productionalize your R analytics**   With Oracle R Enterprise, you can store R scripts in the Oracle Database. This allows you to expose other people in your organization to these R scripts and the analytic results they produce. It was mentioned earlier that you can include graphics and charts produced by the R packages in your applications. The same applies for any of the analytics you perform using R that are stored in R scripts. Using the SQL API functions allows you to seamlessly integrate your R scripts into your applications. These applications can include your analytic dashboards and your day-to-day business applications that your company depends on. You can also build your ORE analytics into your back-end or batch process to build advanced workflows with automatic decision making based on your R analytics.

R Technologies from Oracle

In addition to Oracle R Enterprise, Oracle has a number of other offerings that use the R language or support the use of the R language in different environments. Table 1-3 describes the main R technologies from Oracle.

Oracle Product	Description
Oracle R Distribution	Oracle R Distribution is an Oracle-supported version redistribution of the open source R language. Oracle R Distribution also supports a number of external libraries such as Intel's Math Kernel Library (MKL), AMD's ACML, and Oracle Sun's performance libraries for Solaris (BLAS and LaPack). These libraries are designed to optimize the performance of certain matrix-based R functions on the corresponding hardware.
	Oracle R Distribution is free for everyone to use.
	Oracle support is provided for all customers who are licensed for the Oracle Advanced Analytics option, Oracle Linux, or Oracle Big Data Appliance.
	It is recommended that Oracle R Distribution be used with Oracle R Enterprise.
ROracle	ROracle is an open source R package. It has been designed to allow for the highly optimized reading of data from an Oracle Database and the writing of data to an Oracle Database. The ROracle package provides a DBI-compliant set of functions, and it offers significant performance improvements over alternatives such as RODBC and RJDBC. Additionally, ROracle supports the use of NUMBER, VARCHAR2, TIMESTAMP, and BINARY_DOUBLE data types.
	ROracle is offered for free for everyone to use and can be downloaded from the Oracle website or from one of the CRAN websites or mirrors.

TABLE 1-3. *R Technology Offerings from Oracle*

Oracle Product	Description
Oracle R Advanced Analytics for Hadoop	Oracle R Advanced Analytics for Hadoop (ORAAH) is one of the components of the Oracle Big Data Connectors. ORAAH provides a set of R functions that allows you to connect to and manipulate data stored on HDFS using Hive transparency. ORAAH allows you to build map-reduce analytics and use the prepackaged algorithms exposed through an R interface. Additionally, you can integrate with Apache Spark and other tools and languages for greater performance for multilayer neural networks and for logistic regression.

TABLE 1-3. *R Technology Offerings from Oracle (continued)*

In addition to the offerings listed in Table 1-3, Oracle has been working on integrating the R language into other products. For example, the R language is installed as a component of the OBI environment. A number of interfaces have been created to allow you to use various features of the R language to add analytics and graphics to your analysis and dashboards.

How Customers Are Using Oracle R Enterprise and Oracle Advanced Analytics

Being able to see and understand how other companies have used Oracle Advanced Analytics can help you understand how you can use this option in your company. Oracle Advanced Analytics has a wide customer base spanning many industries and types of projects. Some of the Oracle Advanced Analytics customers have shared the details of their projects at various conferences and in various publications. The following gives you a sample of some of the customers and how they are using Oracle Advanced Analytics to run their businesses more profitably.

StubHub   StubHub is an online marketplace that provides services for buyers and sellers of tickets for sporting, concert, theater, and other live entertainment events. The team of data scientists at StubHub has been able to take their extensive array of predictive and customer analytics, developed using the R language, and embed these into the Oracle Database. By doing so, they were able to fully integrate with their data warehousing architecture and are able to combine high-performance data mining functions with the open source R language to enable predictive analytics, data mining, text mining, statistical analysis, advanced numerical computations, and interactive graphics, all inside the database.

CERN   CERN is the European Organization for Nuclear Research and operates the largest particle physics laboratory in the world. Apart from being the birthplace of the World Wide Web, in more recent times CERN is famous for their particle accelerator experiments. CERN is using Oracle R Enterprise and the Oracle Database to analyze some of the 30 petabytes of new data generated annually from their various experiments.

An Post   An Post is the national postal service for Ireland, which also provides a wide range of banking and financial services through their network of owned and franchised branches. Every day, the An Post staff collects, processes, and delivers more than 2.5 million items of mail to 2.2 million business and residential addresses, using a road fleet of 2738 vehicles and 1645 bicycles. In addition, every week it serves 1.7 million customers through its unique national network of 1100 post offices and more than 2000 PostPoint payment channels at retail outlets nationwide. An Post is using the Oracle Database and Oracle Advanced Analytics to analyze over 2 billion internal transaction messages to optimize cash management by delivering same-day analytics on easy-to-use dashboards and to minimize fraud.

Financiera Uno   Financiera Uno provides financial services, including credit card and financial brokerage, receives deposits from third parties, grants bonds, and acquires and trades deposit certificates. Financiera Uno is using the in-database capabilities of the Oracle Database and Oracle Advanced Analytics within their data warehousing environment. This allows them to quickly develop risk models for their commercial and collection divisions, without the need to extract data to another analytic environment.

Turkcell   Turkcell is one of Turkey's leading mobile phone operators, with over 35 million subscribers. Communications fraud and the use of telecommunications products and services without the intention to pay is a major issue for Turkcell. This type of unusual activity occurs with their anonymous network-branded prepaid cards and is a common technique used by money launderers, particularly because these cards can be used as cash vehicles—for example, to withdraw cash at ATMs. Turkcell is using Oracle Advanced Analytics to quickly build and deploy antifraud models and to rapidly update these models to keep pace with the changing nature of the fraud.

Dunnhumby/84.51° Dunnhumby is a major global loyalty card analytics company that provides services for some of the largest retail brands in the world. By implementing Oracle Advanced Analytics and the Oracle Database, they have been able to reduce the time taken to process their customer data and to generate their customer prediction models from weeks to hours. Using the computing capabilities of the Oracle Database, coupled with the performance of Oracle Advanced Analytics, they have been able to generate predictive models on their structured and unstructured data.

There are many, many more customers who are using Oracle Advanced Analytics to gain a deeper insight into their data and to manage their customers more effectively. Check out the Oracle web pages for Oracle Advanced Analytics for more examples of customers and their projects. Also look out for customer case studies presented at Oracle Open World and other Oracle and Oracle User Group (OUG) conferences around the world.

Summary

This chapter provided an overview of Oracle R Enterprise and how it works with the Oracle Database. Additionally, we looked at some of the advantages of using Oracle R Enterprise and how some of the major companies around the world are using Oracle R Enterprise and the Oracle Advanced Analytics option to help them better understand their businesses. This book is aimed at helping you better understand Oracle R Enterprise. You'll learn how to use most of the features and capabilities of the product, as well as how it can be used with some of the other tools available from Oracle.

CHAPTER
2

Installing
Oracle R Enterprise

Oracle R Enterprise is a component of the Oracle Advanced Analytics option to the Oracle Database Enterprise Edition. Before you can use Oracle R Enterprise, you first need to complete a number of installation steps. The installation can be divided into two main parts. The first of these is the installation on the Oracle Database Server. The second part is the installation on the client machines of what will be used by the data analysts and data scientists. Additionally, this chapter looks at the various prerequisites that need to be completed before the installation can commence.

Installation Prerequisites

The following prerequisites are required before the installation of Oracle R Enterprise:

- You have installed the Enterprise Edition of Oracle Database 12c or 11g R2.

- You know the SID or the Service Name of the Oracle Database or Pluggable Database.

- You have the SYS password or you have your DBA available for the steps that require it.

- You have downloaded the Oracle R Enterprise Server and the supporting packages' installation files for your Server operating system.

- You have installed the Oracle Client software on your client machine.

- You have downloaded the Oracle R Enterprise Client and supporting packages' installation files for your client operating system.

Another useful step is to install the Oracle Sample Schemas. Although these are not necessary for installing and using Oracle R Enterprise, they give you an excellent set of prepared data sets that you can use to work with and learn how Oracle R Enterprise works.

NOTE
Some of the Oracle Sample Schema data will be used in various examples throughout this book. If you would like to follow all of these examples, you will need to talk to your Oracle DBA to get the necessary permissions to the Oracle Sample Schema data.

Setting Up Your Oracle Database

Oracle R Enterprise is a component of the Oracle Advanced Analytics option in the Enterprise Edition of the Oracle Database. The Oracle Advanced Analytics option is available from the 11.2.0.1 version of the Enterprise Edition of the Oracle Database and also in Oracle Database 12c. The Oracle Advanced Analytics option is installed and enabled by default when the database is installed. In addition to the Oracle Advanced Analytics option, you will need to have the Oracle Text option installed and enabled in the database, because this is used by some elements of the in-database Oracle Data Mining features. If the Advanced Analytics option was disabled after the installation of the database, you will need to talk to your DBA to get this option enabled.

To enable the Advanced Analytics option, you can use the `chopt` command. The `chopt` command allows you to enable and disable the following database options:

Database Option	Description
dm	Oracle Data Mining RDBMS files. This is the option for the Advanced Analytics option.
olap	Oracle OLAP.
partitioning	Oracle Partitioning.
rat	Oracle Real Application Testing.

Before you change the option, you need to stop the database service and restart it after the following command has been run on the operating system command line:

```
chopt enable dm
```

If you are using the 11.2.0.1 or the 11.2.0.2 version of the Enterprise Edition of Oracle Database 11g, you need to install patch 11678127 to include some of the necessary features for Oracle Advanced Analytics and Oracle R Enterprise. This patch has been included in the 11.2.0.3 and 11.2.0.4 versions of the Oracle Database, so you do not need to install it.

NOTE
You will need to get your Oracle DBA to check with Oracle Support (MOS) to see if there are any additional patches related to the Oracle Advanced Analytics option and for Oracle R Enterprise for your version of the Oracle Database.

Oracle R Enterprise uses `EXTPROC` to support the embedded execution of R code in the database. `EXTPROC` is the method used by the Oracle Database to allow the execution of a program written in another language such as C or Java—or in our case, R code. `EXTPROC` comes preconfigured with the Oracle Database, and Oracle R Enterprise uses this default configuration. You should consult with your Oracle DBA about the configuration of `EXTPROC` and whether any changes are necessary. For example, the `EXTPROC_DDLS` variable can be set to `ANY` or left blank (the default) in the file `$ORACLE_HOME/ha/admin/extproc.ora`. When `EXTPROC` is set to `ANY` or left blank, this allows the Oracle Database to invoke any external procedure.

When you have completed the Oracle Database installation and ensured the requirements in this section have been met, you are now ready to commence the installation of Oracle R Enterprise on your Server and client machines.

Installing Oracle R Enterprise

Installing Oracle R Enterprise involves two major phases. The first phase involves installing R and Oracle R Enterprise on the Database Server. The second phase involves installing R and Oracle R Enterprise on the client machine.

The installation instructions given in this chapter are for Linux and Windows servers and are aimed at simplifying the installation processes detailed in the Oracle R Installation and Administration Guide. If you are using a different platform, you can check out the specific instructions relating to your platform in that guide.

For the installation of Oracle R Enterprise on the Database Server, Oracle provides an installation script. It is important that you gather the necessary information listed in the upcoming "Pre-installation Requirements" section and that you have the ORE Server and ORE Supporting downloads uncompressed into the same directory. This will significantly simplify the installation process. Details of how to perform these steps will be given in the "Oracle Database Server Installation" section in this chapter.

NOTE
It is important that you ensure that the same version of the Oracle R Enterprise packages are installed on the Database Server and on the Client machine. You will also need to ensure that the Database Server and Client ORE packages are upgraded at the same time. If these are different, you will get some error messages and your ORE code will not run or not run correctly.

Package Name	Package Description
ORE	The top-level package for Oracle R Enterprise
OREbase	Corresponds to the open source R base package
OREcommon	Contains common low-level functionality for Oracle R Enterprise
OREdm	Exposes the in-database Oracle Data Mining algorithms
OREeda	Contains functions for exploratory data analysis
OREembed	Supports the embedded execution of R in the database
OREgraphics	Corresponds to the open source R graphics package
OREmodels	Contains functions for advanced analytical modeling
OREpredict	Enables scoring data in the Oracle Database using R models
OREserver	Contains functions for an Oracle R Enterprise Server
OREstats	Corresponds to the open source R stats package
ORExml	Supports XML translation between R and the Oracle Database

TABLE 2-1.   *Oracle R Enterprise Core Packages*

Oracle R Enterprise Packages

The installation of Oracle R Enterprise consists of a core set of Oracle R Enterprise packages and a set of supporting R packages. Both of these sets of packages need to be installed on the Oracle Database Server and on the client machines.

The Oracle R Enterprise download website has specific download files for the Oracle Database and the client machines. Therefore, you need to be careful that you download the correct version of the files. Table 2-1 lists the Oracle R Enterprise–specific packages.

The supporting packages, shown in Table 2-2, are a set of open source packages that specifically support the core Oracle R Enterprise packages.

Pre-installation Requirements

The following pre-installation requirements detail the items you need to know or need to have in place before you commence the installation of Oracle R Enterprise on your Server and client machines. These requirements are in addition to the prerequisites listed earlier in this chapter.

Package Name	Package Description
`arules`	Allows for frequent item sets and association rules. Provides support for representing, manipulating, and analyzing the transactional data and the patterns of the results.
`Cairo`	Supports graphic rendering on Oracle Enterprise Server.
`DBI`	The database interface definition for communicating between R and the Oracle Database.
`png`	Supports the reading and writing of PNG images for Oracle R Enterprise objects.
`randomForest`	Supports the ORE implementation of randomForests.
`ROracle`	The Oracle Database interface for R-based Oracle Call Interface (OCI).
`statmod`	Provides a variety of statistical modeling functions

TABLE 2-2. *Oracle R Enterprise Supporting Packages*

Oracle Database Server Requirements:

- Verify that your Oracle Database Server platform is supported for Oracle R Enterprise.

- Check that the version of your Oracle Database supports ORE.

- Enable Oracle Advanced Analytics.

- You need the `SYS` password and the name of the SID or Service Name of the Oracle Database.

- You need the tablespace name where the ORE metadata and system objects can be stored. This will typically be the `SYSAUX` tablespace.

- You need to check whether there is sufficient space in this tablespace. If there isn't, ask the DBA to allocate some more.

- Know the name of the temporary tablespace. This will typically be the `TEMP` tablespace.

- Know the default tablespace for the ORE User Schema (for example, the `USERS` tablespace).

- Decide on a password for the ORE system account `RQSYS` (for example, `RQSYS`). This schema is created and only used during the ORE installation process. Once the installation is complete, the `RQSYS` schema will be locked with an expired password. The `RQSYS` schema does not have the `CREATE SESSION` privilege.

- Decide on a name for your first ORE User Schema and a password. This will be created during the ORE installation (for example, `ore_user/ore_user`).

- Check that the `ORACLE_HOME` and `SID` environment variables are set.

Oracle Client Machine Requirements:

- Verify that your client operating system is supported for Oracle R Enterprise.

- Ensure that Oracle Client is installed on the client machine.

NOTE
The sample passwords given in the preceding list are for illustrative purposes, and these will be used in the installation notes that follow. These passwords are not secure, and you will need to discuss with your DBA what passwords should be used. In particular, the `SYS` password should not be shared. If the preceding suggested password `RQSYS` is used, the DBA should change this password afterwards.

Oracle Database Server Installation

This section details the steps required to install Oracle R Enterprise on your Database Server. Before commencing with these installation steps, you need to have completed the steps in the preceding "Pre-installation Requirements" section. Also, some of the information from the pre-installation requirements will be needed during the installation process.

Figure 2-1 outlines the steps involved in the installation of Oracle R Enterprise on your Oracle Database Server. The following sections detail what is required for each of these steps.

Install Oracle R Distribution

To use Oracle R Enterprise on your Oracle Database Server, you need an installation of the R software. Two options are open to you for installing R. The first is to install the version of R that is provided by Oracle. This is called the Oracle R Distribution.

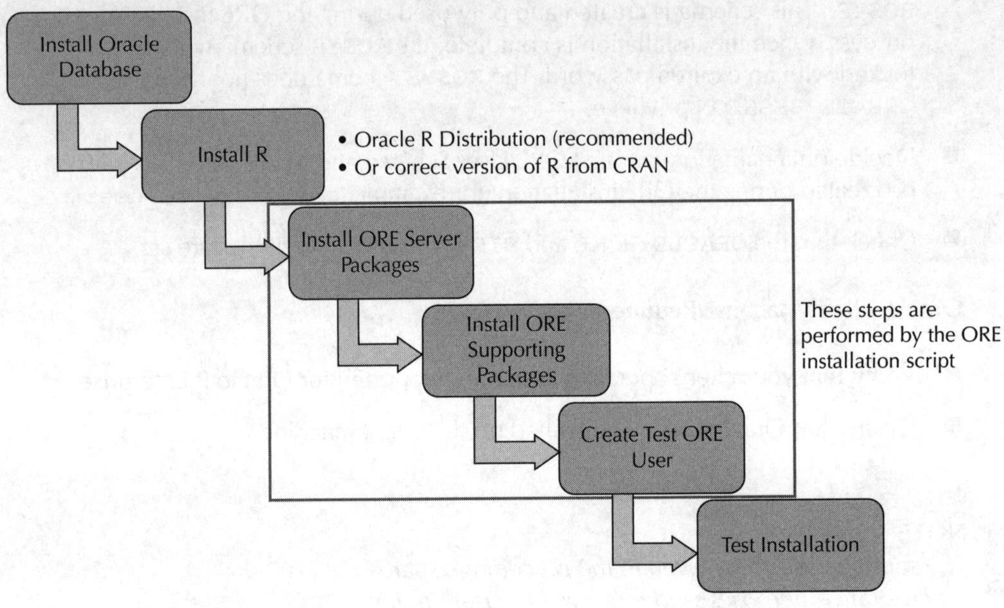

FIGURE 2-1. *Oracle R Enterprise installation steps on the Database Server*

The second option is to install the version of R required for the version of Oracle R Enterprise you are installing. If you choose this second option, it is vital that you install the correct version of R; otherwise, Oracle R Enterprise might not work for you.

Oracle recommends that you use Oracle R Distribution, which is a separately maintained and supported version of R provided by Oracle. Additionally, Oracle has worked to integrate with certain libraries, such as the Intel Math Kernel Library (MKL) and the Sun Performance Library. These libraries improve the performance of certain mathematical functions, including BLAS and LAPACK, to ensure that they utilize the underlying hardware preference.

If you would prefer to use the version of R that is available from the R CRAN website, you will need to check for the correct version of R needed for the version of Oracle R Enterprise you are installing. Check out the Oracle R Enterprise website and the Oracle R Enterprise Installation and Administration Guide for the Oracle R Enterprise/Oracle R Distribution/Open Source R support matrix.

To install the Oracle R Distribution, you need to download the software from the Oracle Open Source Download page (https://oss.oracle.com/ORD).

On this website, select the version of Oracle R Distribution you would like to download. When the download has completed, you can uncompress the file and then run the executable file to perform the installation. You are not required to enter any details during the installation process, and when this is complete, you will have R (the Oracle R Distribution version) installed on your server.

The only post-installation step you need to perform is to add the full path to the Oracle R Distribution bin directory to the `PATH` environment variable.

On Linux, you can use YUM to automatically download and install Oracle R Distribution. To enable YUM to perform this download and install Oracle R Distribution, you need to make the following edits to the YUM repository file located in `/etc/yum.repos.d`. The following example illustrates the steps and what changes you need to perform as the root user:

```
cd /etc/yum.repos.d
vi yum.repos.d
```

For Oracle Linux 5 or Oracle Linux 6, locate the following sections and make the change highlighted in bold. Also, note that olX is either ol5 or ol6 and depends on the version of Oracle Linux you are using.

```
[olX_latest]
enabled=1
[olX_addons]
enabled=1
```

If you are using Oracle Linux 7, there is an additional change to the YUM repository file:

```
[ol7_optional_latest]
enabled=1
```

After making these changes, you are now ready to run the yum.repos.d script to download and install Oracle R Enterprise. This will also download and run any other operating system updates available. To run the download and begin the installation, you can run the following command:

```
yum install R.x86_64
```

This command installs the latest version of Oracle R Distribution. If you need to install a slightly older version of Oracle R Distribution, you can specify the version number. For example, for Oracle R Enterprise version 1.5, you need to install Oracle R Distribution 3.2.0. An example of this is shown here:

```
yum install R.XXX
```

where XXX is the specific version number, e.g., 3.0.1, 3.1.1, etc.

When the update is complete, Oracle R Distribution will be installed. You can now run the R software and use the vast array of statistical functions by running the R command, like so:

```
$  R
```

Details on how to install R or Oracle R Distribution on other platforms such as Exadata can be found in the Oracle R Enterprise Installation and Administration Guide, which is available on the Oracle R Enterprise website.

Install Oracle R Enterprise Server and the Supporting Packages

In this section, we walk through the steps involved with installing the Oracle
R Enterprise Server packages and Supporting packages. The version of Oracle
R Enterprise being installed in here is Oracle R Enterprise 1.5. If you require
a different version of Oracle R Enterprise to be installed, you need to check with the
Oracle R Enterprise website and supporting documentation for any particular
requirements. For example, for Oracle R Enterprise 1.5, you need to have Oracle R
Distribution 3.2.0 installed.

The installation steps detailed in this section assume that you have all the
requested information outlined in the "Pre-installation Requirements" section. You
will need most of this information to complete the installation of these R packages.
The Oracle R Enterprise packages and Supporting packages, when installed on the
Database Server, will support the embedded R execution from the Oracle Database.

The first step is to download and uncompress the Oracle R Enterprise Server and
Supporting packages from the Oracle R Enterprise Download web page. Make sure
you download the version of these files that corresponds with the operating system
of your Database Server.

A user-created installation directory (for example, ORE_Server_Install)
should be where both of these downloaded files are uncompressed. After this is
done, your installation directory should look like the following directory listing:

```
/ORE_Server_Install
    /ore-server-linux-x86-64-1.5.zip
    /ore-supporting-linux-x86-64-1.5.zip
    /server.sh
    /server
    /supporting
```

NOTE
*It is important to have the Server and the Supporting
packages uncompressed into the same directory,
as shown here, as this will simplify the installation
of Oracle R Enterprise. Otherwise, you will have
to install the supporting R packages as a separate
step after completing the installation of the
Server packages.*

The `server.sh` file (or `server.bat` on a Windows server) is the batch file you
run to install the Oracle R Enterprise Server and Supporting packages. You have two
options for running this file. The first is in batch mode, where you can specify all the
arguments on the command line. To see all the available parameters, you can run

```
./server.sh -help
```

An alternative way to run this script is in interactive mode:

```
./server.sh
```

Before running this server installation script, you should have set up the `ORACLE_HOME` and `ORACLE_SID` environment variables.

If you are running Oracle 12c Database, you can set the `ORACLE_SID` to your Pluggable Database (PDB) name. When you are prompted for the `SYS` password during the installation, you may need to add the PDB name after the password. If you are using an Oracle 11g R2 Database, you do not need to add anything after entering the `SYS` password.

The following listing shows the interactive running of the server installation script. The parts highlighted in bold show you what you have to type in for each of the prompts. The "Pre-installation Requirements" section listed the various inputs required.

```
[oracle@localhost ORE_install]$ ./server.sh -i

Oracle R Enterprise 1.4.1 Server.

Copyright (c) 2012, 2014 Oracle and/or its affiliates. All rights reserved.

Checking platform ................. Pass
Checking R ........................ Pass
Checking R libraries .............. Pass
Checking ORACLE_HOME .............. Pass
Checking ORACLE_SID ............... Pass
Checking sqlplus .................. Fail
  Enter SYS password:  XXXXXX@PDB12C
Checking sqlplus .................. Pass
Checking ORACLE instance .......... Pass
Checking CDB/PDB .................. Pass
Checking ORE ...................... Pass

Choosing RQSYS tablespaces
  PERMANENT tablespace to use for RQSYS [list]: SYSAUX
  TEMPORARY tablespace to use for RQSYS [list]: TEMP
Choosing RQSYS password
  Password to use for RQSYS:  RQSYS

Choosing ORE user
  ORE user to use [list]: ore_user
Choosing ORE_USER tablespaces
  PERMANENT tablespace to use for ORE_USER [list]: USERS
  TEMPORARY tablespace to use for ORE_USER [list]: TEMP
Choosing ORE_USER password
  Password to use for ORE_USER:  ore_user

Current configuration
  R Version ...................... Oracle Distribution of R version 3.2.0 (2012-06-22)
  R_HOME ......................... /usr/lib64/R
  R_LIBS_USER .................... /home/oracle/app/oracle/product/12.1.0/dbhome_1/R/library
  ORACLE_HOME .................... /home/oracle/app/oracle/product/12.1.0/dbhome_1
  ORACLE_SID ..................... PDB12C
```

```
Existing R Version ............... None
Existing R_HOME .................. None
Existing ORE data ............... None
Existing ORE code ............... None
Existing ORE libraries .......... None

RQSYS PERMANENT tablespace ....... SYSAUX
RQSYS TEMPORARY tablespace ....... TEMP

ORE user type ................... New
ORE user name ................... ORE_USER
ORE user PERMANENT tablespace .... USERS
ORE user TEMPORARY tablespace .... TEMP
Grant RQADMIN role .............. No

Operation ....................... Install/Upgrade/Setup

Proceed? [yes] yes

Removing R libraries ............... Pass
Installing R libraries ............. Pass
Installing ORE libraries ........... Pass
Installing RQSYS data .............. Pass
Configuring ORE .................... Pass
Installing RQSYS code .............. Pass
Installing ORE packages ............ Pass
Creating ORE script ................ Pass
Installing migration scripts ....... Pass
Installing supporting packages ..... Pass
Creating ORE user .................. Pass
Granting ORE privileges ............ Pass

Done
[oracle@localhost ORE_install]$
```

HINT
When prompted to enter the tablespace names, you should use all uppercase letters. When prompted to enter the ORE username and password, you should use all lowercase letters.

You now have Oracle R Enterprise installed on your Oracle Database Server. The next step is to install and configure Oracle R Enterprise on your client machines.

Client Installation

Any data analysts or data scientists who will be using Oracle R Enterprise will need to have the R software installed on their machines, as well as having the necessary Oracle R Enterprise and Supporting R packages installed on their client machines. Figure 2-2 illustrates the client installation process.

It is important that the version of R installed on a client machine matches the version of R or Oracle R Distribution installed on the Oracle Database Server. If a

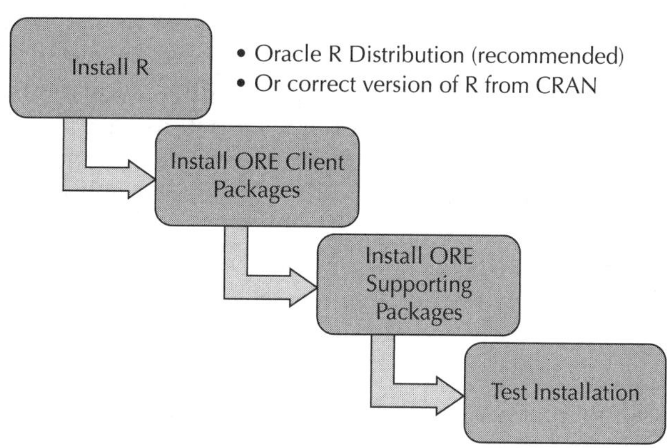

FIGURE 2-2.   *Client installation of Oracle R Enterprise*

different version of R is used, you will get an error when you try to establish an ORE connection to the database.

The only client machine pre-installation requirement is that the Oracle Instant Client or the Oracle Database Client be installed. These can be obtained from the Oracle Download web page. This software allows for efficient networking and communications with the Oracle Database.

Installing R on a Client Machine

When it comes to installing R on the client machine, you have two options, just like when installing R on the Oracle Database Server. You can download and install the Oracle R Distribution or the corresponding version of R that matches the version of R installed on the Database Server.

Oracle recommends that you use Oracle R Distribution, which is a separately maintained and supported version of R from Oracle.

To install Oracle R Distribution on a Windows client machine, you need to download the software from the Oracle Open Source Download page (https://oss.oracle.com/ORD).

NOTE

In the previous section, Oracle R Enterprise 1.5 was installed on the Oracle Database Server. This version of Oracle R Enterprise requires the installation of Oracle R Distribution 3.2.0. These same versions of the software will need to be installed on the client machines.

If you prefer to use the version of R that is available from the R CRAN website, you need to check for the correct version of R that is needed for the version of Oracle R Enterprise you are installing. Check out the Oracle R Enterprise website and the Oracle R Enterprise Installation and Administration Guide for the Oracle R Enterprise/Oracle R Distribution/Open Source R support matrix.

The only post-installation step you need to perform is to add the full path to the Oracle R Distribution bin directory (or your R bin directory) to the `PATH` environment variable.

You can now perform a quick check of whether Oracle R Distribution or R has been installed. Open a command window and try the following command:

```
> R
```

The R command-line interface applications will open. Alternatively, you can open the R GUI, shown in Figure 2-3, by typing

```
> rgui
```

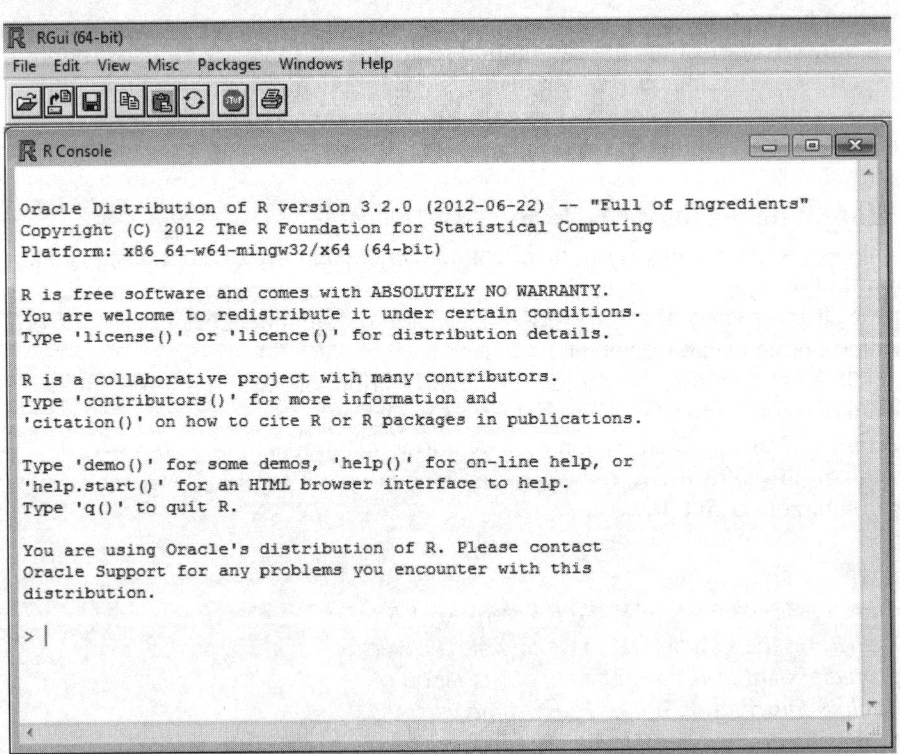

FIGURE 2-3. *The R GUI interface*

Install the Oracle R Enterprise Client and Supporting Packages

To install Oracle R Enterprise on your client machine, you will need to download and unzip the Oracle R Enterprise Client and Oracle Supporting packages from the Oracle R Enterprise website. Care should be taken to download the correct version of these packages and that the version matches the one installed on the Oracle Database Server.

After downloading the compressed files, you can uncompress them into the same directory (for example, `ORE_Client_Install`). After you have uncompressed these files, your directory should contain the following (for ORE 1.5):

```
...\ORE_Client_Install
        \client
            \ORE_1.5.zip
            \OREbase_1.5.zip
            \OREcommon_1.5.zip
            \OREdm_1.5.zip
            \OREeda_1.5.zip
            \OREembed_1.5.zip
            \OREgraphics_1.5.zip
            \OREmodels_1.5.zip
            \OREpredict_1.5.zip
            \OREstats_1.5.zip
            \ORExml_1.5.zip
        \supporting
            \arules_1.1-9.zip
            \Cairo_1.5-8.zip
            \DBI_0.3.1.zip
            \png_0.1-7.zip
            \randomForest_4.6-10
            \Roracle_1.2-1.zip
            \statmod_1.4.21.zip
```

To install these packages, you have two options. The first is to use the `install.packages` function in R. To use this function, you need to start R and then run the commands shown next to install the core Oracle R Enterprise packages and the Supporting packages:

```
> ## Install the Oracle R Enterprise Client Packages
> ##
> ## Need to ensure your Client has the correct version of R
> ## or Oracle R Distribution
> ##
> install.packages("C:/app/ORE_Client_Install/client/ORE_1.5.zip")
> install.packages("C:/app/ORE_Client_Install/client/OREbase_1.5.zip")
> install.packages("C:/app/ORE_Client_Install/client/OREcommon_1.5.zip")
> install.packages("C:/app/ORE_Client_Install/client/OREdm_1.5.zip")
> install.packages("C:/app/ORE_Client_Install/client/OREeda_1.5.zip")
> install.packages("C:/app/ORE_Client_Install/client/OREembed_1.5.zip")
> install.packages("C:/app/ORE_Client_Install/client/OREgraphics_1.5.zip")
> install.packages("C:/app/ORE_Client_Install/client/OREmodels_1.5.zip")
> install.packages("C:/app/ORE_Client_Install/client/OREpredict_1.5.zip")
> install.packages("C:/app/ORE_Client_Install/client/OREstats_1.5.zip")
> install.packages("C:/app/ORE_Clien_Install/client/ORExml_1.5.zip")
```

```
> ## Install the ORE Supporting packages
> install.packages("C:/app/ORE_Client_Install/supporting/arules_1.1-9.zip")
> install.packages("C:/app/ORE_Client_Install/supporting/Cairo_1.5-8.zip")
> install.packages("C:/app/ORE_Client_Install/supporting/DBI_0.3.1.zip")
> install.packages("C:/app/ORE_Client_Install/supporting/png_0.1-7.zip")
> install.packages("C:/app/ORE_Client_Install/supporting/randomForest_4.6-10.zip")
> install.packages("C:/app/ORE_Client_Install/supporting/ROracle_1.2-1.zip")
> install.packages("C:/app/ORE_Client_Install/supporting/statmod_1.4.21.zip")
```

An alternative approach is to use the command-line option. This is illustrated in the following code listing, which is run from the operating system command line:

```
R CMD INSTALL C:/app/ORE_Client_Install/client/OREbase_1.5.zip
R CMD INSTALL C:/app/ORE_Client_Install/client/OREcommon_1.5.zip
R CMD INSTALL C:/app/ORE_Client_Install/client/OREdm_1.5.zip
R CMD INSTALL C:/app/ORE_Client_Install/client/OREeda_1.5.zip
R CMD INSTALL C:/app/ORE_Client_Install/client/OREembed_1.5.zip
R CMD INSTALL C:/app/ORE_Client_Install/client/OREgraphics_1.5.zip
R CMD INSTALL C:/app/ORE_Client_Install/client/OREmodels_1.5.zip
R CMD INSTALL C:/app/ORE_Client_Install/client/OREpredict_1.5.zip
R CMD INSTALL C:/app/ORE_Client_Install/client/OREstats_1.5.zip
R CMD INSTALL C:/app/ORE_Client_Install/client/OP3xml_1.5.zip

R CMD INSTALL C:/app/ORE_Client_Install/supporting/arules_1.1-9.zip
R CMD INSTALL C:/app/ORE_Client_Install/supporting/Cairo_1.5-8.zip
R CMD INSTALL C:/app/ORE_Client_Install/supporting/DBI_0.3.1.zip
R CMD INSTALL C:/app/ORE_Client_Install/supporting/png_0.1-7.zip
R CMD INSTALL C:/app/ORE_Client_Install/supporting/randomForest_4.6-10.zip
R CMD INSTALL C:/app/ORE_Client_Install/supporting/Roracle_1.2-1.zip
R CMD INSTALL C:/app/ORE_Client_Install/supporting/statmod_1.4.21.zip
```

You have now completed the Oracle R Enterprise installation on the client machine.

NOTE
The Oracle R Enterprise client installation assumes you have already installed Oracle Database Client or Oracle Instant Client on your machine. This is required by the ROracle package.

Verifying the Installation of ORE

After completing the server and client installation of Oracle R Enterprise, you are now ready to perform initial tests to make sure the installation has been completed correctly. The following code example illustrates the creation of a database connection using the ore.connect command. This connects to the ORE_USER schema created during the Oracle R Enterprise Server installation. In this example, we are connecting to an Oracle Database using the service name:

```
> # First you need to load the ORE library
> library(ORE)

> # Create an ORE connection to your Oracle Schema
> ore.connect(user="ore_user", password="ore_user", host="localhost",
              service_name="PDB12C", port=1521, all=TRUE)
```

We can now perform some simple checks. The first is to check that we are connected to the database. The response to this is TRUE to indicate that we have an open connection to the database; otherwise, we would get FALSE.

```
> # Test that we are connected
> ore.is.connected()
 [1] TRUE
```

Next, we can list all the objects that exist in the Oracle Schema (ORE_USER). This includes all the tables and views. The ORE_USER schema was created during the Oracle R Enterprise Server installation. At this point, we have no objects in this schema, which is indicated with the `character(0)` response:

```
> # List the objects that are in the Oracle Schema.
> # No objects exist if a new schema
> ore.ls()
 character(0)
```

An additional test to verify the embedded R execution involves running the following `ore.doEval` function. To run this function, the ORE_USER will need to have the RQADMIN database privilege granted to them:

```
> ore.doEval(function() .libPaths() )
```

After finishing our initial checks, we can now disconnect from the Oracle Database, like so:

```
> # Disconnect from the Database
> ore.disconnect()
```

The `ore.connect` command is discussed in more detail in Chapter 3.

Installing RStudio

The R language comes with a command-line interface and a very simple GUI interface. As an alternative, many data analysts and data scientists use the popular tool RStudio (www.rstudio.com). RStudio is available in open source and commercial editions. Additionally there is an RStudio Server edition that allows for all your R work to take place on a centralized server.

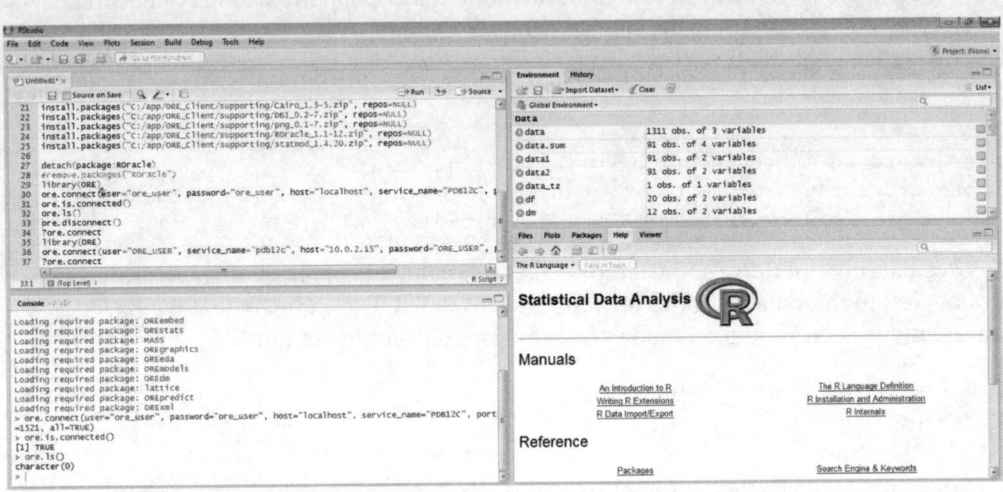

FIGURE 2-4. *RStudio*

RStudio provides an integrated development environment (IDE) that allows us to work with all the components of our R projects in one place. Figure 2-4 shows an example of RStudio, where we can work with R scripts, use the R console, view all the variables and data sets we have in our environment, have easy access to the R help system, and display any charts and graphs we may produce.

RStudio is available as an open source tool, and it is recommended that you download and use this tool on your client machine. There is a very simple installation process. Just go to the RStudio web page (www.rstudio.com) and then download and run the RStudio Desktop installer. When you run RStudio, you get a screen very similar to Figure 2-4, but some of the sections will be empty until you start using the tool.

Using Oracle Pre-built Appliances

To use Oracle R Enterprise, you need access to an Oracle Database (11*g* R2 or 12*c*). If you don't have ready access to a suitable Oracle Database environment or are not allowed to install Oracle R Enterprise on your Oracle Database Server, then you are a bit stuck. One option open to you is to build a virtual machine on your client machine. This involves installing the operating system, installing the Oracle Database, and setting up schemas and data sets, which may or may not be something you are comfortable with.

As an alterative, you could use one of the Oracle pre-built appliances that come pre-configured with loads of Oracle software installed and with some sample data sets. These pre-built appliances provide a great way to try the software before you have to install it in your development environments. You can import these appliances into Oracle VirtualBox to have your own personal Oracle virtual machine.

If you want to try out the various features of Oracle R Enterprise, you can use one of these pre-built appliances as a learning environment. Oracle provides a number of pre-built appliances that are suitable for you to use with Oracle R Enterprise, with the Oracle OBIEE Sample App and the Oracle Big Data Lite appliances having Oracle R Enterprise already installed and configured for you.

Oracle Database Developer Pre-built Appliance

The Oracle Database Developer appliance comes with the latest version of the Oracle Database, but it also has the following items installed and configured for you:

- Oracle XML DB

- Oracle SQL Developer (including the Oracle Data Miner tool)

- Oracle APEX

This appliance also has a suite of hands-on labs and tutorials already set up for you. This appliance is what is used for many of the Oracle Technology Network (OTN) Developer Days Hands-on Database Developer sessions. Although Oracle R Enterprise is not installed in this version of the appliance, you can easily install Oracle R Enterprise using the instructions given earlier in the "Oracle Database Server Installation" section.

You can use this appliance as a Database Server and as your Client machine. If you would prefer to have this appliance act as a Database Server, you need to set up port forwarding in the virtual machine settings. You can then use your R and Oracle R Enterprise client installation to connect to the Oracle Database that is running in the virtual machine.

Oracle OBIEE Sample App Pre-built Appliance

The Oracle OBIEE Sample App pre-built appliance allows you to set up a virtual machine that has an Oracle Database and the full Oracle Business Intelligence suite of products installed and configured for you to use. This appliance also comes with a number of data sets already loaded into the database and has a large collection of analytics, reports, and dashboards already built for you to explore. Some of these analytics, reports, and dashboards are illustrated in Figure 2-5.

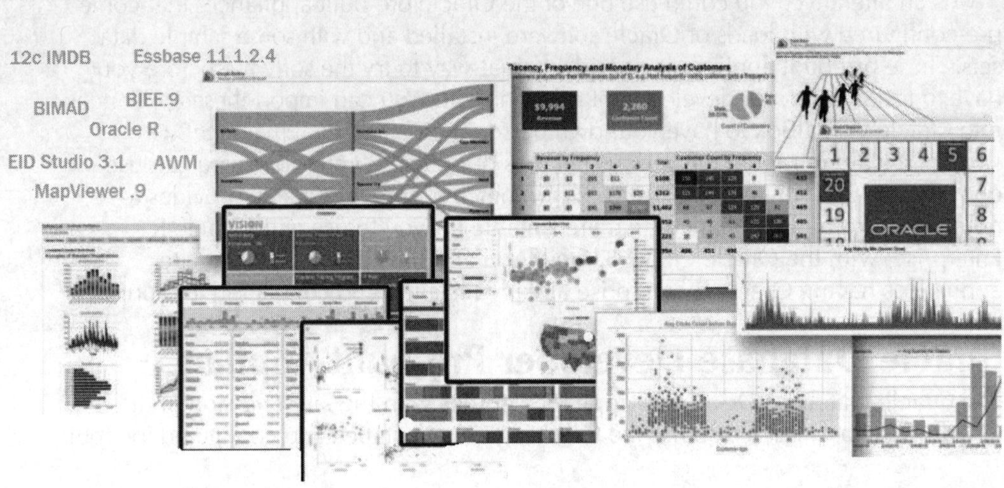

FIGURE 2-5. *The Oracle OBIEE Sample App pre-built appliance*

The Oracle OBIEE Sample App pre-built appliance comes configured with the following software:

- Oracle Business Intelligence Foundation Suite

- Essbase

- Oracle MapViewer

- Oracle BICS Data Sync tool

- Oracle APEX

- Endeca

- Cloudera

- Oracle Big Data SQL

- Oracle R Enterprise

This pre-built appliance comes with Oracle R Enterprise installed and configured. This allows you to use Oracle R Enterprise to perform various analytics using the supplied sample data sets. The sample OBIEE dashboards also have a number of examples that use the advanced analytics capabilities of Oracle R Enterprise and show you how these have been included in the dashboards. These capabilities greatly expand the functionality available in the Oracle Database, within the OBIEE and the various other Oracle products.

Oracle Big Data Lite Pre-built Appliance

The Oracle Big Data Lite pre-built appliance is another virtual machine that comes with Oracle R Enterprise already installed and configured for you to use. The Oracle Big Data Lite appliance is an environment built to allow you to get started with the Oracle Big Data platform. It includes the Big Data Appliance and Oracle Database, Hadoop using Cloudera, and many of the other Oracle products for managing your data. This appliance has the following additional software installed and configured and includes a number of data sets:

- Oracle Big Data Discover

- Cloudera Distribution, including Apache Hadoop

- Cloudera Manager

- Oracle Big Data Connectors

- Oracle X Query for Hadoop

- Oracle NoSQL Database Enterprise Edition

- Oracle Big Data Spatial and Graph

- Oracle SQL Developer

- Oracle Data Integrator

- Oracle Golden Gate

- Oracle R Enterprise

This pre-built appliance comes with Oracle R Enterprise installed and configured, which allows you to use Oracle R Enterprise to perform various analytics using the supplied sample data sets and to use the advanced analytics capabilities of R within your Big Data environment.

Summary

In this chapter, we worked through the various pre-installation requirements necessary to install Oracle R Enterprise. We also worked through the various steps required to install Oracle R enterprise on your Oracle Database Server and also how to install Oracle R Enterprise on a client machine. Oracle provides a number of pre-built virtual machine appliances that come pre-configured with Oracle R Enterprise. These are a great way to quickly get up and running with a test environment before you have to install Oracle R Enterprise in your development, test, and production environments. In the next chapter, we look at some of the typical functions you will perform when starting out with Oracle R Enterprise.

CHAPTER 3

Getting Started with Oracle R Enterprise

I n this chapter, we explore some of the more common Oracle R Enterprise functions you will use in all your analytics projects. In later chapters, we explore some of the more detailed and advanced features of Oracle R Enterprise.

In this chapter, you learn how to create and manage your connection to the Oracle Database, how to execute SQL statements in the database, how to analyze your tables and views in the Oracle Database, how to create objects in the database, how to copy database objects to your local R environment, and how to use and manage an ORE datastore.

Creating and Managing ORE Connections to the Database

Before you can use Oracle R Enterprise, the first task you need to perform is to create a connection to a schema in the Oracle Database. The following sections explore the various aspects relating to establishing a connection—from creating a basic type of connection to managing all aspects of the connection.

Creating an ORE Connection Using `ore.connect`

One of the first functions you will use with Oracle R Enterprise is the `ore.connect` function, which allows you to create a connection to the database and to create ORE proxy objects for the tables and views in your schema.

Your R session is only allowed to have one open `ore.connect` session at a time. If you try to create a new ORE connection to the Oracle Database, the currently open connection will be closed before the new connection is opened.

Two types of connections can be made with `ore.connect`. The main type of connection is to ORACLE, which is the default value. We will be using this type of connection throughout the book. The second type of connection we can have is to HIVE, which you will use when you are connecting using Oracle R Advanced Analytics for Hadoop (ORAAH).

Table 3-1 lists the parameters for the `ore.connect()` function.

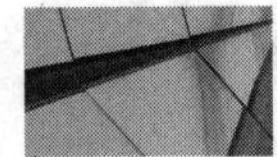

TIP
Over time, as you work on your various analytics projects, the number of database objects will grow larger. This has the effect of slowing down the `ore.connect` *function and creating unnecessary objects in your environment. When this occurs, set* `type=FALSE` *and then use the* `ore.sync` *function to create proxy* `ore.frame` *objects for the schema objects that you need only for your analytics work.*

Parameter Name	Description
user	This is the schema name you want to connect to in the Oracle Database.
password	This is the password for the Oracle Schema you are connecting to.
sid	This is the Database SID name. You will use this for all 12c databases and 11g R2 databases that have been set up with a SID.
service_name	This is the Service Name of the database. You will use this for all 12c databases and 11g R2 databases that have been set up with a Service Name.
host	This is the host name of the Oracle Database server. This can be the full host name or the IP address of the server.
port	This is the port number for the Oracle Database. The typical value for this is 1521. You will need to confirm the correct number with your Oracle DBA.

conn_string	This can be used as an alternative to specifying the various connection parameters. Here is an example:
	
	`conn_string = "dev-server:1521:del01`
	`(ADDRESS=(PROTOCOL=tcp) (HOST=dev-server) (PORT=1521))`
	`(CONNECT_DATA=(SERVICE_NAME=dev.xyz-example.com)))"`
	
	This parameter can also be used when you are using Oracle Wallet to manage your passwords.

all	When `all=TRUE`, the `ore.connect` function will perform an `ore.sync` and `ore.attach` automatically. This makes all the tables and views that are available in the Oracle schema visible in your R session. The default value is `FALSE`.
type	The default value for this parameter is ORACLE. This is the typical connection you will make. You do not need to use this in your `ore.connect` if you are connecting to an Oracle Database. If you are connecting to HIVE, when using ORAAH, you will need to explicitly state this in the `ore.connect` function.

TABLE 3-1.   *Parameters for the `ore.connect` Function*

The following is an example of establishing a connection to the ORE_USER schema, specifying all the parameters for the `ore.connect` function. Because this connection will be to an Oracle Database, no value is specified for the `type` variable because the default is ORACLE.

```
> # First you need to load the ORE library
> library(ORE)
```

```
> # Create an ORE connection to your Oracle schema
> ore.connect(user="ore_user", password="ore_user", host="localhost",
              service_name="PDB12C", port=1521, all=TRUE)
```

In this example, we have set `all=TRUE`. This will create ORE proxy objects for each of the tables and views in the ORE_USER schema. It does this by reading the metadata of these objects and then using this metadata to create the ORE proxy objects.

If your Oracle Database is the 11*g* R2 version and is set up with a SID, then the `ore.connect` function would be the following:

```
> # Create an ORE connection to your Oracle schema using a SID
> ore.connect(user="ore_user", password="ore_user", host="localhost",
              sid="ORCL", port=1521, all=TRUE)
```

A useful way to check whether you have an open connection is to use the `ore.is.connected` function. You can easily utilize this function in your R and ORE scripts to check for an open connection. In the following example, the code checks to see whether we have an open ORE connection. If not, then we open a connection to the Oracle Database.

```
> if (!ore.is.connected())
  {
      message("Not currently connected.  Connecting Now")
      ore.connect(user="ore_user", password="ore_user", host="localhost",
                  service_name="PDB12C", port=1521, all=TRUE)
  } else {
    message("Already connected")
  }
```

Syncing Data Using `ore.sync`

When you use `ore.connect` to establish a connection to your schema in the Oracle Database and you have the setting `all=TRUE`, the connection will create an ORE proxy object for each of the tables and views in the schema.

If the `all=FALSE` setting is used, the `ore.connect` will not examine the schema objects and no ORE proxy objects will be created. You can see this when you list the available objects after a connection, as shown in the following example:

```
> # List the objects in the Oracle schema. No objects exist if a new schema
> ore.ls()
 character(0)
```

You can use the `ore.sync` function to identify the schema objects you want included in your ORE session and which ORE proxy objects will be created. For example, if we have tables or views called PRODUCTS and CUSTOMERS in our schema, we can include these in our ORE session, as illustrated in the following example:

```
> ore.sync(table=c("PRODUCTS", "CUSTOMERS"))
> ore.ls()
 [1] "CUSTOMERS" "PRODUCTS"
```

TIP
Specifying the schema objects you want to use in your analysis reduces the amount of memory that needs to be allocated to your R session. It also speeds up the ore.connect *when you are connecting to a schema with a large number of objects.*

The ore.sync function has a number of parameters, as shown in Table 3-2. The following example illustrates how you can use ore.sync to include objects that you have access to from another schema:

```
> ore.sync(schema="SH", table=c("COUNTRIES", "SALES"))
```

Parameter Name	Description
schema	The schema name where the objects exists. By default, this is the schema name for the current connection. If a different schema name is used, the connection schema should have access to the objects in the other schema. Do not use this parameter when using the query parameter.
table	The names of the tables and views for which ore.frame objects will be created. The default value is NULL.
use.keys	This is used when you want the table's primary keys to be used for ordering the data in the ore.frame object. The default value is TRUE.
query	Instead of listing the tables and views to include, you can write a query to return a particular data set. This data set will be represented by an ore.frame. When you're using this parameter, the query must be based on the data in the connection schema. You do not use the schema parameter when using the query parameter.

TABLE 3-2. *Parameters for the* ore.sync *Function*

But when you use the `ore.ls` function to list the objects, these additional tables are not listed because they are not part of the current connection schema. Instead, you have to specify the name of the schema in the function call. Here's an example:

```
ore.ls("SH")
```

You can now assign these ORE proxy objects to an R variable for use in your data analytics. You will use the `ore.get` function to perform this assignment. The R variable now points to the object in the database, and all functions and operations performed on this R variable will, via the transparency layer, be performed in the Oracle Database:

```
> ds<- ore.get("PRODUCTS")
> class(ds)
 [1] "ore.frame"
 attr(,"package")
 [1] "OREbase"
> dim(ds)
 [1] 72 22
```

If the table or view exists in a schema other than your current connection schema, you need to include the schema name in the `ore.get` function:

```
> ds2<-ore.get("COUNTRIES", "SH")
```

The following example illustrates using the `ore.sync` function to create ORE proxy objects that are based on a query. The call to `ore.sync` does not include the schema name because it will only use the current connection schema. This is a very useful method for building up various subsets of your data.

```
> ore.sync(query = c("COUNTRY_COUNT" = "SELECT cc.country_name, count(c.cust_id)
                        FROM    customers c,
                                countries cc
                        WHERE   c.country_id = cc.country_id
                        GROUP BY cc.country_name"))
```

If you have multiple queries listed in the one `ore.sync` command, each query will have a different name. These objects now appear when you use `ore.ls` and they are assigned to local R variables to be used in your analytics.

Adding Objects to the Search Space Using `ore.attach`

The `ore.attach` function allows you to add objects from your schema and other schemas to the search space path in R. In the previous section, we used the `ore.sync` function to create ORE proxy objects for the tables and views in the database. We also had an example of using the `ore.get` function to assign the ORE proxy object to a local R variable.

When we use the `ore.attach` function, we make these ORE proxy objects visible and useable for the user. If we issue the `ore.attach` command with no parameters, it will add all the synchronized objects to the R search path. The following example illustrates this and shows how we can query the PRODUCTS table directly. This example displays the dimension details of the object and the first five records.

```
> dim(PRODUCTS)
[1] 72 22
> head(PRODUCTS, 5)
  PROD_ID                          PROD_NAME                          PROD_DESC
1      13            5MP Telephoto Digital Camera       5MP Telephoto Digital Camera
2      14            17" LCD w/built-in HDTV Tuner      17" LCD w/built-in HDTV Tuner
3      15                      Envoy 256MB - 40GB                 Envoy 256MB - 40Gb
4      16                                 Y Box                              Y Box
5      17 Mini DV Camcorder with 3.5" Swivel LCD Mini DV Camcorder with 3.5" Swivel LCD
...
```

We can also assign objects from another schema to the R search path by adding the schema name as a parameter to `ore.attach`, like so:

```
> ore.attach("SH")
```

The only condition to issuing this `ore.attach` is that a corresponding `ore.sync` had been issued previously.

TIP
The `ore.connect` command automatically calls the `ore.sync` and `ore.attach` functions for all the tables and views in the schema you are connecting to.

When you are finished working with the database objects, you might want to remove them from the R search path. You can do this using the `ore.detach` function. When a schema name is passed as a parameter, the objects from the current schema/connection are removed. If you want to remove objects from a specific schema, you can include the schema name, as shown here:

```
> ore.detach("SH")
> ore.detach()
```

Running a SQL Command

The `ore.exec` function allows you to execute SQL statements in your schema. These statements will typically be DDL and DML statements that do not return a value. You can also use this command to set any optimizer settings and session-level settings, to use the in-memory option, and so on.

The following example illustrates using `ore.exec` to drop some views, to create some views, to create a table, and to put the table into memory:

```
> ore.exec("DROP VIEW customers_v")
> ore.exec("DROP VIEW products_v")
> ore.exec("DROP VIEW countries_v")
> ore.exec("DROP VIEW sales_v")
> ore.exec("CREATE VIEW customers_v AS SELECT * FROM sh.customers")
> ore.exec("CREATE VIEW products_v AS SELECT * FROM sh.products")
> ore.exec("CREATE VIEW countries_v AS SELECT * FROM sh.countries")
> ore.exec("CREATE VIEW sales_v AS SELECT * FROM sh.sales")
> # create a view for Customers who live in USA
> ore.exec("CREATE TABLE customers_usa
            AS SELECT * FROM customers_v WHERE COUNTRY_ID = 52790")
> # put the new Customers table in memory
> ore.exec("ALTER TABLE customers_usa inmemory")
```

The `ore.exec` function should only be used on SQL statements when there is no return value.

The views and table created in the preceding example are not included in the R environment because no ORE proxy objects have been created for them—plus, they have not been added to the R search space. You can see this when you use the `ore.ls` function. These proxy objects do not exit. You will need to run the `ore.sync` function to make these objects accessible to your R environment, as shown here:

```
> ore.ls()
 [1] "CUSTOMERS_USA"
> ore.sync()
> ore.ls()
 [1] "COUNTRIES_V"    "CUSTOMERS_USA" "CUSTOMERS_V"    "PRODUCTS_V"    "SALES_V"
```

Working with Data in the Oracle Database

In the previous sections, we looked at connecting to an Oracle schema, listing and viewing some of the objects that may exist in the schema, performing some simple functions on these objects, and running some SQL statements to create a number of objects (views and a table) in the Oracle schema. In this section, we look at performing some additional functions using Oracle R Enterprise to interact with the database.

When working with data in an Oracle table or view, you can use the ORE proxy object to perform your analysis and such, or you might prefer to use a local R variable to refer to the object in the database. The following example shows this kind of assignment and displays some basic information and statistics about the data:

```
> # create a local variable ds that points to SALES_V in the database
> ds <- ore.get("SALES_V")
> # We can verify we are pointing at the object in the database
> class(ds)
 [1] "ore.frame"
 attr(,"package")
 [1] "OREbase"
> # How many rows and columns are in the table
> dim(ds)
 [1] 918843       7
> # Display the first 6 records from the table
> head(ds)
     PROD_ID CUST_ID    TIME_ID CHANNEL_ID PROMO_ID QUANTITY_SOLD AMOUNT_SOLD
1         13     987 1998-01-10          3      999             1     1232.16
2         13    1660 1998-01-10          3      999             1     1232.16
3         13    1762 1998-01-10          3      999             1     1232.16
4         13    1843 1998-01-10          3      999             1     1232.16
5         13    1948 1998-01-10          3      999             1     1232.16
6         13    2273 1998-01-10          3      999             1     1232.16
Warning messages:
1: ORE object has no unique key - using random order
2: ORE object has no unique key - using random order

> # Get the Summary statistics for each attribute in SALES_V
> summary(ds)
     PROD_ID          CUST_ID          TIME_ID         CHANNEL_ID        PROMO_ID
 Min.   : 13.00   Min.   :     2   Min.   :1998-01-01   Min.   :2.000   Min.   : 33.0
 1st Qu.: 31.00   1st Qu.:  2383   1st Qu.:1999-03-13   1st Qu.:2.000   1st Qu.:999.0
 Median : 48.00   Median :  4927   Median :2000-02-17   Median :3.000   Median :999.0
 Mean   : 78.18   Mean   :  7290   3rd Qu.:2001-02-15   Mean   :2.862   Mean   :976.4
 3rd Qu.:127.00   3rd Qu.:  9163   Max.   :2001-12-31   3rd Qu.:3.000   3rd Qu.:999.0
 Max.   :148.00   Max.   :101000                        Max.   :9.000   Max.   :999.0
 QUANTITY_SOLD   AMOUNT_SOLD
 Min.   :1   Min.   :    6.40
 1st Qu.:1   1st Qu.:   17.38
 Median :1   Median :   34.24
 Mean   :1   Mean   :  106.88
 3rd Qu.:1   3rd Qu.:   53.89
 Max.   :1   Max.   : 1782.72
```

HINT

In the preceding example, you will notice some warning messages displayed after the results for the head(ds) *function. These messages are for information purposes only. If you would prefer for these messages not to be displayed, you can use the command* options(ore.warn.order=FALSE). *I typically run this command after I have created my connection to the Oracle Database.*

If you would prefer to work with the data on your local machine (PC or laptop), you can use the ore.pull function to create a local copy of the data in a data frame. You need to be careful when using this function because, depending on the volume of data, it can take a lot of time to move the data from the Oracle Database to your local R session. If the volume of data is large, this will also impact the available RAM on your local machine, and in some cases the data may not fit into RAM. Plus, you will not be using any of the performance features available by default in the database. This function should only be used on rare occasions. An example of using the `ore.pull` function to make a local copy of the SALE_V database object is illustrated in the following example. You can see that we are using a local data frame to store the data instead of using an ORE frame that points to the data in the database.

```
> # Create a local copy of the SALES_V data
> sales_ds <- ore.pull(SALES_V)
 Warning message:
 ORE object has no unique key - using random order
> # Check to see that this is a local data frame and not an ORE object
> class(sales_ds)
 [1] "data.frame"
> # Get details of the local data
> dim(sales_ds)
 [1] 918843       7
```

HINT
The `ore.pull` function should only be used in situations where a local copy of the data is needed on your machine. If possible, the data should be left in the database and the other ORE functions should be used to process the data. By doing this, you utilize all the benefits and scalability of the database.

WARNING
You may have noticed some warning messages in the last two code examples, telling us about objects that do not have a unique key. These are informational messages and point out things you may want to address.

Because it is a view, SALE_V does not have a primary key associated with it. ORE will return or display the data as it is retrieved from the underlying database objects. The data is not stored in any order in the underlying tables, so it will come back in whatever order it is found.

This is very similar to the CUSTOMERS_USA table we created earlier. This table was created without a primary key. When using some of the ORE and R functions, you may need the data to be ordered. If a table has a primary key, when the data is being retrieved, the primary key attributes will be used to perform the ordering. This automatically happens when you use the `ore.sync` function. One of the parameters of this function is `use.keys`, and the default is TRUE. Using this approach can be an expensive operation if the data volume is large because the data needs to be sorted. In these kinds of scenarios, you might prefer to have the data returned unsorted.

One option we have to add ordering to our data is to use the `ore.exec` function to create a primary key, as shown in the following example. After creating the primary key, we will need to run the `ore.sync` function to re-create the ORE proxy object to pick up the primary key for the ordering:

```
> ore.exec("ALTER TABLE customers_usa ADD CONSTRAINT cust_usa_pk PRIMARY KEY
          (cust_id)")
> usa_ds2<-ore.get("CUSTOMERS_USA")
```

When we run this code, we do not get any warning messages stating "ORE object has no unique key – using random order."

An alternative approach is to add the unique key details as part of your R session. The following example illustrates how you can do this. The following example also assumes that the code to create the primary key on the table has not been run, because this example illustrates an alternative approach.

```
> usa_ds <-ore.get("CUSTOMERS_USA")
> # Check what the unique identifier is for the object.
> # We should get no unique key for our data
> row.names(head(usa_ds))
 Error: ORE object has no unique key
 In addition: Warning message:
 ORE object has no unique key - using random order
> # Define and assign the unique key for the data set. In our data this is CUST_ID
> row.names(usa_ds)<-usa_ds$CUST_ID
> # Display the first 6 records.  You will not get the unique key message.
> head(usa_ds)
```

When you are working with data sets that are local to your R environment, sometimes it can be useful to move them temporarily to the database. Doing so allows you to utilize the in-database performance and scalability features, thus enabling you to perform more complex analysis in a shorter period of time.

You can use the `ore.push` function to take a local data frame and move it to your schema in the database. A temporary table will be created in your schema with a name beginning with ORE$. This will be followed by some set of numbers. The following example takes the MTCARS data set that comes with R and pushes it to a temporary table in the database:

```
> cars_ore_ds<-ore.push(mtcars)
```

The `cars_ore_ds` variable will now be an ORE object pointing to a table in the database. You can see this table if you log into your schema in the database.

You can now perform all of your typical data manipulation and analytics operations on this data, and all of these operations will be performed in the Oracle Database.

When you disconnect your ORE connection using `ore.disconnect`, all temporary tables and objects (like the one we just created) will be removed from the database. If you would like to persist the table and data to work on at a later time or to share with others on your team, you will need to use the `ore.create` function. This is illustrated in the next section.

Storing Data in the Database

As we work with our various data sets, we will want to be able to manage the persistence of these data sets in the database. To do this, Oracle R Enterprise gives us the `ore.create` and `ore.drop` functions to create and drop tables, respectively, in the database schema.

Using these functions allows us to persist and manage our data sets through our data science projects, to utilize the performance and scalability of the database, and to share our data with other data analysts and users of the data.

Using `ore.create` to Create Tables

You have already seen examples of how you can create tables in your schema. We have used the `ore.exec` function to execute a SQL statement in the database to create a table with a subset of data from another object. We have also used the `ore.push` function to move a data set temporarily to the database for additional analysis.

The `ore.create` function allows us to persist the data to the database. This function creates a table in your schema that contains the data that is in an R data frame. This table becomes visible to all users of that schema, and it can also be shared with other schemas in the database.

In a previous example, it was shown how you can take a local R data frame and push it to the database as a temporary table. In the following example, this same data frame will instead be created as a table in the schema:

```
> ore.create(mtcars, "CARS_DATA")
> ore.ls()
```

In this example, the `ore.create` function takes two parameters. These are the name for the data frame we want to persist in the schema and the name of the table in the database schema.

When we run the `ore.ls` function, we will now see that the new table is listed. The `ore.create` function also performs an `ore.sync` and `ore.attach` for this new object. This makes it available for use without us needing to run any additional functions.

Using `ore.drop` to Remove a Table

We have the `ore.drop` function to drop and remove a database table or a database view from the schema. The following example illustrates the dropping of the CARS_DATA table that we created using the `ore.create` function in the previous section:

```
> ore.drop("CARS_DATA")
> ore.ls()
```

When we inspect the list of objects displayed by the `ore.ls` function, we will see that the CARS_DATA table is no longer listed.

Similarly, we can use the `ore.drop` function to remove a database view from the schema. When dropping or removing a view from the database, you need to state the view parameter explicitly, as shown next. This is needed to drop the view in the schema.

```
> ore.drop(view="SALES_V")
```

An alternative way of using the `ore.drop` function is to state explicitly that we are dropping a table or a view from the schema. The following examples illustrates how the preceding examples can be used in one command:

```
> ore.drop(table="CARS_DATA", view="SALES_V")
```

Example Combining `ore.create` and `ore.drop`

The following ORE code example illustrates how to combine some of the ORE functions illustrated in this chapter to manage the updating and creating of a table in the database based on a local R data frame:

```
> if (ore.exists("CARS_DATA")) {
    message("Updating table in schema.  Dropping and Recreating with new data")
    ore.drop("CARS_DATA")
    ore.create(mtcars, "CARS_DATA")
  } else {
    message("Creating table in your schema. It did not exist")
    ore.create(mtcars, "CARS_DATA")
  }
```

Storing ORE Objects in the In-database R Datastore

When you are working with R, you will create many objects. These objects reside in memory as part of your R global environment. When you go to exit from your R session, you will probably perform some cleanup of these objects, such as using the rm function to remove them from memory and your R workspace. However, some other objects you will want to preserve for the next time you open R. You can save these when you exit your R session by saving them to your session workspace. You will be prompted to do this when exiting R.

Many of the objects you create using ORE you will have pushed to the database so that you can utilize the in-database performance and scalability features. As mentioned previously, when you disconnect your ORE session, all the temporary objects created in the database will also be dropped and removed from the database.

It would be useful if you could save these temporary objects for later use without having to go through the extra steps of creating tables to store the data. Additionally, when using ORE you can create other types of objects, such as data mining models, that you will want to use later. What you don't want to do is to go through the steps of creating these objects all over again.

A fantastic feature of Oracle R Enterprise is that we can create an ORE datastore in our database. In this ORE datastore, we can store all these temporary and working objects we have created. We can share the ORE datastore with other data analysts and data scientists, but perhaps the most important feature of the ORE datastore is that we can use it when we are performing the embedded ORE execution in SQL. The examples given in this section cover creating an ORE datastore, saving objects to it, retrieving those objects, getting the details of the ORE datastore, sharing the ORE datastore with other users, deleting objects, and finally deleting the ORE datastore. Other examples will be given in later chapters.

Table 3-3 outlines the set of functions available in Oracle R Enterprise that allows us to create and manage an ORE datastore.

HINT

You can create as many ORE datastores as you want in your Oracle Database. Plan in advance how many ORE datastores you want to have. Consider one ORE datastore per project or subject area of the business. Try to avoid having 100+ ORE datastores.

The first of these functions you will need to use is the ore.save function. This function allows you to save your ORE objects to a datastore for later use.

Function	Description
`ore.datastore`	Lists information about the ORE datastore that exists in your schema. This defaults to the current schema. When a name is provided, this function returns the details of that ORE datastore. The details displayed for each ORE datastore include the name, the number of objects, the size of the ORE datastore, the date created, and any description that has been assigned to the ORE datastore.
`ore.datastoreSummary`	Provides detailed information about the objects in a specified ORE datastore.
`ore.delete`	Deletes the ORE datastore from the database. This will also remove all the ORE objects contained in the ORE datastore.
`ore.grant`	Grants access to the ORE datastore to other users in the database if the ORE datastore had been created as grantable.
`ore.load`	Loads the objects from the ORE datastore back into the R environment. These objects are available for use immediately. Either all the objects can be retrieved or only the objects listed.
`ore.lazyLoad`	Loads the objects from the ORE datastore when they are first used by your R code. Objects are only restored one at a time.
`ore.revoke`	Revokes access that a schema has to an ORE datastore.
`ore.save`	Creates an ORE datastore and stores the listed objects in the ORE datastore for future use.

TABLE 3-3.   *Functions for Using the In-database ORE Datastore*

Apart from listing the objects you want to save in an ORE datastore, you also need to decide on the name of the ORE datastore, as well as if objects should be appended to an existing ORE datastore or if an existing ORE datastore is to be overwritten. You can save individual objects, a group of objects, or all available objects that are available in the ORE datastore. In this case, an object can be an ORE object or an object in your R environment.

The following example illustrates saving an individual object, CARS_DATA, in an ORE datastore call ORE_DS:

```
> ore.save(CARS_DATA, name="ORE_DS", description="Example of ORE Datastore")
```

When creating a new ORE datastore, you should try to give a meaningful description. The description can be up to 2000 characters, which enables you to give a description that clearly explains what the objects in the datastore are being used for.

To add any more objects to the ORE datastore, you will need to add append=TRUE to the end of the ore.save command, like so:

```
> ore.save(cars_ds, name="ORE_DS", append=TRUE)
```

The append parameter allows you to add objects to an existing ORE datastore. You will need to check to see if an object exists in the ORE datastore before running the ore.save function. If the object already exists, you can use the overwrite=TRUE parameter setting, as shown here:

```
> ore.save(cars_ds, name="ORE_DS", overwrite=TRUE)
```

If you need to share the ORE objects you are storing in the ORE datastore with another database user, you need to create the ORE datastore with the grantable=TRUE option. More details on sharing an ORE datastore are provided later in this section.

```
> ore.save(list=c("cars_ds", "iris_ds", "random_values"), name="ORE_DS3",
           grantable=TRUE)
```

The following example shows you how to delete one object from an ORE datastore. If you want to delete multiple objects, you need to form a list of objects as illustrated here:

```
> # Delete one object from the ORE Data Store
> ore.delete("ORE_DS", list="cars_ds")
> # Delete multiple objects from the ORE Data Store
> ore.delete("ORE_DS", list=c("cars_ds", "CARS_DATA"))
```

If you need to save all the objects in your current R environment to the ORE datastore, you can use the list parameter to pass in the names of these objects. This allows you to save these objects to the database, adding them to the data security provided by the database and to your backups. The following example illustrates adding the local R environment objects to an ORE datastore called ORE_DS2:

```
> ore.save(list=ls(), name="ORE_DS2", description="DS for all R Env Data")
```

Oracle R Enterprise has two functions that give details about ORE datastores. These functions are `ore.datastore` and `ore.datastoreSummary`. The `ore.datastore` function lists all the ORE datastores available for the user.

```
> ore.datastore()
    datastore.name object.count      size        creation.date              description
1          ORE_DS            2      5104 2016-04-04 10:33:25 Example of ORE Datastore
2         ORE_DS2            5 51466509 2016-04-04 10:30:19      DS for all R Env Data
```

The `ore.datastoreSummary` function displays the details of what objects are contained in a particular datastore:

```
> ore.datastoreSummary("ORE_DS2")
    object.name       class      size length row.count col.count
1       cars_ds data.frame      3798     11        32        11
2   cars_ore_ds  ore.frame      1675     11        32        11
3      sales_ds data.frame  51455575      7    918843         7
4        usa_ds  ore.frame      2749     23     18520        23
5       usa_ds2  ore.frame      2712     23     18520        23
```

Being able to save your various R and ORE objects to an in-database datastore helps you in securing your data and being able to utilize the performance and scalability features of the database when you want to reuse these objects.

As you build up your analytics environment, you will want to store data in various ORE datastores and be able to retrieve these objects so that you can continue with your analytics at a later time. Oracle R Enterprise provides you with the `ore.load` and `ore.lazyLoad` functions to load or restore the objects from an ORE datastore into your environment.

The `ore.load` function restores objects to your R environment. The function requires the name of an ORE datastore. In this case, all the objects in the ORE datastore will be restored, as shown in the following example:

```
> ore.load("ORE_DS")
```

As you add more and more objects to your ORE datastore, it may take some time to restore all the objects when you run the `ore.load` function. In such scenarios, it will be better to restore only the objects you require. In this case, you will provide a list of the objects you want restored.

```
> ore.load("ORE_DS2", c("cars_ds", "sales_ds", "usa_ds"))
```

An alternative approach is to load only the objects as and when they are required. This requires you to use the `ore.load` function before an object in the ORE datastore is used for the first time. Alternatively, you can use the `ore.lazyLoad` function. The `ore.lazyLoad` function does not immediately retrieve the specified objects from an ORE datastore. Instead, objects are retrieved when they are first referenced. The `ore.lazyLoad` function takes the ORE datastore name as a parameter to the `ore.lazyLoad` function. You can pass the name of the ORE datastore, or the ORE datastore name and the list of objects. The following examples are the `ore.lazyLoad` alternatives to the `ore.load` examples given earlier:

```
> ore.lazyLoad("ORE_DS2")
> ore.lazyLoad("ORE_DS2", c("cars_ds", "sales_ds", "usa_ds"))
```

As you build up a variety of ORE objects in your ORE datastores, at some point you may want to grant other users of the Oracle Database and ORE access to them. To grant access and remove access to the ORE datastores, you can use the `ore.grant` and the `ore.revoke` functions, respectively, to manage these privileges. Before you can grant other users access to the ORE datastore, you need to ensure that your datastore has been created with `grantable=TRUE`. When you use the `ore.save` function to create or update your ORE datastore, the datastore status will be set to private. This private setting is defined by the default TRUE setting for the `grantable` parameter in the `ore.save` function. This means that only you can use that ORE datastore. When you have an ORE datastore that you want to share with other database users, you need to have defined this by setting the `grantable` parameter to TRUE, as illustrated in the following example:

```
> # set up some data to use to demo Grant and Revoke
> cars_ds <- mtcars
> iris_ds <- iris
> random_values <- sample(seq(100),10)
> # Delete the ORE data store if it already exists. Otherwise skip this step
> ore.delete("ORE_DS3")
> # Create a ORE data store that can be shared with other users.
> ore.save(list=c("cars_ds", "iris_ds", "random_values"), name="ORE_DS3", grantable=TRUE)
```

You saw earlier how you can use the `ore.datastore` function to list all the datastores you have access to. You can also use this function to see which of these datastores can be shared with other database users. To do this, you can specify the `type` parameter (default is `"all"`) as `type="grantable"`. This will list all the ORE datastores that can be shared with other users.

```
> # List all the ORE data stores
> ore.datastore(type="all")
> # List all the ORE data stores that can be shared
> ore.datastore(type="grantable")

    datastore.name object.count size      creation.date description
  1        ORE_DS3            3 9649 2015-11-26 15:52:14        <NA>
```

This ORE datastore, called ORE_DS3, can now be shared with other users of the Oracle Database. To do so, you can use the `ore.grant` function to grant specific users access to the datastore and the objects stored within it. When you use the `ore.grant` function, you can grant all database users access to the datastore by setting the `user` parameter to NULL. Alternatively, you can list the individual users you want to have access to the datastore. This second method is recommended because it ensures controls and security on who can access the data. The following example illustrates using the `ore.grant` function to grant ORE_USER2 access to the datastore ORE_DS3. This is the recommended approach. The second command illustrates using the `ore.grant` function to give every database user access to the ORE_DS3 datastore.

```
> # Grant the ORE_USER2 database user access to the ORE_DS data store
> ore.grant("ORE_DS3", type="datastore", user="ORE_USER2")
> # Grant all database users access to the ORE_DS data store
> ore.grant("ORE_DS3", type="datastore", user=NULL)
```

In these examples, you have seen how you can create an ORE datastore, store objects in it, and share this datastore with other users in the database. If you are one of those other database users, you may want to access this data and use it for your own analysis. You have already seen an example of using the `ore.load` function to load the objects in an ORE datastore. For a shared ORE datastore, you can still use this function and add an additional parameter to specify the owner of the shared datastore. The following code example illustrates how you can examine what sharable ORE datastores you have access to. In this example, I have connected to the ORE_USER2 schema and can use the `ore.datastore` and `ore.datastoreSummary` functions to examine the shared datastores and what objects they contain. I can then use the `ore.load` function to load the objects in the ORE_DS3 datastore into a working R environment for that connection.

```
> # list all the ORE data stores I have access to
> ore.datastore(type="all")
> # list the contents of the ORE_DS3 data stores owned by the ORE_USER
> ore.datastoreSummary("ORE_DS3", owner="ORE_USER")
> # Load the objects from the ORE_DS3 data store owned by ORE_USER
> ore.load("ORE_DS3", owner="ORE_USER")
```

The `ore.revoke` function allows you to revoke access to one of your ORE datastores that has been shared with all or some of the other users in the database. The `ore.revoke` function takes the ORE datastore name, the type being a `datastore`, and the user who is being revoked access to the datastore. You can list the individual database users, or if you want to revoke access to all users you can specify the NULL value for the `user` parameter. The following example illustrates these two types of scenarios:

```
> # Revoke all access to the ORE_DS3 from all database users
> ore.revoke("ORE_DS3", type="datastore", user=NULL)
> # Revoke access to the ORE_DS3 datastore from the ORE_USER database user
> ore.revoke("ORE_DS3", type="datastore", user="ORE_USER2")
```

To delete an ORE datastore and all the objects within the ORE datastore, you use the `ore.delete` function. You saw an example of using this function earlier, but in this previous example the function was used to delete an object with an ORE datastore. To delete an ORE datastore, you need to provide its name, as shown here:

```
> ore.delete("ORE_DS")
```

Disconnecting from the Database

When you are finished working with your ORE connection, you will need to issue the `ore.disconnect` command to exit your ORE connection cleanly and disconnect from the Oracle Database. Any temporary objects created in your schema, and not explicitly saved, will be removed before your connection to the database is closed. All temporary ORE objects will have a name beginning with ORE$.

```
> ore.disconnect()
```

ORE will issue an implicit `ore.disconnect` command when you quit your R session or issue a new ORE connection using `ore.connect`.

However, if a session was abnormally disconnected—for example, the session dies or gets killed by the user, the machine hibernates, and so on—then any temporary objects that were created during your ORE session will remain as objects in the database. These objects will have an object name beginning with ORE$. You can locate these objects in your Oracle Schema using the following SQL:

```
SELECT object_name, object_type, last_ddl_time
FROM   user_objects
WHERE  object_name like 'ORE$%';
```

Summary

Oracle R Enterprise is a very powerful tool available to data analysts and data scientists where they can utilize the performance and scalability of the Oracle Database. In this chapter, we looked at some of the more common functionality available in Oracle R Enterprise to allow you to manage your connection to the database and show you how to interact with objects in the database. The functionality and the examples given in this chapter illustrate how you can quickly get up and running with your data analytics and data science projects.

In each of the following chapters, we will build upon the functionality illustrated in this chapter as we look at the more advanced capabilities of Oracle R Enterprise.

CHAPTER 4

The Transparency Layer

The transparency layer is a core feature of Oracle R Enterprise and allows data scientists to work with data in the Oracle Database in a seamless manner. The R code that a data scientist writes, when connected using Oracle R Enterprise, can use the equivalent in-database functions, thereby utilizing the computing capabilities of the Oracle Database and the database server. In this chapter, we explore some of the features of the transparency layer, how you can discover some of what is happening in the transparency layer, and some of the characteristics of objects and data types as they move from the database to the R environment.

Overview of the Transparency Layer

Over the last two chapters you saw examples of using the transparency layer, such as connecting to the database to access and process the data in various tables and views. One part of the transparency layer allows you to work with objects in your Oracle Database, such as tables and views, as if they are objects or a data frame in your local R environment. You will have seen over the last two chapters how easy it is to use ORE to seamlessly access and use the data stored in the Oracle Database. With the minimum of changes to their R programs, the data scientist can be using the data stored in an Oracle Database and using the database server as a high performance compute engine.

Over the course of the next two chapters, and even throughout this book, we will explore many more of the core features of Oracle R Enterprise and the transparency layer. For example, we will cover the various ways you can work with your database-resident data to prepare, join, and filter data; perform a variety of transformations; work with graphics; sample data; and so on. The ORE transparency layer allows the R developer to work with database-resident data as if it was in their local R environment.

Another part of the transparency layer allows you to run R functions transparently to process and analyze data in the Oracle Database, using the database as a high-performance and scalable compute engine. The database server typically has significantly more computing resources than what is available to the data scientist on their client machine. This allows the data scientist to work with significantly larger volumes of data than they would typically be able to. For example, in one company, I've seen the data scientists being able to work with data sets consisting of almost one billion records when using Oracle R Enterprise. Previously they had to spend many days processing data, sampling data, and building analytic and predictive models on subsets of the data. Now with Oracle R Enterprise they can work with the entire data set.

The major benefit of the transparency layer is that it has a number of core R packages that have been overloaded by the Oracle R Enterprise packages to translate R functions into the equivalent underlying in-database SQL functions.

These SQL functions are run on the data in the database, and the generated results are returned to the R user and displayed in R format. You will see examples in later chapters where we use algorithms that are not part of Oracle R Enterprise, but we can install these R packages and enable Oracle R Enterprise to run them.

The transparency layer does not execute each R function or the equivalent SQL function immediately. The equivalent SQL functions are accumulated. It is only when a result is required by the calling R script for display or for immediate computation that the accumulated SQL code will be executed. This allows the Oracle Database to apply its extensive range of query optimizations to the SQL to ensure optimal execution.

Figure 4-1 illustrates the type of processing that happens with the transparency later. The R aggregate function is used to summarize data in a table in the Oracle Database (1). The transparency layer then converts this into the equivalent SQL function (2). It is only when the results are required to be displayed in the R environment that the SQL will be executed in the database (3) and generate the query results (4). These results are then passed back through the transparency layer (5) to be displayed in the typical R format (6).

The transparency layer of Oracle R Enterprise contains packages that are overloaded versions of the functions in the open source R base, graphics, and stats packages. Tables and views in the Oracle Database are represented by an `ore.frame` object, and this is a subclass of the R `data.frame` object. Similarly, for other R objects there is an equivalent Oracle R Enterprise object that inherits from the R object type.

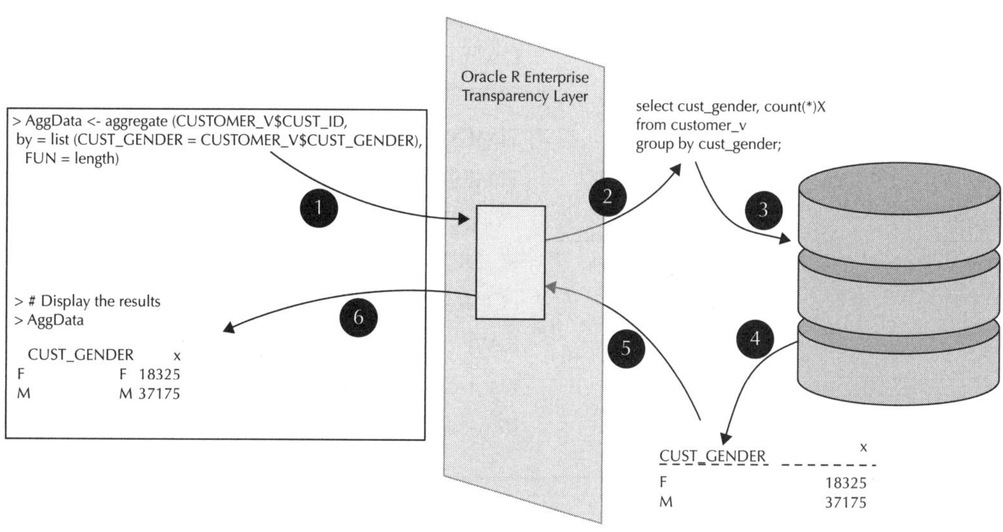

FIGURE 4-1.   *The transparency layer*

The transparency layer has a number of classes and data types that map the R data types to the data types in the Oracle Database. The transparency layer will perform the necessary mappings between the data types depending on the direction in which the data is being moved. For example, if you have an R object that is being moved to the Oracle Database, then all necessary data type conversions will be performed. This is similar for when data is being moved from the database to the local R environment. From time to time you may need to explicitly use a function to map a particular variable. Oracle R Enterprise has a number of functions that allow you to perform conversions. Table 4-1 lists the R, ORE, and SQL data type mappings.

In addition to the data types listed in Table 4-1, the transparency layer supports the use of the CLOB and BLOB Oracle data types within your local R environment.

R Data Type	ORE Data Type	SQL Data Type
Character mode vector	ore.character	VARCHAR2
		INTERVAL YEAR TO MONTH
Integer mode vector	ore.integer	NUMBER
Logical mode vector	ore.logical	The number 0 for FALSE and 1 for TRUE
Numeric mode vector	ore.number	BINARY_DOUBLE
		BINARY_FLOAT
		FLOAT
		NUMBER
Date	ore.date	DATE
POSIXct	ore.datetime	TIMESTAMP
POSIXlt		TIMESTAMP WITH TIME ZONE
		TIMESTAMP WITH LOCAL TIME ZONE
Difftime	ore.difftime	INTERVAL DAY TO SECOND
None	Not supported	LONG
		LONG RAW
		RAW
		User-defined data types
		Reference data types

TABLE 4-1. *R, ORE, and SQL Data Type Mappings*

The `ore.push` and the `ore.create` functions implicitly coerce R class types to ORE class types, and the `ore.pull` function coerces ORE class types to R class types.

When you are using R, a data.frame has an explicit order that is defined by its elements using integer indexing. When you are working with data in tables or views in an Oracle Database, the data or records do not have a defined order—this is an artifact of relational algebra. When working with Oracle R Enterprise, you can have ordered and unordered ORE data frame objects. If a table has a primary key, you can use this to define the order for the ORE data frame. This is the default ordering that is used in the `ore.sync` function. Alternatively, you can specify the attribute or attributes that define the order after the ORE data frame has been defined. Sometimes—and it really depends on if you are working with a large table— performing the ordering can be an expensive operation due to the need to order the data. You need to consider the types of functions you will be performing on the data set. Some R functions require an ordered data set and some don't. So if you are working with a large data set and the R functions do not require an ordered data set, it would be quicker to process the data set as an unordered ORE data frame.

Looking Behind the Scenes of the ORE Transparency Layer

If you have the role of DBA, data architect, or database performance expert, or any other role that involves using Oracle R Enterprise, one of the things you will be curious about is what happens in the transparency layer. One of the questions you may be asking is, "Can I see what is happening in the transparency layer?" The answer to this question is the typical IT answer to everything: "It depends!" To examine the transparency layer and see what is happening when you run your R code involves looking at two areas. The first of these areas involves seeing what information is made available to you by examining the objects created by Oracle R Enterprise. The second area involves examining what is happening in the Oracle Database.

To help us explore the transparency layer and see some of the available information, we will work through two examples. The first example involves the creation of a new object, and the second example looks at when an aggregation is performed on data in the database.

In the first example, we will look at what happens when we take an R data frame and push it to the Oracle Database. In this case, we will use the MTCARS data set that comes standard with R. If you have R installed, then you have this data set.

Why do we want to push a data frame to the Oracle Database? Well, there are lots of reasons, and most of these involve wanting to use the power of the Oracle Database server to process the data.

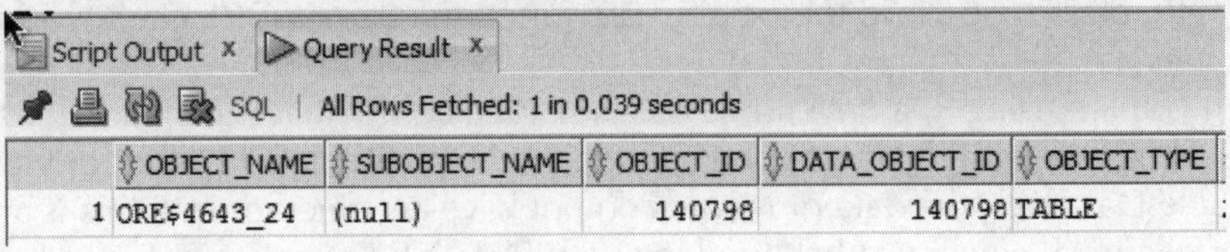

Script Output ✕   Query Result ✕

SQL | All Rows Fetched: 1 in 0.039 seconds

	OBJECT_NAME	SUBOBJECT_NAME	OBJECT_ID	DATA_OBJECT_ID	OBJECT_TYPE
1	ORE$4643_24	(null)	140798	140798	TABLE

FIGURE 4-2. *Temporary table created by the ORE transparency layer*

The following example uses the `ore.push` function to move the MTCARS data frame to the Oracle Database. The function creates a temporary table object in our schema, with a name beginning with `ORE$`, and inserts a record in the table for each row in the R data frame. This temporary table will only exist for the lifetime of our ORE session connection to the schema in the Oracle Database.

```
> cars_dataset <- ore.push(mtcars)
```

The `cars_dataset` variable is a local variable in our R session that contains an R object that serves as a proxy for the database in the table in our schema. We can check this out by looking at the class of the object, which we are told is an ore.frame:

```
> class(cars_dataset)
[1] "ore.frame" attr(,"package")
[1] "OREbase"
```

When we look in our schema for this object, we see that it has a name starting with `ORE$`. (In our current example, it is called `ORE$4643_24`.) We can use the following SQL to list objects created in our Oracle schema today (see Figure 4-2):

```
select *
from user_objects
where trunk(created) = trunk(sysdate);
```

When we query this database object using a `SELECT *` statement, we see that all the data that is in the MTCARS data set is also in this database object, `ORE$4643_24`.

When it comes to the ORE transparency layer, you may be interested in seeing what it's doing and what kind of information ORE has about this object/table in our sample schema. To view this information in our local R environment, we need to use an R function called `str`. When we use this function on the `cars_dataset` ore.frame, we get the following information:

```
> str(cars_dataset)
'data.frame':    32 obs. of  11 variables:
Formal class 'ore.frame' [package "OREbase"] with 12 slots
  ..@ .Data    : list()
```

```
  ..@ dataQry  : Named chr "( select /*+ no_merge(t) */ VAL012 NAME001,VAL013
NAME002, VAL001 ,VAL002 ,VAL003 ,VAL004 ,VAL005 ,VAL006 ,VAL007 ,VAL008 ,VAL0"|
__truncated__
  .. ..- attr(*, "names")= chr "4643_25"
  ..@ dataObj  : chr "4643_25"
  ..@ desc     :'data.frame':    11 obs. of  2 variables:
  .. ..$ name  : chr  "mpg" "cyl" "disp" "hp" ...
  .. ..$ Sclass: chr  "numeric" "numeric" "numeric" "numeric" ...
  ..@ sqlName  : Named chr  "VAL012" "VAL013"
  .. ..- attr(*, "names")= chr  "asc" ""
  ..@ sqlValue : chr  "VAL001" "VAL002" "VAL003" "VAL004" ...
  ..@ sqlTable : chr "\"ORE_USER\".\"ORE$4643_24\""
  ..@ sqlPred  : chr ""
  ..@ extRef   :List of 1
  .. ..$ :<environment: 0x000000001ba84ba8>
  ..@ names    : chr
  ..@ row.names: int
  ..@ .S3Class : chr "data.frame"
```

You'll notice here that some of the information displayed is truncated. To overcome this, we need to query each of the items individually, as shown next. These examples show you how to display the object/table name in the database, list the attribute/variable names to be used in the ORE data frame, list the data types of each attribute/variable, and finally how to query the ORE transparency layer to retrieve the data from the table in the database.

```
# What is the name of the table in the Database
> cars_dataset@sqlTable
# Get the names of the attributes/variables
> cars_dataset@desc$name
# Get the data types of the attributes/variables
> cars_dataset@desc$Sclass
# Return the SQL Query used to retrieve the data from the table in the Database
> cars_dataset@dataQry
# Display the first 5 records from the ORE table
> head(cars_dataset, 5)
```

Let's look at the last R command, where we display five records from the data set. If we want to see the query that was run in the Oracle Database, we can create a data frame for the query. The following R code shows you how to set this up to retrieve the SQL query:

```
> df <- head(cars_dataset, 5)
> df@dataQry
```

When we look inside the Oracle Database using SQL and the data dictionary views of the database, we can see the actual query that was run. The following output is what is shown in `v$sql` for when we ran this R command. When examining the query displayed by the transparency layer in our R environment, we can see it is very similar to the SQL that is displayed in `v$sql`. The main differences are due to the layout or format of the actual query.

```
with OBJ4643_25 as
( select /*+ no_merge(t) */ VAL012 NAME001,VAL013 NAME002, VAL001 ,VAL002 ,VAL003
 ,VAL004 ,VAL005 ,VAL006 ,VAL007 ,VAL008 ,VAL009 ,VAL010 ,VAL011
 from "ORE_USER"."ORE$4643_24" t  ),
OBJ4643_29 as (
       select *
       from (select * from  OBJ4643_25 order by NAME001 asc,NAME002)
       where  rownum <= 5 )
select  *  from  OBJ4643_29 t order by NAME001 asc,NAME002
```

These examples show you how to examine some of what is happening in the transparency layer of Oracle R Enterprise.

In our next example, we are going to look at the transparency layer when we run a query on a table that already exists in our Oracle schema. In this particular scenario, we will be using a view that is defined over the CUSTOMERS table in the SH schema.

```
# Aggregate the data in the CUSTOMER_V (a view based on the sh.customer table)
#   Aggregate based on each value of Customer Gender
> AggData <- aggregate(CUSTOMER_V$CUST_ID,
                    by = list(CUST_GENDER = CUSTOMER_V$CUST_GENDER),
                    FUN = length)
# Display the results
> AggData
  CUST_GENDER     x
F           F 18325
M           M 37175
```

Again, we can use the `str` function to examine each of the elements of the ORE transparency layer for this function call:

```
> str(AggData)
> AggData@dataQry
> AggData@dataObj
> AggData@desc$name
> AggData@sqlName
> AggData@sqlValue
> AggData@sqlTable
> AggData@sqlPred
> AggData@extRef
> AggData@row.names
> AggData@.Data
```

When we look at the @dataQry slot from the ORE transparency layer, we see the structure of the query it will perform in the database:

```
> AggData@dataQry
4643_39
"( select \"CUST_GENDER\" NAME001, \"CUST_GENDER\" VAL001,count(*) VAL002
from \"ORE_USER\".\"CUSTOMER_V\" where (\"CUST_GENDER\" is not null) group
by \"CUST_GENDER\" )"
```

When we look inside the Oracle Database and use the v$sql view, we see the actual query that was run to retrieve the results:

```
with OBJ4643_39 as
    ( select "CUST_GENDER" NAME001, "CUST_GENDER" VAL001,count(*) VAL002
      from "ORE_USER"."CUSTOMER_V"
      where ("CUST_GENDER" is not null) group by "CUST_GENDER" ),
OBJ4643_42 as
    ( select /*+ no_merge(t) */ 1 NAME001, count(*) VAL001 from OBJ4643_39 t  )
select   *   from   OBJ4643_42 t order by NAME001
```

Summary

The Oracle R Enterprise transparency layer is a fundamental feature of Oracle R Enterprise. It allows you to work in a seamless manner with objects and data in your Oracle Database and for this data to appear as local objects in your R environment. The transparency layer also allows you to work seamlessly with the Oracle Database as a compute engine, where most of the typical R functions you want to run on your data get translated into equivalent SQL functions, if possible. These SQL functions are then run on the data. Any results generated are then, via the transparency layer, converted into R format. If you have been following along with the examples in the previous chapters, then you have already been using the transparency layer. In the following chapters, you will see how easy it is to use and how you can benefit from using the Oracle Database and the database server.

CHAPTER 5

The Oracle R Enterprise Packages

The Oracle R Enterprise consists of a suite of R language packages that support a range of functionality that includes the transparent manipulation of database data using standard R syntax, predictive analytics, embedded R execution from R, and R script deployment with access from SQL. The transparency layer was discussed in Chapter 4. In this chapter, we have a look at the main components of the Oracle R Enterprise suite of packages, how to explore the contents of these packages so that you can find the function you require, and how to get help with using Oracle R Enterprise.

Additionally, Oracle R Enterprise comes with a suite of demonstration scripts that shows you how you can use the various capabilities available in Oracle R Enterprise. An example is given of how to use these demonstrations.

The Oracle R Enterprise Package

When you install Oracle R Enterprise, a number of R packages are installed in your R environment. These are listed in Table 5-1. These packages, when installed on the Oracle Database Server, support the running of R functions in the database using the Oracle R transparency layer that was discussed in Chapter 4, as well as predictive analytics, embedded R execution, and R script deployment from SQL.

These packages support the use of R in the Oracle Database under three main categories. These are the ORE Statistics Engine, ORE Predictive Analytics, and ORE Graphics. Underpinning all of these categories is the ability to run R in the Oracle Database by either using the transparency layer to translate an R function into a corresponding SQL function in the Oracle Database or by calling an R function using the Oracle `extproc` capability of the database to span external processes.

The Oracle R Enterprise set of packages overloads the existing statistical functions that come with the base packages in R. When we make a call to one of these functions, and if we are working with an ORE data frame where the data exists in the database, the Oracle R Enterprise version of the function will be used. The transparency layer translates the function into the underlying SQL function. This SQL function is executed and a proxy object for the results is returned to the R environment from where it was called. By using Oracle R Enterprise, you can now utilize the scalability and performance features of the Oracle Database. You are no longer constrained by the processing capabilities of the computer your data scientist is using. In Chapter 6, we look at some of the typical statistical functions that can be used on your data.

Oracle R Enterprise also gives you the capability to run in-database predictive analytics. With Oracle R Enterprise, you have the option of using the in-database data mining algorithms that are part of the Oracle Advanced Analytics, but you also have the ability to use any of the huge number of predictive analytics algorithms available in R. Oracle R Enterprise comes with a set of functions to build predictive models and to apply these models to new data. In addition to using the in-database

Package Name	Package Type	Package Description
ORE	Core	The top-level package for Oracle R Enterprise.
OREbase	Core	Corresponds to the open source R base package.
OREcommon	Core	Contains common low-level functionality for Oracle R Enterprise.
OREdm	Core	Exposes the in-database Oracle Data Mining algorithms.
OREeda	Core	Contains functions for exploratory data analysis.
OREembed	Core	Supports the embedded execution of R in the database.
OREgraphics	Core	Corresponds to the open source R graphics package.
OREmodels	Core	Contains functions for advanced analytical modeling.
OREpredict	Core	Enables scoring data in the Oracle Database using R models.
OREserver	Core	Contains functions for an Oracle R Enterprise Server.
OREstats	Core	Corresponds to the open source R stats package.
ORExml	Core	Supports XML translation between R and the Oracle Database.
arules	Supporting	Allows for frequent item sets and association rules. Provides support for representing, manipulating, and analyzing the transactional data and the patterns of the results.
Cairo	Supporting	Supports graphic rendering on Oracle Enterprise Server.
DBI	Supporting	The database interface definition for communicating between R and the Oracle database.
png	Supporting	Supports the reading and writing of PNG images for Oracle R Enterprise objects.
randomForest	Supporting	Supports the ORE implementation of randomForest.
ROracle	Supporting	The Oracle Database interface for R-based OCI.
statmod	Supporting	Provides a variety of statistical modeling functions.

TABLE 5-1.   *Oracle R Enterprise Packages*

algorithms, Oracle R Enterprise comes with a number of additional algorithms that have been specifically tuned to work with the Oracle Database. We explore the various predictive analytics algorithms that are part of Oracle R Enterprise in Chapter 7 and Chapter 8.

Another benefit of Oracle R Enterprise is the ability to use the charting and graphics capabilities of R. The Oracle R Enterprise graphics package allows us to incorporate many of these graphics into our front-end analytics tools such as Oracle Business Intelligence and BI Publisher. We explore in Chapter 13 how to incorporate the various graphics produced using Oracle R Enterprise into your analytic dashboards.

Exploring the ORE Package Functions and Package Version

In the previous section we explored the various elements of the Oracle R Enterprise packages. When it comes to working with Oracle R Enterprise in your R environment, you will want to quickly see what specific Oracle R Enterprise functions might be suitable for the task you want to complete. To help you to quickly search the available functions, you can use the R function call `apropos`.

The `apropos` function allows you to search the available list of functions and objects using a subset of a string. In our case, we would like to look for all functions that exist of the Oracle R Enterprise package. Therefore, we would search for "ore". Performing this test will only show the list of functions that are prefixed with "ore". There are many other functions available. The following example illustrates how you can use the `apropos` function and the results it returns containing the Oracle R Enterprise–specific functions:

```
> apropos("^ore")
 [1] "ore.attach"          "ore.connect"          "ore.const"
 [4] "ore.corr"            "ore.create"           "ore.crosstab"
 [7] "ore.datastore"       "ore.datastoreSummary" "ore.delete"
[10] "ore.detach"          "ore.disconnect"       "ore.doEval"
[13] "ore.drop"            "ore.esm"              "ore.exec"
[16] "ore.exists"          "ore.frame"            "ore.freq"
[19] "ore.get"             "ore.getXlevels"       "ore.getXnlevels"
[22] "ore.glm"             "ore.glm.control"      "ore.grant"
[25] "ore.groupApply"      "ore.hash"             "ore.hiveOptions"
[28] "ore.hour"            "ore.indexApply"       "ore.is.connected"
[31] "ore.lazyLoad"        "ore.lm"               "ore.load"
[34] "ore.ls"              "ore.make.names"       "ore.mday"
[37] "ore.minute"          "ore.month"            "ore.neural"
[40] "ore.odmAI"           "ore.odmAssocRules"    "ore.odmDT"
[43] "ore.odmGLM"          "ore.odmKMeans"        "ore.odmNB"
[46] "ore.odmNMF"          "ore.odmOC"            "ore.odmSVM"
```

```
[49]  "ore.predict"          "ore.pull"           "ore.pull"
[52]  "ore.pull"             "ore.push"           "ore.push"
[55]  "ore.randomForest"     "ore.rank"           "ore.recode"
[58]  "ore.revoke"           "ore.rm"             "ore.rollmax"
[61]  "ore.rollmean"         "ore.rollmin"        "ore.rollsd"
[64]  "ore.rollsum"          "ore.rollvar"        "ore.rowApply"
[67]  "ore.save"             "ore.scriptCreate"   "ore.scriptDrop"
[70]  "ore.scriptList"       "ore.scriptLoad"     "ore.second"
[73]  "ore.showHiveOptions"  "ore.sort"           "ore.stepwise"
[76]  "ore.summary"          "ore.sync"           "ore.tableApply"
[79]  "ore.toXML"            "ore.univariate"     "ore.year"
[82]  "OREShowDoc"
```

HINT
If you do not get the preceding list of functions, you probably haven't loaded the Oracle R Enterprise package. Make sure you load the ORE package before running this command using `library(ORE)`.

You can also explore each of the ORE packages listed in Table 5-1 and see all the typical R functions that have been overloaded. To access the high-level R documentation for an Oracle R package, you can use the help function or alternatively use the question mark. The following example illustrates both of these ways of accessing the help function for a package:

```
> help("OREstats")
> ?OREstats
```

To see the functions contained in a package, you can use the `ls` function. For example, the following lists all the functions contained in the OREstats package:

```
> ls("package:OREstats")
```

As you can imagine, there will be a lot of functions listed using this code. Within this list of functions you will see functions that have "ore" as part of the name. These are Oracle R Enterprise–specific functions. The other functions listed are functions from some of the base R packages that have been overloaded to work with the Oracle R Enterprise transparency layer and that allow these functions to be executed in the Oracle Database.

When you are working with Oracle R Enterprise, there are two parts to the installation of a package, as discussed in Chapter 2: the client installation and the server installation. It is important to have the same version of the Oracle R Enterprise package installed on both the client and the server. If you don't, you may end up getting some errors or inconsistencies with the behavior. To verify the version of Oracle R Enterprise installed on the client and on the server (if you are using R and ORE directly on the server), you can use the R function `packageVersion`. This function checks the currently installed version of the package that is part of your R environment:

```
> packageVersion("ORE")
 [1] '1.5'
```

To verify the version of ORE installed on the Oracle Database server, you can use the `ore.doEval` function. This function performs the commands within it on the Oracle Database server and returns the results to the R client.

```
> ore.doEval(function() packageVersion("ORE"))
```

When checking the installed version of Oracle R Enterprise on the Oracle Database server, you can also use this example, but it really depends on how R was installed on your server. To verify the version of Oracle R Enterprise installed as part of the Oracle Database, you can use SQL to verify this. The following SQL query can be run from any schema in the Oracle Database:

```
SELECT value
FROM   sys.rq_config
WHERE  name = 'VERSION';

VALUE
-----------------
1.5
```

If there is a difference in the version numbers of Oracle R Enterprise on the client or the server, then one of these platforms will need to be upgraded or downgraded.

ORE Settings and Options

When working with R, you have a large number of global environment options you can configure to suit your particular environment. You can set global environment options to fix the width that controls the maximum number of characters or columns to display on each line, to specify the number of decimal points to return for a number, and to specify the level of error reporting. For example, to set the width of the display to 100 characters and to set the number of decimal points to 5, you can use the following R code:

```
> options(width = 100)
> options(digits = 5)
```

You can examine the various global environment options settings for your
R session using the following:

```
> geo <- options()
> geo
```

When you are working with data in your Oracle Database and your R client
session, the data might be slightly altered in certain scenarios when it is mapped
between these two environments. One such scenario is working with attributes that
have a Date data type. There could be differences in the time zones being used. In
this case, you will need to define the TZ and ORA_SDTZ global environment
variables. These need to be defined before you establish your connection to the
database. If you try to set these global environment variables after you have created
your connections to the data, they will have no effect.

```
> Sys.setenv(TZ = "GMT")
> Sys.setenv(ORA_SDTZ = "GMT")
```

Oracle R Enterprise comes with the five global environment variables described
in Table 5-2. You can use these ORE-specific options to define how the data and the
query results are to be processed.

For instance, the following gives an example of setting the degree of parallelism
to eight for embedded R execution, checking the current value, and then resetting
the degree of parallelism back to the default value:

```
> # What is the current degree of parallelism
> options("ore.parallel")
 $ore.parallel
 NULL

> # Set the degree of parallelism to 8
> options(ore.parallel=8)

> # Check the that the degree of parallelism is set to 8
> options("ore.parallel")
 $ore.parallel [1]
 8

> # Set the degree of parallelism back to the default for your ORE connection
> options(ore.parallel=NULL)
```

You saw in Chapter 3 that some warning messages can be displayed when we
do not have a way of uniquely identifying each of the records. For example, when
we query the CUSTOMERS_USA table, we get a warning message saying "ORE
object has no unique key – using random order."

ORE Global Environment Variable	Description
`ore.na.extract`	The default value is FALSE. When FALSE, the NA value will result in the removal of the corresponding row or element. When TRUE, rows or elements with an NA will produce rows or elements with NA values. This is similar to how R treats missing values in data frames and vector objects.
`ore.parallel`	Allows you to specify the degree of parallelism to use for your Oracle R Enterprise session for the following commands. The default value is NULL. The degree of parallelism can be set using the following options: **N** N is the degree of parallelism. N should be a number greater than or equal to 2. **TRUE** This will use the default degree of parallelism for the database session. **NULL** This is for the database default for the operation. **FALSE** This is where no parallelism is to be used. Defaults to 1.
`ore.sep`	This is the character to be used as a separator between multiple column row names of an `ore.frame`. The default character is |.
`ore.trace`	If set to TRUE, this ensures that Oracle R Enterprise functions will print output at each iteration of the function. The default value is FALSE.
`ore.warn.order`	The default value is TRUE. This environment variable determines if Oracle R Enterprise should display warning messages when ORE objects lack certain information, such as row names, objects that need ordering, and so on. When this environment variable is set to FALSE, these warning messages are not displayed.

TABLE 5-2. *Oracle R Enterprise Global Environment Variables*

In Chapter 3, a couple of different ways were illustrated for how to handle this data. However, when you are building up your data science scripts, sometimes it is okay to have data sets with a primary key and hence sorted R objects. In this kind of scenario, you would perhaps prefer not to have these warning messages being displayed. To do this, you can use the ore.warn.order global environment option to turn off these messages, as illustrated in the following code:

```
> # Check the current value of ore.warn.order
> options("ore.warn.order")
 $ore.warn.order
 [1] TRUE


> # Display the first 4 columns for the first 6 records
> #    from the CUSTOMER_USA table
> head(CUSTOMERS_USA[,1:4])

    CUST_ID CUST_FIRST_NAME CUST_LAST_NAME CUST_GENDER
 1   43228            Abner        Everett           M
 2   47006            Abner        Everett           M
 3   12112            Abner        Everett           M
 4   16581            Abner         Kenney           M
 5   13895            Abner         Kenney           M
 6   21006            Abner         Kenney           M
Warning messages:
1: ORE object has no unique key - using random order
2: ORE object has no unique key - using random order

> # Set the ore.warn.order option to FALSE
> #    to turn off the warning messages
> options(ore.warn.order=FALSE)


> # Display the details from the CUSTOMER_USA table again
> #    This time we do not get the warning messages
> head(CUSTOMERS_USA[,1:4])

    CUST_ID CUST_FIRST_NAME CUST_LAST_NAME CUST_GENDER
 1   43228            Abner        Everett           M
 2   47006            Abner        Everett           M
 3   12112            Abner        Everett           M
 4   16581            Abner         Kenney           M
 5   13895            Abner         Kenney           M
 6   21006            Abner         Kenney           M


> # Set the value ore.warn.order back to TRUE
> options(ore.warn.order=TRUE)
```

Getting Help for ORE

When you are working with any language, there will be times when you need to get some help with a command or how to perform a certain task. The R language comes with a built-in help system. This can be accessed by using the `help` function or by placing a question mark before the function you are looking for help with. For example, the following two R commands are equivalent and will display the built-in help documentation for the function. Oracle R Enterprise provides a complete set of documentation for all the Oracle R Enterprise functions.

```
> help(ore.connect)
> ?ore.connect
```

You saw in an earlier section in this chapter how you might go about finding a possible Oracle R Enterprise function.

When you need help that is beyond what is given in this book and in the Oracle R Enterprise documentation in R, where can you go to get reliable help? Three main options are open to you. The first of these is to access the Oracle R Enterprise support that is available as part of the discussion forums on the Oracle Technology Network (OTN) Community web page. This space and other related spaces can be found under Business Intelligence | Data Warehousing. Here, you will find discussion forums for R technologies and for Oracle Data Mining. These discussion forums are a great place to get a quick response to your queries or an answer to the problems you are having because they are monitored by the relevant Oracle product development teams and by many active community members. You can access these OTN Community spaces and discussion forums at the following web address:

https://community.oracle.com/community/business_intelligence/data_warehousing/r

The second place to find information are the blogs maintained by the Oracle development teams. These give details of features, instructions on how to perform certain tasks, and updates of changes to the products with each new release. It would be worth bookmarking the following blogs or adding them to your daily news feeds:

- **Oracle R Technologies**   https://blogs.oracle.com/R/

- **Oracle Data Mining**   https://blogs.oracle.com/datamining/

The third place to find information is on each of the product web pages on the Oracle website. On the following web pages you will find the latest details about the product, as well as access to the documentation, presentations, and other documents/tutorials to help you with learning the product:

- **Oracle R Technologies**   http://www.oracle.com/technetwork/database/database-technologies/r/r-technologies/overview/index.html

- **Oracle R Enterprise**   www.oracle.com/technetwork/database/database-technologies/r/r-enterprise/overview/index.html

- **Oracle Data Mining/Oracle Advanced Analytics**   http://www.oracle.com/technetwork/database/options/advanced-analytics

ORE Demo Script

The R language comes with a number of demonstration scripts that are built into several of the R packages. Also, as you install each new R package, it would be worth checking out whether it comes with any demonstration scripts.

Oracle R Enterprise comes with an extensive set of demonstration scripts that illustrate a significant number of the features in Oracle R Enterprise. If you are new to Oracle R Enterprise, it would be worth spending some time working through these demonstrations. This allows you to quickly get an idea of the capabilities of Oracle R Enterprise. The following is the currently available list of demonstrations, and this list will probably grow with each new release of Oracle R Enterprise:

```
> demo(package="ORE")

Demos in package 'ORE':
aggregate               Aggregation
analysis                Basic analysis & data processing operations
basic                   Basic connectivity to database
binning                 Binning logic
columnfns               Column functions
cor                     Correlation matrix
crosstab                Frequency cross tabulations
datastore               Datastore operations
datetime                Date/Time operations
derived                 Handling of derived columns
distributions           Distribution, density, and quantile functions
do_eval                 Embedded R processing
esm                     Exponential smoothing method
freqanalysis            Frequency cross tabulations
glm                     Generalized Linear Models
graphics                Demonstrates visual analysis
group_apply             Embedded R processing by group
```

```
hypothesis               Hyphothesis testing functions
matrix                   Matrix related operations
nulls                    Handling of NULL in SQL vs. NA in R
odm_ai                   Oracle Data Mining: attribute importance
odm_ar                   Oracle Data Mining: association rules
odm_dt                   Oracle Data Mining: decision trees
odm_glm                  Oracle Data Mining: generalized linear models
odm_kmeans               Oracle Data Mining: enhanced k-means clustering
odm_nb                   Oracle Data Mining: naive Bayes classification
odm_nmf                  Oracle Data Mining: non-negative matrix factorization
odm_oc                   Oracle Data Mining: o-cluster
odm_svm                  Oracle Data Mining: support vector machines
pca
push_pull                RDBMS <-> R data transfer
randomForest
rank                     Attributed-based ranking of observations
reg                      Ordinary least squares linear regression
row_apply                Embedded R processing by row chunks
sampling                 Random row sampling and partitioning of an ore.frame
script
sql_like                 Mapping of R to SQL commands
stepwise                 Stepwise OLS linear regression
summary                  Summary functionality
table_apply              Embedded R processing of entire table
```

The Oracle R Enterprise demonstration scripts use some of the standard data sets that come with R. Most of these demonstration scripts use the `iris` data set, but some of the others use the `mtcars` and other data sets. You can use the following R code to get a listing of the available data sets in your installation of R:

```
> library(help="datasets")
```

To run one of the Oracle R Enterprise demonstration scripts, you need to run the demo function. This function accepts two parameters: the name of the demonstration and the name of the package. It would be useful to have a printout or a copy of the Oracle R Enterprise demonstration scripts because this will make it easier for you when you want to run several of the demonstrations.

HINT

You need to have an ORE connection open to run Oracle R Enterprise demonstration scripts. The reason for this is that these scripts will take standard R data sets and push them to the database. All the analysis that is done will be performed on the data set that is now in the database.

The following example illustrates what is demonstrated when you run the analysis demonstration script:

```
> demo("analysis", package = "ORE")

 demo(analysis)
 ---- ~~~~~~~~
Type  <Return>     to start :
> #
> #     O R A C L E   R   E N T E R P R I S E   S A M P L E   L I B R A R Y
> #
> #     Name: analysis.R
> #     Description: Demonstrates basic analysis & data processing operations
> #     The setup of a table in the database is repeated in each script
> #
> #
>
> ## Set page width
> options(width = 80)

> # Push the built-in iris data frame to the database
> IRIS_TABLE <- ore.push(iris)

> # Display the class of IRIS_TABLE
> class(IRIS_TABLE)
[1] "ore.frame" attr(,"package")
[1] "OREbase"

> # Number of unique specifies
> length(unique(iris$Species))
[1] 3

> length(unique(IRIS_TABLE$Species))
[1] 3

> # What are the unique species ?
> levels(iris$Species)
[1] "setosa"     "versicolor" "virginica"

> levels(IRIS_TABLE$Species)
[1] "setosa"     "versicolor" "virginica"

> # Alternatively..
> unique(iris$Species)
[1] setosa     versicolor virginica
Levels: setosa versicolor virginica

> unique(IRIS_TABLE$Species)
[1] setosa     versicolor virginica
Levels: setosa versicolor virginica

> # Count of observations with species = "setosa"
> nrow(iris[iris$Species == "setosa", ])
```

```
[1] 50

> nrow(IRIS_TABLE[IRIS_TABLE$Species == "setosa", ])
[1] 50

> # Count of rows where species == "setosa" and Petal.Width=0.3
> # Notice the use of a single & to represent a conjunction (AND)
> nrow(iris[iris$Species == "setosa" & iris$Petal.Width == 0.3, ])
[1] 7

> nrow(IRIS_TABLE[IRIS_TABLE$Species == "setosa" &
+                 IRIS_TABLE$Petal.Width == 0.3, ])
[1] 7

> # Exclude observations with Petal.Width > 0.3
> iris_new = iris[iris$Petal.Width <= 0.3, ]
> nrow(iris_new)
[1] 41
> class(iris_new)
[1] "data.frame"

> # On an ore.frame the result is just a logical query
> iris_new = IRIS_TABLE[IRIS_TABLE$Petal.Width <= 0.3, ]
> nrow(iris_new)
[1] 41

> # Look at the class of iris_new to confirm that it is indeed
> # a logical query
> class(iris_new)
[1] "ore.frame"
attr(,"package")
[1] "OREbase"

> # Missing is NA in R.
> # Lets count observations where Petal.Length is missing
> #
>
> nrow(iris[is.na(iris$Petal.Length), ]) [1] 0
> nrow(IRIS_TABLE[is.na(IRIS_TABLE$Petal.Length), ])
[1] 0

> # Or the other way round..
> nrow(iris[!is.na(iris$Petal.Length),])
[1] 150
> nrow(IRIS_TABLE[!is.na(IRIS_TABLE$Petal.Length), ])
[1] 150
>
```

Summary

In this chapter, we explored some of the capabilities of the Oracle R Enterprise suite of packages. These capabilities support a range of functionality, including the transparent manipulation of database data using standard R syntax, predictive analytics, embedded R execution from R, and R script deployment with access from SQL. Over the course of Chapters 3 to 5, we have explored many of the everyday features you will use with your projects that involve Oracle R Enterprise. These include how to connect to the database, how to move data to the database, how to run R functions on the data in the database, how to explore the Oracle R Enterprise packages, how to find functions in these packages, and how to get help. In the upcoming chapters we will be building on the topics covered in Chapters 3–5, and we will be exploring some of the more advanced features such as building predictive analytics models, creating Oracle R Enterprise scripts, and being able to use the full in-database embedded R execution capabilities of Oracle R Enterprise.

CHAPTER
6

Exploring Your Data

In the previous chapters of this book, you saw many examples of how you can use various Oracle R Enterprise features to explore and process your data. Some of these functions involved selecting, updating, and ordering data; creating objects; and using the in-database Oracle R Enterprise datastore. As your skills with Oracle R Enterprise evolve and you become more experienced, you will want to perform some more advanced data manipulations to help you explore and understand your data in greater detail.

This chapter covers some of the more common topics and tasks you typically perform on your data when exploring and preparing it as part of your data science projects. The topics in the following sections cover the most typical tasks. This is not an exhaustive list of tasks that you can perform with Oracle R Enterprise. However, these tasks can be used in addition to the typical R functions used as part of your exploratory data analysis and data preparation. After completing these tasks, I encourage you to explore the other functions available in Oracle R Enterprise. With each release of Oracle R Enterprise, we are going to find more and more Oracle R Enterprise functions that have been enabled to utilize the equivalent functions in the Oracle Database.

This chapter has been laid out into sections that cover what you will typically experience in your data science projects. These projects begin with some data exploration (ORE EDA functions will be shown), sampling of your data sets, creating various transformations on the data to reformat it or to generate new attributes or features, sorting and organizing the data in a variety of ways, depending on how you want to prepare it, as well as how to partition or divide the data set into a number of subpartitions and how to aggregate data. These subpartitions can be used for different purposes. For example, if you are building a classification model, you will need to create a data set for training the model and another data set for testing your model.

Exploratory Data Analysis (EDA)

The R language has a vast array of functions you can use when exploring your data. Some of these have been used in the previous chapters, and there are lots of books and websites available to you to learn about them. Instead of exploring all of the various EDA functions here, we will instead look at some of the ORE-specific functions, which are listed in Table 6-1.

In addition to the functions listed in Table 6-1, Oracle R Enterprise has, via the transparency layer, mapped most of the typical statistical functions found in the R base package and the R stat package.

The `ore.summary` function calculates descriptive statistics using a large number of statistical functions based on numerical attributes. By default, the statistical functions used include the frequency or count of nonmissing values,

ORE Function	Description
ore.corr	Used to perform correlation analysis across numeric columns.
ore.crosstab	Used to build cross-tabulations; supports multiple columns. Also allows optional aggregations, weighting, and ordering options.
ore.esm	Builds an exponential smoothing model on data in an ordered ore.vector function.
ore.freq	Using the output of the ore.crosstab function, it determines whether two-way cross-tabulation or N-way cross-tabulation tables should be used for the results.
ore.rank	Allows you to investigate the distribution of values along numeric columns.
ore.sort	Allows you to sort the data in a variety of ways.
ore.summary	Provides a series of descriptive analytics based on the data in an ORE data frame.
ore.univariate	Provides distribution analysis of numeric columns in an ORE data frame. Gives all the statistics from an ore.summary function plus signed rank test and extreme values.

TABLE 6-1.   *Oracle R Enterprise Exploratory Data Analysis Functions*

mean, minimum value, and maximum value. In addition to these statistical functions, there are many more, as listed next:

```
"n" or "freq" (Count of non-missing values)
"count" or "cnt" (Count of all observations)
"nmiss" (Count of missing values)
"mean" or "avg" (Average of values)
"min" (Minimum of values)
"max" (Maximum of values)
"css" (Corrected sum of squares)
"uss" (Uncorrected sum of squares)
"cv" (Coefficient of variation)
"sum" (Sum of values)
"sumwgt" (Weighted sum of values)
"range" (Range of values)
"stddev" or "std" (Standard deviation of values)
"stderr" or "stdmean" (Standard error for the mean)
"variance" or "var" (Variance of values)
"kurtosis" or "kurt" (Kurtosis)
"skewness" or "skew" (Skewness)
"loccount<" or "loc<" (Number of observations whose values are less than the supplied mu)
"loccount>" or "loc>" (Number of observations whose values are greater than the
supplied mu)
```

```
"loccount!" or "loc!" (Number of observations whose values are not equal to the
supplied mu)
"loccount" or "loc" (Number of observations whose values are equal to the supplied mu)
Percentiles Types: "p0", "p1", "p5", "p10", "p25" or "q1", "p50" or "q2" or "median",
"p75" or "q3", "p90", "p95", "p99", "p100"
"qrange" or "iqr" (Interquartile range, Q3-Q1)
"mode" (Most frequently occurring value)
"lclm" (Two-sided left confidence limit with confidence level of the interval equal to
0.95)
"rclm" (Two-sided right confidence limit with confidence level of the interval equal
to 0.95)
"clm" (Two-sided confidence interval with confidence level of the interval equal to
0.95)
"t" (Student's t-test statistic)
"probt" or "prt" (Two-tailed p-value for student's t-test)
```

The following example illustrates how you can use the ore.summary function at a basic level for one numeric attribute. If you want to include additional numeric attributes, you can include them in the var list.

```
> # EDA - Examples
> #
> # Use the CUSTOMERS_V data. It is in our schema in the Database
> full_dataset <- CUSTOMERS_USA
> names(full_dataset)
> # Generate the summary statistics
> ore.summary(full_dataset, var="CUST_YEAR_OF_BIRTH")

    FREQ     N    MEAN MIN  MAX
1 18520 18520 1958.838 1913 1990
```

This example illustrates how the ore.summary uses the default list of statistical functions. If you want to use some of the other functions available with ore.summary, you will need to list out all the statistical functions, as shown in the following example:

```
> ore.summary(full_dataset, var="CUST_YEAR_OF_BIRTH",
                   stats=c("n", "nmiss", "min", "max", "range", "std"))

    FREQ     N NMISS  MIN  MAX RANGE      STD
1 18520 18520     0 1913 1990    77 14.98443
```

The ore.summary function also allows you to group the calculations. Adding a grouping produces statistics for the numeric attribute based on all the values in the grouping attribute. The following example illustrates the calculation of the statistics for each of the values in the CUST_GENDER attribute. The first row of results provides the overall statistics for the CUST_YEAR_OF_BIRTH attribute.

This is the same as what we had in the previous example. Then, for rows 2 and 3, we get the statistics for the values "M" and "F" in the CUST_GENDER attribute.

```
> ore.summary(full_dataset, class="CUST_GENDER", var="CUST_YEAR_OF_BIRTH")

   CUST_GENDER  FREQ TYPE     N       MEAN  MIN  MAX
 1           F  6197    0  6197  1959.183  1913  1990
 2           M 12323    0 12323  1958.665  1913  1990
 3        <NA> 18520    1 18520  1958.838  1913  1990
```

We can add more levels to the grouping set of attributes that are listed for `class`. For each attribute listed, we will get different grouping levels. For example, if we add CUST_CITY to the class list, we will get the statistics for the males and females for each city in the data set. This is illustrated here, with a partial set of output:

```
> ore.summary(full_dataset, class=c("CUST_CITY", "CUST_GENDER"),
                  var="CUST_YEAR_OF_BIRTH", ways=2)

     CUST_CITY CUST_GENDER  FREQ TYPE    N      MEAN  MIN  MAX
 1         Opp           F    10    0   10  1963.800  1944  1983
 2         Opp           M    14    0   14  1952.357  1942  1972
 3        Alma           F    37    0   37  1958.000  1922  1986
 4        Alma           M    74    0   74  1957.257  1926  1986
 5        Earl           F    15    0   15  1958.133  1931  1984
 6        Earl           M    38    0   38  1958.342  1936  1980
 7        Elba           F    34    0   34  1962.353  1935  1985
 8        Elba           M    80    0   80  1956.575  1925  1982
 9        Gays           F    15    0   15  1959.933  1935  1983
 10       Gays           M    39    0   39  1961.359  1923  1984
 ...
```

In addition to the `ore.summary` function, the `ore.univariate` function gives us statistics for our numeric variables. Some of these additional statistics include signed rank tests, extreme values reporting, and more. Here is an example of how to use this function, along with the default statistics produced:

```
> ore.univariate(full_dataset, var="CUST_YEAR_OF_BIRTH")

        SKEW        KURT   N SUMWGT      MEAN       SUM    STDDEV       VAR          USS
CSS        CV     STDERR
 1 -29450213 -7477842093 18520  18520  1958.838  36277682  14.98402  224.5209  71066264568
4158127 0.7649443 0.1101082
```

The `ore.corr` function allows you to perform a correlation analysis on your data. The correlation analysis can include the Pearson, Spearman, and Kendall correlations on your numeric attributes. By default, the `ore.corr` function will create a Pearson correlation analysis. The following example illustrates the correlation analysis of CUST_POSTAL_CODE and CUST_CITY. In the Oracle Database table CUSTOMERS_USA, these attributes are defined with a character data type, but these are really a number value and we can remap them to numeric.

```
> # Use the CUSTOMERS_V data. It is in our schema in the Database
> full_dataset <- CUSTOMERS_USA
> # add an index to the data frame
> row.names(full_dataset) <- full_dataset$CUST_ID
> # Remap the following to numeric data type
> full_dataset$CUST_POSTAL_CODE <- as.numeric(full_dataset$CUST_POSTAL_CODE)
> full_dataset$CUST_CITY_ID <- as.numeric(full_dataset$CUST_CITY_ID)
```

You can then perform the correlation analysis using the following:

```
> # Correlation analysis using Pearson
> ore.corr(full_dataset, var="CUST_POSTAL_CODE, CUST_CITY_ID")

                ROW          COL    PEARSON_T   PEARSON_P PEARSON_DF
1 CUST_POSTAL_CODE CUST_CITY_ID -0.01246904 0.08972686      18518
```

You would expect this to be highly correlated, and this is indicated by the value under the PEARSON_P column. You can add attributes to the `var` list, and the correlation analysis of each pair of attributes will be calculated.

If you would like to perform a Spearman or Kendall correlation analysis, you can do so by changing the default value for the `stats` setting, as shown here:

```
> # Correlation analysis using Spearman
> ore.corr(full_dataset, var="CUST_POSTAL_CODE, CUST_CITY_ID", stats="spearman")

                ROW          COL SPEARMAN_T SPEARMAN_P SPEARMAN_DF
1 CUST_POSTAL_CODE CUST_CITY_ID 0.00420496  0.5671802       18518
```

The `ore.crosstab` function allows you to create some cross-tabulation analyses based on the attributes in your data set. The cross-tabulations will create a frequency count table based on the attributes you specify.

The following example shows how you can use `ore.crosstab` to create a simple frequency count of the males and females in your data set:

```
> # Use the CUSTOMERS_V data. It is in our schema in the Database
> full_dataset <- CUSTOMERS_USA
> # add an index to the data frame
> row.names(full_dataset) <- full_dataset$CUST_ID
> # Crosstab example
> ore.crosstab(~CUST_GENDER, data=full_dataset)

  CUST_GENDER ORE$FREQ ORE$STRATA ORE$GROUP
F           F     6197          1         1
M           M    12323          1         1
```

You can add any number of attributes to be included in the crosstab calculations, and you can also add different groups for the calculations. For example, suppose you want to get the calculations of the number of males and females for each age range. This is illustrated in the following example, along with a sample of the output:

```
> full_dataset$AGE <- as.numeric(format(Sys.time(), "%Y")) -
                      full_dataset$CUST_YEAR_OF_BIRTH
> # Analyze Age by Customer Gender
> ore.crosstab(AGE~CUST_GENDER, data=full_dataset)

      AGE CUST_GENDER ORE$FREQ ORE$STRATA ORE$GROUP
26|F   26           F        1          1         1
26|M   26           M        9          1         1
27|F   27           F       10          1         1
27|M   27           M       12          1         1
28|F   28           F        7          1         1
28|M   28           M       25          1         1
29|F   29           F       14          1         1
29|M   29           M       29          1         1
30|F   30           F       45          1         1
30|M   30           M       76          1         1
31|F   31           F       62          1         1
31|M   31           M       90          1         1
32|F   32           F      102          1         1
32|M   32           M      123          1         1
33|F   33           F      110          1         1
33|M   33           M      175          1         1
34|F   34           F      114          1         1
34|M   34           M      170          1         1
35|F   35           F      119          1         1
...
```

You can add attributes to be included in the cross-tabulation analysis. The following example creates two sets of outputs. The first set of output has the calculations for the Customer Age by Customer Gender values. The second set of output has the Customer City by Customer Gender values.

```
> # Analyze Age by Customer Gender and Customer City by Customer Gender
> ore.crosstab(AGE+CUST_CITY~CUST_GENDER, data=full_dataset)
```

When you're generating data using the `ore.crosstab` function, it can be useful to be able to order the data so that the output appears in ascending or descending order based on the frequency counts. The following two examples illustrate how you can put the output in ascending order (shown in the first `ore.crosstab` function call) and in descending order (shown in the second `ore.crosstab` function call):

```
> # Order the data in ascending Frequency count order
> ore.crosstab(AGE+CUST_CITY~CUST_GENDER | FREQ, data=full_dataset)
> # Order the data in descending Frequency count
> order ore.crosstab(AGE+CUST_CITY~CUST_GENDER | -FREQ, data=full_dataset)
```

The `ore.rank` function analyzes your data and calculates the distribution of the values of numeric attributes. You can specify for the ranking to be based on the entire data set, within groupings of attributes, and for the rankings to be based on percentages and percentiles.

When you use the `ore.rank` function, you can create additional attributes that capture the value calculated for the ranking. This is particularly useful if you would like to use this ranking value later in your analysis and for outputting and organizing your data on reports and dashboards.

The following examples illustrate some of the typical ways you can use the `ore.rank` function. The output listing is not included because all the records in the data set are returned. The first example of using `ore.rank` creates a new attribute in the output that is called Rank_CL to indicate the rank of the CUST_CREDIT_LIMIT values. The second example uses a `group.by` to create ranks within each of the values of the attribute CUST_CITY. The third example builds upon the previous ranking by changing it to percentage rank and dense ranking when ties occur.

```
> # EDA - ore.rank
> #
> # Use the CUSTOMERS_V data. It is in our schema in the Database
> full_dataset <- CUSTOMERS_USA
> # add an index to the data frame
> row.names(full_dataset) <- full_dataset$CUST_ID
> # Basic use of ore.rank
> head(ore.rank(full_dataset, var="CUST_CREDIT_LIMIT=Rank_CL"),50)
> # Rank based on grouping on CUST_CITY attribute
> head(ore.rank(full_dataset, var="CUST_CREDIT_LIMIT=Rank_CL", group.by="CUST_CITY",
ties="dense"),50)
> # Percentage Rank on grouping
> head(ore.rank(full_dataset, var="CUST_CREDIT_LIMIT=Rank_CL", group.by="CUST_CITY",
percent=TRUE, ties="dense"),50)
```

When processing the data set, you many want to sort it so that the records are ordered based on the ranks that have been calculated. The following example illustrates how you can create a data set that contains the original data plus the new attribute that contains the rank values. You can then use the `ore.sort` function to create an ordered data set based on the values in the rank attribute.

```
> # Create a Sorted dataset of the Ranked Data
> ranked_data <- ore.rank(full_dataset, var="CUST_CREDIT_LIMIT=Rank_CL",
                          group.by="CUST_CITY", percent=TRUE, ties="dense")
> sorted_ranked_data <- ore.sort(ranked_data, by=c("CUST_CITY", "Rank_CL"))
> head(sorted_ranked_data,30)
```

Data Sampling

When you start working with your data sets, you can easily use R to extract the data from the database and analyze this data locally on your laptop or PC. But as you venture into the Big Data world, the size of the data sets, including the number of records and the number of attributes or features, can increase dramatically. In these situations, the data sets become too large to work with on the local machine.

Traditionally with R you would extract the data to your local machine, using ROracle or RJDBC, and then create different subsets of the data locally. When working with Big Data, we need an alternative approach. With Oracle R Enterprise, we can use a variety of data sampling techniques that are executed in the Oracle Database. This is achieved by the transparency layer of Oracle R Enterprise. The typical data sampling techniques available in Oracle R Enterprise are outlined in Table 6-2.

When you use the data sampling techniques outlined in Table 6-2, the data sampling and corresponding process will occur in the Oracle Database. The resulting sampled data set will then exist in the Oracle Database, and you can access this via an ORE proxy object. You can then choose to leave the sampled data in the Oracle Database or pull the data set to your local machine.

The following examples illustrate how you can use the data sampling techniques outlined in Table 6-2. The first sampling technique we will look at is random sampling. Before you run the sampling technique, you need to set the seed value.

Sampling Technique	Description
Random	This technique takes a random sample from the input data set and creates a subset that contains a specified number of records. This method takes as input the number of records to be in the sample data set.
Stratified	This technique looks to create a randomized selection of data that is based on a particular attribute. For example, if the attribute contains the values 0 and 1, the sampled data set will have records selected in proportion to the number of records for 0 and 1 in the original data set. This is a very common technique used for creating data sets to be used in building and testing classification data mining models.
Split	You use the split sampling technique to divide your data set into a number of smaller data sets. For example, you can use this to create training and test data sets. This approach is different from the stratified sampling technique in that there is no attribute used to proportion the partitioning of the data.
Cluster	Cluster sampling allows you to base a sample of data on randomly selected groups determined by values in a certain attribute.
Systematic	Systematic sampling selects rows from the data set at regular intervals. You can also give a starting position for the first record to be selected.

TABLE 6-2.   *Data Sampling Techniques*

Although the seed value is not technically required, it is useful to set the seed value when you require repeatability with your results. The seed value is used by the random number generator to initialize its algorithm. The following example illustrates how you can create a random sample of the CUSTOMERS_V data set and generate a subset that contains a specified number of records. In this example, the CUSTOMERS_V object contains 55,500 records, and we want to create a sample data set that contains 1000 records.

```
> # Use the CUSTOMERS_V data. It is in our schema in the Database
> # Random Sampling Example
> #
> full_dataset <- CUSTOMERS_V
> # add an index to the data frame
> row.names(full_dataset) <- full_dataset$CUST_ID
> # Check the class of the object. It should be an ore.frame pointing
> #   to the object in the Database
> class(full_dataset)
 [1] "ore.frame"
 attr(,"package")
 [1] "OREbase"
> # Set the sample size
> SampleSize <- 1000
> # Create the sample data set
> sample_dataset <- full_dataset[sample(nrow(full_dataset), SampleSize), ,
                                  drop=FALSE]
> # Check to class of the sample data set. As an ore.frame object
> #   the sample data set is located in the Database. No data movement
> #   has occurred in creating it.
> class(sample_dataset)
 [1] "ore.frame"
 attr(,"package")
 [1] "OREbase"
> # Check the number of rows in the sample data set
> nrow(sample_dataset)
 [1] 1000
```

NOTE
The sampling functions require that the data sets are ordered and have an attribute defined for the ordering. If your data is from a table in your schema and your table has a primary key, this will define the ordering. When your table does not have a primary key or you are using a view, you will need to define an attribute for the ordering. This is illustrated in the preceding example using the following:

```
# add an index to the data frame
row.names(full_dataset) <- full_dataset$CUST_ID
```

After completing this example, you will have a sample data set with 1000 records randomly selected from the full data set. You can also see that the sample data set is an `ore.frame`, which means that the sample data set resides in the database, and all the work to create this data set was completed in the database via the ORE transparency layer. There was no data movement, and we used the performance and scalability features of the Oracle Database.

With stratified sampling, you are looking to produce a sample data set that is based on the values from one or more particular attributes. This is a very common sampling technique that is used with building Classification data mining models. With stratified sampling, you want the sampled data set to have the same proportions as the original data set.

The following example illustrates how to create a stratified sample set based on the proportion of values for the CUST_GENDER attribute. This example uses the same data set of CUSTOMER_V, and again it will create a sample data set of 1000 records. The data set is split into subgroups according to the value of the split attributes (CUST_GENER), and it selects a random sample from this subgroup in proportion to the number of records for that group. The output from each of these sampled subgroups is then merged using `rbind` to form an `ore.frame` object.

```
> # Stratified Sampling example
> #
> full_dataset <- CUSTOMERS_V
> # add an index to the data frame
> row.names(full_dataset) <- full_dataset$CUST_ID
> # Check the class of the object. It should be an ore.frame pointing
> #   to the object in the Database
> class(full_dataset)
 [1] "ore.frame"
 attr(,"package")
 [1] "OREbase"
> # Set the sample size
> SampleSize <- 1000
> # Calculate the total number of records in the full data set
> NRows_Dataset = nrow(full_dataset)
> # Create the Stratified data set based on using the CUST_GENER attribute
> stratified_sample <- do.call(rbind,
            lapply(split(full_dataset, full_dataset$CUST_GENDER),
            function(y) {
                NumRows <- nrow(y)
                y[sample(NumRows, SampleSize*NumRows/NRows_Dataset), , drop=FALSE]
            }))
> class(stratified_sample)
 [1] "ore.frame"
 attr(,"package")
 [1] "OREbase"
> nrow(stratified_sample)
 [1] 999
```

In this particular example, the sampled data set only contains 999 records, although we asked for 1000 records. When you are performing stratified sampling, the data set is divided and proportioned based on the values of the attribute being used. This can result in the sampled data set having a slightly smaller number than what was asked for. If you change the attribute (for example, to COUNTRY_ID), you will get a sample data set with a slightly different number of records.

With split sampling, we want to create two data sets out of the main data set. When performing split sampling, you specify the size of one of the data sets. This is done by specifying the number of records you want to have in one of the partitioned data sets. You can then assign all the other records to be in another data set. This is achieved by grouping the data.

```
> # Split Sampling
> #
> full_dataset <- CUSTOMERS_V
> # add an index to the data frame
> row.names(full_dataset) <- full_dataset$CUST_ID
> # Check the class of the object. It should be an ore.frame pointing
> #   to the object in the Database
> class(full_dataset)
 [1] "ore.frame"
  attr(,"package")
 [1] "OREbase"
> # Get number of records in full data set
> nrow(full_dataset)
 [1] 55500
> # Set the sample size to be 40% of the full data set
> #     The Testing data set will have 40% of the records
> #     The Training data set will have 60% of the records
> SampleSize <- nrow(full_dataset)*0.40
> # Create an index of records for the Sample
> Index_Sample <- sample(1:nrow(full_dataset), SampleSize)
> group <- as.integer(1:nrow(full_dataset) %in% Index_Sample)
> # Create a partitioned data set of records not selected to be in sample
> Training_Sample <- full_dataset[group==FALSE,]
> # Get the number of records in the Training Sample data set
> nrow(Training_Sample)
 [1] 33300
> # Create a partitioned data set of records who were selected to be in the sample
> Testing_Sample <- full_dataset[group==TRUE,]
> # Get the number of records in the Testing Sample data set
> nrow(Testing_Sample)
 [1] 22200
```

You can see from this example that our full data set contained 55,500 records. We set the sample size for one of the partitioned data sets to be 40 percent of this number of records. The Testing data set was created with a random selection of the records (where group==TRUE), and the remaining records were assigned to the Testing data set (where group==FALSE).

Cluster sampling allows us to create our partitioned data sets on records that are based around the randomly selected values of an attribute in our full data set. In the following example, the sampled data set is created in two steps. The first step involves creating a subset of the data based on the randomly select number of groups. In our example, this is based on a random selection of countries found in the COUNTRY_ID attribute. We randomly select three countries from all the unique values in COUNTRY_ID. The second step involves selecting random records from this subset to give to our final sample data set.

```
> # Cluster Sampling
> #
> full_dataset <- CUSTOMERS_V
> # add an index to the data frame
> row.names(full_dataset) <- full_dataset$CUST_ID
> # Set the sample size
> SampleSize <- 1000
> # Create the Clustered subset that will contain 3 randomly selected countries
> Cluster_SubSet <- do.call(rbind,
                         sample(split(full_dataset, full_dataset$COUNTRY_ID), 3))
> nrow(Cluster_SubSet)
> # Create the final Cluster Sample data set based on the Sample Size value
> Cluster_Sample <- Cluster_SubSet[sample(nrow(Cluster_SubSet), SampleSize), ,
                                   drop=FALSE]
> # Check the number of records produced and the number of distinct split values
> nrow(Cluster_Sample)
> unique(Cluster_Sample$COUNTRY_ID)
```

NOTE
You need to be careful of the value you use for the sample size. If the number of records produced by the first step of selecting data based on the attribute values is less than the final sample size, you will get an error message.

With systematic sampling, the data is sampled at regular intervals, selecting the rows that occur at the defined interval. For example, suppose you want to sample every fifth row. For this method, you need to define two variables. The first variable is the starting position to commence the sampling. The second variable is the interval setting. In the following example, the starting position is record 1000 and the interval setting is every 20 records. With this sampling technique, you do not specify the size of the sampled data set. The size of the sampled data set is based on the initial number of records, the starting position, and the interval setting.

```
> # Systematic Sampling
> #
> full_dataset <- CUSTOMERS_V
> # add an index to the data frame
> row.names(full_dataset) <- full_dataset$CUST_ID
> # Set the Starting position
> StartPosition <- 1000
> # Set the Interval setting
```

```
> IntervalSetting <- 20
> # Create the sample data set based on the Starting Position
> # and the Interval setting
> sample_dataset <- full_dataset[seq(StartPosition, nrow(full_dataset),
                                 by = IntervalSetting), , drop=FALSE]
> nrow(sample_dataset)
 [1] 2726
```

This section has explored the various data sampling techniques, as listed in
Table 6-1, that utilize the ORE transparency layer to create sampled data sets that
exist in your schema in the Oracle Database. By using these techniques, you have
zero data movement between the Oracle Database and the client machines. All the
work is performed in the Oracle Database, and thus the full scalability and
performance features of the Oracle Database are utilized.

Data Aggregation

A common task when preparing data for your data science projects is to perform
a number of calculations on the data to produce aggregate values. Common
functions include min, max, and mean, and these functions, when used with
ORE, get remapped into the Oracle Database's equivalent SQL using the ORE
transparency layer.

In addition to these common functions for producing aggregate values, you
can use the aggregate function. This function is particularly useful because
you can produce aggregated results based on different groups of attributes and
the distinct values in these attributes. In the following example, the data in our
CUSTOMERS_V ore.frame object will be aggregated, producing a count of
the number of customers from each country. The count is indicated by setting
FUN = length.

```
> # Aggregating Data
> AggData <- aggregate(full_dataset$CUST_ID,
                       by = list(COUNTRY_ID = full_dataset$COUNTRY_ID),
                       FUN = length)
> AggData
> # sort the Aggregated Data in ascending order
> ore.sort(data = AggData, by = "x")
> # sort the Aggregated Data in descending order
> ore.sort(data = AggData, by = "x", reverse = TRUE)
       COUNTRY_ID      x
 52769     52769    597
 52770     52770   7780
 52771     52771    712
 52772     52772   2010
 52773     52773    403
```

```
52774        52774     831
52775        52775     832
52776        52776    8173
52777        52777     383
52778        52778    2039
52779        52779    3833
52782        52782     624
52785        52785     244
52786        52786     708
52787        52787      75
52788        52788      91
52789        52789    7557
52790        52790   18520
52791        52791      88
```

You can use this aggregated data in a variety of ways, including creating additional attributes in your data set, performing additional calculations, and in turn adding these newly created values as attributes to the data set. For example, you can very quickly create a new set of attributes by pivoting the data, converting rows to columns.

In the example just given, the aggregation was based on one particular attribute. When you get into more complex levels of aggregation, you will want to aggregate by more than one attribute. In the following example, this is shown by having an addition item in the by list of the aggregate function:

```
> AggData2 <- aggregate(full_dataset$CUST_ID,
                     by = list(COUNTRY_ID = full_dataset$COUNTRY_ID,
                          CUST_GENDER = full_dataset$CUST_GENDER),
                     FUN = length)
> AggData2
> # sort the Aggregated Data in by CUST_GENDER and then the count value
> ore.sort(data = AggData2, by = c("CUST_GENDER", "x"))
```

In addition to the aggregate function, Oracle R Enterprise has a number of windowing-type functions. With these windowing-type functions, you can perform a calculation based on a predetermined number of records. With windowing, the calculation will only be for the records that fall within the window range. When the window moves to the next set of records, the calculation will be performed again. This continues until all the records in the data set have been covered.

Oracle R Enterprise has a specific set of functions that can allow you to perform these kinds of windowing functions. These ORE functions are prefixed with "ore.roll" and are listed in Table 6-3.

When you call one of these ore.roll functions, you need to pass in an ordered ore.frame and the attribute that contains the value for the calculation and the size of the window. The calculation will be performed only on the values within the window of selected records. The following illustrates how you can

Function	Description
ore.rollmax	Performs a rolling maximum calculation for the rolling window
ore.rollmean	Performs a rolling mean calculation for the rolling window
ore.rollmin	Performs a rolling minimum calculation for the rolling window
ore.rollsd	Performs a rolling standard deviation calculation for the rolling window
ore.rollsum	Performs a rolling sum calculation for the rolling window
ore.rollvar	Performs a rolling variance calculation for the rolling window

TABLE 6-3. *ORE Windowing Functions*

calculate the mean value of CREDIT_LIMIT from CUSTOMERS_V with a window size of 5:

```
> # Rolling calculations
> x <- ore.rollmean(full_dataset$CUST_CREDIT_LIMIT, 5)
> head(x)

[1] 6833.333 5500.000 4700.000 3200.000 1500.000 1800.000
```

These ore.roll functions are particularly useful when you are working with time series data.

Data Transformations

When exploring your data, you will regularly want to create some additional attributes. These new attributes will be used to store values of some common calculations, to store newly generated values based on defined rules, and to combine or add attributes from another data set. A sizable number of possible data transformations can be applied to your data. It would be impossible to include examples of all of these in this book. Lots of books and websites go into lots of detail on these tasks.

The aim of this section is to illustrate to you some of the more common tasks you can use on your data, and particularly those that utilize the ORE transparency layer. These tasks include creating derived attributes that are based on other attributes in the data set, creating binned data based on defined business rules, and how to combine multiple data sets that are ORE data frame objects pointing to objects in the Oracle Database.

Derived Attributes

A derived attribute is created based on some calculation or transformation that is applied to one or more of the attributes in your data set. The aim is to generate a new attribute that will contain a value that is used as part of your data science project. Instead of calculating these values each time you perform your analytics, you can instead create them once and then have them available for the next time you want to use them. These new derived attributes will become part of your data set (in the `ore.frame` object) and can be saved as a table in your schema or as an object in your ORE datastore.

When using R, you have a number of ways to go about creating new attributes that are based on some of the other attributes in the data set. These attributes can contain values that are based on some of the wide variety of statistical and mathematical functions available in R, or values defined based on some subsetting. The following example illustrates the creation of three attributes. The data set is based on the PRODUCTS_V object that was created back in Chapter 3. In this example, a new attribute is created to store a tax rate, a second attribute to store the tax amount based on the product price, and a third attribute to store the product price including the tax amount:

```
> # Adding Derived Attributes
> products <- PRODUCTS_V
> class(products)
> # Add the following Tax related values to the products ORE data frame
> products$TAX <- 0.21
> products$TAX_AMT <- products$PROD_LIST_PRICE * products$TAX
> products$PROD_TOTAL_PRICE <- products$PROD_LIST_PRICE + products$TAX_AMT
> # List the attributes and display the first 6 records.
> names(products)
> head(products)
```

When you view the data set, you will find that the new attributes have been added to the end of the data set. You can now easily use these new values in your various analytics.

Alternatively, you could use the `transform` function, which allows you to group together a number of transformations into one function call. Using the same calculations from the previous example, the following code example uses the `transform` function to perform the exact same operations:

```
> products <- PRODUCTS_V
> # Adding Derived Attributes using the Transform function
> products <- transform(PRODUCTS_V,
                  TAX = 0.21,
                  TAX_AMT = PROD_LIST_PRICE * 0.21,
                  PROD_TOTAL_PRICE = (PROD_LIST_PRICE * 0.21) + PROD_LIST_PRICE)
> # List the attributes and display the first 6 records.
> names(products)
> head(products)
```

You can see that this example has less code, and depending on your background, you will see advantages or disadvantages in using either of these approaches—or perhaps you have your own preferred method.

What these examples illustrate is that the data set resides in the Oracle Database. There is no data movement from the Oracle Database to the client machine, and all the data transformations are applied and stored in the Oracle Database.

Binning Attributes

Using a technique similar to the one just shown, we can look at adding binning to our data transformations. Binning allows us to group together certain values or ranges of values of an attribute and assign each group a defined value or label. We can use this to produce different categories, which allows us to perform our analytics on these categories in a more meaningful way than looking at a large range of values.

The following example illustrates how we can transform values into binned values. The customer data contained in the CUSTOMERS_V `ore.frame` will be examined and a new attribute will be created that assigns the customers to one of the age ranges, as defined by the following rules:

when age between 0 and 18 then 'Too Young'

when age between 19 and 54 then 'Adult'

when age between 55 and 64 then 'Pension Planners'

when age between is 65 or higher then 'Pensioner'

Just like the previous examples, there can be many different ways to do this. The following example illustrates how we can create a new attribute that contains the binned values. This involves defining a function to perform an age calculation, and then the `transform` function is used to create the new attribute.

```
> # Binning - Bin Age into categories
> customers <- CUSTOMERS_V
> # Determine the current year in YYYY format and convert to numeric data type
> current_year <- as.numeric(format(Sys.time(), "%Y"))
> # Function to calculate the age difference based on the years.
> age_diff <- function(x,y) {
               x-y
             }
> # Add the new attribute with the binned values
> customers <- transform(customers,
  AGE_BIN = ifelse(age_diff(current_year, CUST_YEAR_OF_BIRTH) >= 65, 'Pensioner',
     ifelse(age_diff(current_year, CUST_YEAR_OF_BIRTH) >= 55, 'Pension Planner',
     ifelse(age_diff(current_year, CUST_YEAR_OF_BIRTH) >= 19, 'Adult', 'Too Young'
))))
> head(customers, 50)
```

Combining Data

After working with your various data sets, at some point you will want to merge these data sets into one data set to be your main data set for analysis. You can use the `merge` function to combine two data sets. The `merge` function takes the names of the two data sets or ORE data frames, the join attribute from the first data set, and the join attribute from the second data set. This is a bit like specifying the WHERE clause of a SQL SELECT statement. The `merge` function adds the attributes of the second data set to the attributes of the first data set. The join attribute from the second data set is not included in the merged data set.

In the following example, we want to enrich the customer data set to have the geographic region that the customer's home country belongs to. The attribute that contains this information is in the COUNTRY_REGION attribute of COUNTRIES_V. The first step is to create an ORE data frame that consists of the COUNTRY_ID and COUNTRY_REGION attributes. The COUNTRY_ID region attribute is needed to perform the join with our customer data set.

```
> # Combining Data
> # create a subset of the COUNTRIES_V data to primary key and one attribute
> country_regions <- COUNTRIES_V[, c("COUNTRY_ID","COUNTRY_REGION")]
> # Merge the 2 data sets. This will add the COUNTRY_REGION attribute
> #  to our countries data set
> customers <- merge(customers, country_regions, by.x="COUNTRY_ID", by.y="COUNTRY_ID")
> head(customers)
```

The following listing is a subset of what is displayed when the last statement in the preceding code is run—that is, `head(customers)`. You will see that the COUNTRY_REGION attribute is now part of the merged data set.

```
  CUST_VALID    AGE_BIN COUNTRY_REGION
1          I      Adult         Europe
2          A      Adult         Europe
3          I  Pensioner         Europe
4          I      Adult         Europe
5          I  Pensioner       Americas
6          A  Pensioner           Asia
...
```

Sorting Your Data

One of the final steps you may perform on your data is to organize it so that the records are listed in a particular order. This may involve ordering by one particular attribute—for example, when sorting data for time series analysis. When sorting data, you can use any combination of attributes from the data set, and you can specify if the data should be sorted in ascending or descending order.

The following code example illustrates some of the various ways you can sort your data:

```
> # Sorting Data
> ?ore.sort
> # Sort the data set by COUNTRY_REGION (in ascending order by default)
> ore.sort(data = customers, by = "COUNTRY_REGION")

> # Sort the data by COUNTRY_REGION in descending order
> ore.sort(data = customers, by = "COUNTRY_REGION", reverse=TRUE)

> # Sort the data set by COUNTRY_REGION and AGE_BIN
> ore.sort(data = customers, by = c("COUNTRY_REGION","AGE_BIN"))

> # Sort the data by COUNTRY_REGION ascending and by CUST_YEAR_OF_BIRTH in descending
order
> #  You will notices a different way for indicating Descending order. This is to be
used
> #    when sorting your data using a combination of 2 or more attributes.
> cust_sorted <- ore.sort(data = customers, by = c("COUNTRY_REGION","-CUST_YEAR_OF_
BIRTH"))

> # Sorted data is stored in an ORE data frame called 'cust_sorted'
> #   This allows you to perform additional data manipulations on the data set
> #  The following displays 3 of the attributes from the sorted data set
> head(cust_sorted[,c("AGE_BIN","COUNTRY_REGION","CUST_YEAR_OF_BIRTH")], 20)
```

Summary

Exploring your data to gain additional insights is a very important part of any data science project. Additionally, you will need to modify and process your data in a variety of ways. In this chapter, most of the typical Oracle R Enterprise–specific functions have been explored with examples of how you can use these functions to process the data that is still resident in your Oracle Database. You will use a combination of these functions, along with your typical R functions, for exploring and preparing your data, particularly with preparing your data for input to more advanced analytical functions and algorithms.

CHAPTER 7

Building Models Using ODM Algorithms

Oracle R Enterprise and Oracle Data Mining together form the Oracle Advanced Analytics option for the Oracle Database Enterprise Edition. Oracle Data Mining provides a suite of data mining algorithms that are built into the Oracle Database. Typically you will access and use the Oracle Data Mining algorithms using the GUI that comes with SQL Developer or by using the PL/SQL packages and the SQL functions. Oracle R Enterprise has made these in-database data mining algorithms available to the user via a set of R functions. These functions are part of the OREdm R package that is part of Oracle R Enterprise.

In this chapter, examples will be given on how you can use the Oracle Data Mining algorithms using the Oracle R Enterprise set of functions, including how to build models, how to test models, and how to score new data with these models, all using R code. The last section of this chapter looks at how you can persist these data mining models to allow you to reuse them at a later time.

Oracle Data Mining

The Oracle Advanced Analytics option comprises Oracle Data Mining and Oracle R Enterprise. Oracle Data Mining contains a suite of advanced data mining algorithms that are embedded in the database to allow you to perform advanced analytics on your data. The data mining algorithms are integrated into the kernel of the Oracle Database and operate natively on data stored in database tables. This removes the need for extraction or transfer of data into stand-alone mining/analytic servers, as is typical with most data mining applications. This can significantly reduce the time frame of data mining projects by having near-zero data movement.

In addition to the suite of data mining algorithms, which are listed in Table 7-1, Oracle has a variety of interfaces you can apply to use these algorithms. These interfaces include PL/SQL packages that allow you to build and apply models to new data, a variety of SQL functions for real-time scoring of data, and the Oracle Data Miner tool, which provides a graphical workflow interface for creating your data mining projects.

The data sets used in this chapter are the sample data sets installed when you set up and configure the Oracle Data Miner GUI using SQL Developer. The quickest and simplest way to set up this sample data is to create an Oracle Data Miner connection in SQL Developer. A number of database views will be created that select data from the SH schema. Some tables will also be created that contain sample data. When setting up and configuring an Oracle Data Miner connection using SQL Developer, you will need the SYS password. You may require the assistance of your Oracle DBA when performing this step.

All Oracle schemas that are set up and configured to use Oracle Data Mining will have the necessary database privileges to connect to the Oracle Database using Oracle R Enterprise. See Chapter 14 for details of what database privileges a schema requires in order to use Oracle R Enterprise.

Data Mining Technique	Data Mining Algorithms
Anomaly Detection	One-Class Support Vector Machine
Association Rule Analysis	Apriori
Attribute Importance	Minimum Description Length
Classification	Decision Tree
	Generalized Linear Model
	Naïve Bayes
	Support Vector Machine
Clustering	Expectation Maximization
	k-Means
	Orthogonal Partitioning Clustering
Feature Extraction	Non-Negative Matrix Factorization
	Singular Value Decomposition
	Principal Component Analysis
Regression	Generalized Linear Model
	Support Vector Machine

TABLE 7-1.   *Data Mining Algorithms Available in Oracle Data Mining*

The ODM Algorithms Available in ORE

Oracle R Enterprise has exposed most of the Oracle Data Mining algorithms API functions. These functions begin with `ore.odm` and include the name of the algorithm or an acronym for the algorithm as part of their name.

Table 7-2 lists the different Oracle Data Mining algorithms that have been made available in the OREdm package that is part of Oracle R Enterprise.

The model and associated objects you create using the OREdm package are transient or temporary objects in the Oracle Database and do not persist past the R session they are built in. If you would like the model and objects to persist for reuse at a later time, you will need to explicitly save the model and objects in an ORE datastore. An example of saving a model is given later in this chapter in section "Saving Your Data Mining Models."

Automatic Data Preparation in Oracle Using the OREdm Package

With all data mining algorithms, you need to perform some data cleaning and data transformations. This is to prepare the data for input to the data mining algorithm.

ODM Algorithm	Description
`ore.odmAI`	Uses the Minimum Description Length algorithm to generate Attribute Importance.
`ore.odmAssocRules`	Uses the Apriori algorithm to perform Association Rule Analysis.
`ore.odmDT`	Uses the Decision Tree algorithm to create a classification model.
`ore.odmGLM`	Uses the Generalized Linear Model algorithm to create either a classification or regression model.
`ore.odmKMeans`	Uses the k-Means algorithm to create a clustering model.
`ore.odmNB`	Uses the Naïve Bayes algorithm to create a classification model.
`ore.odmNMF`	Uses the Non-Negative Matrix Factorization algorithm for Feature Extraction.
`ore.odmOC`	Uses the Orthogonal Partitioning Cluster algorithm to create a clustering model.
`ore.odmSVM`	Uses the Support Vector Machine algorithm to create a classification or regression model.

TABLE 7-2.   *The In-database Oracle Data Mining Algorithms Available in the OREdm Package*

Some algorithms may require data to be prepared in a particular way. With the in-database data mining algorithms in the Oracle Database, which are part of Oracle Data Mining, Oracle has built a lot of the necessary processing into the database, and the required data transformations are automatically performed on the data. This reduces the amount of time you need to spend on preparing the data for data mining and frees up this time for you to concentrate on your data mining project and its goals. Oracle Data Mining calls this *Automatic Data Preparation (ADP)*.

During the building of a model, Oracle takes the specific data transformations that each algorithm requires and applies them to the input data. In addition to these embedded data transformations, you can supplement these with additional transformations of your own, or you can choose to manage all the transformations yourself by turning ADP off.

Automatic Data Preparation (ADP) looks at the requirements of each algorithm and the input data set and applies the necessary data transformations, which may include binning, normalization, and outlier treatment.

Table 7-3 summarizes the Automatic Data Preparation (ADP) that is performed for each algorithm.

Algorithm	What Automatic Data Preparation Is Performed
Apriori	No ADP transformations are performed.
Decision Tree	The Decision Tree algorithm determines what ADP data transformations are necessary.
GLM	Numerical attributes are normalized with outlier-sensitive normalization.
k-Means	Numerical attributes are normalized with outlier-sensitive normalization.
MDL	All attributes are binned with supervised binning.
Naïve Bayes	All attributes are binned with supervised binning.
NMF	Numerical attributes are normalized with outlier-sensitive normalization.
O-Cluster	Numerical attributes are binned with a specialized form of equal-width binning, which computes the number of bins per attribute automatically. Numerical columns with all nulls or a single value are removed.
Support Vector Machines	Numerical attributes are normalized with outlier-sensitive normalization.

TABLE 7-3.   *Automatic Data Preparation for Oracle Data Mining Algorithms*

When using the Oracle R Enterprise functions to call the Oracle Data Mining algorithms, you will have a parameter setting called `auto.data.prep`. In most of the function calls, this parameter is set to a default value of TRUE. In others, it will be set to FALSE. You need to check and verify this `auto.data.prep` parameter for each of the ORE Oracle Data Mining functions.

Building Models and Scoring Data Using the OREdm Package

The OREdm R package that is part of Oracle R Enterprise provides a series of functions that allows you to use the in-database Oracle Data Mining algorithms. These in-database algorithms are built into the kernel of the Oracle Database and utilize all the performance and scalability features of the database.

Most of the Oracle Data Mining algorithms are available via R functions using Oracle R Enterprise. In this section, examples are given of how you can use these algorithms to explore your data, build models, test your models, and score new data with these models.

Attribute Importance

The `ore.odmAI` function can be used to determine Attribute Importance. It uses the in-database algorithm Minimum Description Length (MDL) to determine the relative importance of each attribute for a defined target attribute. Attribute Importance can be used to explore your data and will typically be used during exploratory data analysis and dimensional reduction. Attributes are ranked according to their significance in predicting the target attribute. Any attribute with a positive value will be the most interesting to you. Any attribute with a negative or zero value indicates that it does not have any relationship with the target attribute.

Here is the syntax of the `ore.odmAI` function:

```
> ore.odmAI (formula,
             data,
             auto.data.prep = TRUE,
             na.action=na.pass)
```

There are two core parameters for the `ore.odmAI` function. The first parameter is the formula used to identify the target attribute and to specify what attributes will be used. The second parameter is the data set that will be an `ore.frame` that points to the table or view in the Oracle schema that contains the data you want to analyze. The following example illustrates how to use the `ore.odmAI` function on a view in the Oracle schema and the output produced by the function:

```
> # Attribute Importance
> ?ore.odmAI()
> ore.odmAI(AFFINITY_CARD ~., MINING_DATA_BUILD_V)

  Call: ore.odmAI(formula = AFFINITY_CARD ~ ., data = MINING_DATA_BUILD_V)
  Importance:             importance rank
  HOUSEHOLD_SIZE          0.15894540    1
  CUST_MARITAL_STATUS     0.15816584    2
  YRS_RESIDENCE           0.09405210    3
  EDUCATION               0.08626079    4
  AGE                     0.08490351    5
  OCCUPATION              0.07520934    6
  Y_BOX_GAMES             0.06303995    7
  HOME_THEATER_PACKAGE    0.05645872    8
  CUST_GENDER             0.03526474    9
  BOOKKEEPING_APPLICATION 0.01920475   10
  CUST_ID                 0.00000000   11
  COUNTRY_NAME            0.00000000   11
  CUST_INCOME_LEVEL       0.00000000   11
  BULK_PACK_DISKETTES     0.00000000   11
  FLAT_PANEL_MONITOR      0.00000000   11
  PRINTER_SUPPLIES        0.00000000   11
  OS_DOC_SET_KANJI        0.00000000   11
```

When you examine the output produced by the `ore.odmAI` function, you see that the last seven attributes listed contain a zero value for importance and have the same rank. These attributes can be ignored in the data set because, based on the MDL algorithm, they do not contribute toward predicting the target attribute. Using this function and the algorithm helps users to quickly explore our data as part of our feature-reduction exercise.

The `ore.odmAI` function has two additional parameters. The first of these is `auto.data.prep`. This uses the Automatic Data Preparation (ADP) feature that is part of the Oracle Advanced Analytics option, which was discussed earlier in this chapter. It is advisable that you leave the parameter with the default value of TRUE. The second additional parameter is `na.action`, which is used to specify how missing data should be handled. The default value is `na.pass`, and this allows missing values to be included in the data set. If this parameter is set to `na.omit`, it will remove rows with missing values from the data set when executing `ore.odmAI`.

The `ore.odmAI` function and the underlying MDL algorithm are only used to explore the data set. There is no model produced, and it cannot be reused on another data set.

Association Rule Analysis

Association Rule Analysis is an unsupervised data mining technique that looks for frequent item sets in your data. This data mining technique is often used in the retail sector to discover what products are frequently purchased together. A traditional example used to illustrate Association Rule Analysis is that bread and milk are two products that are typically purchased together in a grocery store. As mentioned, this type of data mining is very common in the retail sector and is sometimes referred to as Market Basket Analysis. By analyzing what products previous customers have bought, we can then prompt a new customer with products they might be interested in. For example, every time you look at a product (such as a data mining book on a book website), you are presented with a list of other products that previous customers bought, in addition to the product you are looking at. By using Association Rule Analysis, you can start to answer questions about your data and the patterns that may exist in the data.

For Association Rule Analysis, you can use the `ore.odmAssocRules` function. This function uses the Apriori algorithm that is embedded in the Oracle Database as part of the Oracle Advanced Analytics option. The `ore.odmAssocRules` function has the following syntax and default values:

```
> ore.odmAssocRules(formula,
        data,
        case.id.column,
        item.id.column = NULL,
        item.value.column = NULL,
```

```
    min.support = 0.1,
    min.confidence = 0.1,
    max.rule.length = 4,
    na.action = na.pass)
```

The data set you use for Association Rule Analysis needs to consist of
transactional records, and the algorithm will look at the co-occurrence of items
(or in the following example, products). First, you need to construct the input data
set. This is done by creating a view over the transactional data, creating a single
attribute as the identifier of each record and product name. This information is then
passed into the ore.odmAssocRules function along with the values for the
Support and Confidence measures. You many need to spend some time adjusting
these measures. If you set them too high, you will get too few or no association rules
being produced, whereas if you set them too low, you will end up getting way too
many rules being produced. The following code example illustrates the generation
of an Association Rule Analysis model for data that comes from the SH schema:

```
> # Association Rule Analysis
> ?ore.odmAssocRules()
> # Build an Association Rules model using ore.odmAssocRules
> ore.exec("CREATE OR REPLACE VIEW AR_TRANSACTIONS
      AS
      SELECT s.cust_id || s.time_id  case_id,
             p.prod_name
      FROM   sh.sales s,
             sh.products p
      WHERE s.prod_id = p.prod_id")
> # You need to sync the meta data for the newly created view to be visible in
> #  your ORE session
> ore.sync()
> ore.ls()
> # List the attributes of the AR_TRANSACTION view names(AR_TRANSACTIONS)
> # Generate the Association Rules model
> ARmodel <- ore.odmAssocRules(~., AR_TRANSACTIONS, case.id.column = "CASE_ID",
           item.id.column = "PROD_NAME", min.support = 0.06, min.confidence = 0.1)
> # List the various pieces of information that is part of the model
> names(ARmodel)
> # List all the information about the model summary(ARmodel).
> summary(ARmodel)
> # To examine the individual elements of the model
> ARmodel$name
> ARmodel$settings
> ARmodel$attributes
> ARmodel$inputType
> ARmodel$formula
> ARmodel$extRef
> ARmodel$call
```

When setting up the parameters for the `ore.odmAssocRules` function, you need to be careful of what values you use for `min.support` and `min.confidence`. The default values for both of these is 0.1. You may need to run the `ore.odmAssocRules` function a number of times with different values, particularly for `min.support`. The higher the value for `min.support`, the fewer the number of association rules produced. Similarly, the lower the value for `min.support`, the greater the number of association rules produced. In the example just given, `min.support` is set to 0.06, which is lower than the default value. At this setting, the Association Rule Analysis model produces 42 rules, and these are the top association rules that match the values set for `min.support` and `min.confidence`. Depending on the number of association rules you want to produce for your scenario, you need to run the `ore.odmAssocRules` function several times, adjusting these values for each run, until you are producing approximately the number of association rules you need for your analysis.

The following illustrates the output of the Association Rule Analysis model and the contents of the `ore.odmAssocRules` object when you use the `summary` function:

```
> summary(ARmodel)
Call:
    ore.odmAssocRules(formula = ~., data = AR_TRANSACTIONS, case.id.column = "CASE_ID",
        item.id.column = "PROD_NAME", min.support = 0.06, min.confidence = 0.1)

Settings:
                                value
asso.min.confidence              0.1
asso.min.support                 0.06
odms.item.id.column.name prod.name
prep.auto                        off

Rules:
    RULE_ID NUMBER_OF_ITEMS                                 LHS                                        RHS     SUPPORT CONFIDENCE
1        38               2          CD-RW, High Speed Pack of 5   CD-R with Jewel Cases, pACK OF 12 0.06122021  0.9064860
2        38               2 CD-R, Professional Grade, Pack of 10   CD-R with Jewel Cases, pACK OF 12 0.06122021  0.9064860
3        37               2     CD-R with Jewel Cases, pACK OF 12          CD-RW, High Speed Pack of 5 0.06122021  0.8566820
4        37               2 CD-R, Professional Grade, Pack of 10          CD-RW, High Speed Pack of 5 0.06122021  0.8566820
5        39               2          CD-RW, High Speed Pack of 5 CD-R, Professional Grade, Pack of 10 0.06122021  0.8412211
6        39               2     CD-R with Jewel Cases, pACK OF 12 CD-R, Professional Grade, Pack of 10 0.06122021  0.8412211
7        10               1                          Music CD-R   CD-R with Jewel Cases, pACK OF 12 0.06349073  0.8407031
8        26               1         O/S Documentation Set - French      O/S Documentation Set - English 0.06028406  0.8379297
9        27               1 CD-R, Professional Grade, Pack of 10   CD-R with Jewel Cases, pACK OF 12 0.07146201  0.8279909
10       22               1          CD-RW, High Speed Pack of 5   CD-R with Jewel Cases, pACK OF 12 0.07277541  0.8268773
...
```

When working with these in-database data mining models, you can extract their results to your local R client environment. This allows you to use some of the existing packages that are available for examining the data. For example, with the Association Rule Analysis model created earlier, you can extract the association rules from the `ore.rules` object for the model as well as the item sets from the `ore.itemsets` object for the model. These objects are produced by the model, and they use the functionality available in other R packages to examine and analyze this data in more detail. The following example illustrates how you can use some of the functions available in the arules R package to inspect the association rules and item sets:

```
> library(arules)
> # Extract the Association Rules to local client and inspect the rules
> local_ARrules <- ore.pull(rules(ARmodel))
> inspect(local_ARrules)
> # extract a subset of the Association Rules
> rules1 <- subset(rules(ARmodel), min.confidence=0.7, orderby="lift")
> rules1

> # Extract the Itemsets to local client and inspect
> local_ARitemsets <- ore.pull(itemsets(ARmodel))
> inspect(local_ARitemsets)
> # extract a subset of the itemsets
> itemsets1 <- subset(itemsets(ARmodel), min.support=0.12)
> itemsets1
```

Decision Tree

Decision Tree is a very popular technique for building a model for classification-type problems. Classification is a supervised data mining technique that takes a data set of pre-labeled data and builds a classification model using defined algorithms. The pre-labeled data set is called the *Training data set,* which consists of the data for which we already know the outcome. For example, if we want to run a customer churn analysis, we would take all our customers who have registered up to a certain date. We can write some code that can easily determine which of these customers have remained as customers (that is, they are still active) and those customers who are no longer active customers (that is, they have left). We will create a new attribute for each customer; this attribute is typically called the *target attribute.* It is this target variable that contains the label (0 or 1) used by the classification algorithm to build models. We can then use one of these models to score a new group of customers and determine which ones are likely to stay and which ones will leave (churn). This process is commonly referred to by the following:

We learn from the past to predict the future.

A number of algorithms are available in Oracle R Enterprise that can be used for classification problems. The examples shown in this section illustrate how you can build a Decision Tree data mining model using the `ore.odmDT` function.

The first step in building a classification data mining model is to prepare the data input for the data mining algorithm. This may require you to integrate data from various sources, perform a variety of data transformations on the data, and decide how to handle missing data, generate additional attributes, and so on. When your data is ready, you can then input it to the data mining algorithm. The following code example uses the DATA_MINING_BUILD_V and the DATA_MINING_APPLY_V view objects that are part of the Oracle Data Mining sample data.

For the Decision Tree, you can use the `ore.odmDT` function. This function uses the in-database Decision Tree algorithm that is embedded in the Oracle Database. The `ore.odmDT` function has the following syntax and default values:

```
> ore.odmDT(formula,
            data,
            auto.data.prep = TRUE,
            cost.matrix = NULL,
            impurity.metric = "gini",
            max.depth = 7,
            min.rec.split = 20,
            min.pct.split = 0.1,
            min.rec.node = 10,
            min.pct.node = 0.05,
            na.action = na.pass)
```

As mentioned earlier, you need two different data sets. One of these will be used for building or training the Decision Tree model and another data set for testing the Decision Tree model. Data sampling was covered in Chapter 6, and the following example uses the split sampling technique illustrated in Chapter 6 to create the Training and Testing data sets:

```
> # Create the Training and Test data sets using Split Sampling
> full_dataset <- MINING_DATA_BUILD_V
> # add row indexing to the data frame
> row.names(full_dataset) <- full_dataset$CUST_ID
> # Set the sample size to be 40% of the full data set
> #    The Testing data set will have 40% of the records
> #    The Training data set will have 60% of the records
> SampleSize <- nrow(full_dataset)*0.40
> # Create an index of records for the Sample
> Index_Sample <- sample(1:nrow(full_dataset), SampleSize)
> group <- as.integer(1:nrow(full_dataset) %in% Index_Sample)
> # Create a partitioned data set of those records not selected to be in sample
> Training_Sample <- full_dataset[group==FALSE,]
> # Create partitioned data set of records who were selected to be in the sample
> Testing_Sample <- full_dataset[group==TRUE,]
> # Check the number of records in each data set
> nrow(Training_Sample)
> nrow(Testing_Sample)
> nrow(full_dataset)
```

IMPORTANT
The Training and Testing data sets created in the preceding code are used in other sections in this chapter that cover the various data classification techniques, including Decision Tree, Support Vector Machines, Naïve Bayes, and Generalized Linear Model.

After creating the data sets, you can now use the Training data set to build the Decision Tree model using the `ore.odmDT` function:

```
> # Build a Decision Tree model using ore.odmDT
> DTmodel <- ore.odmDT(AFFINITY_CARD ~., Training_Sample)
> class(DTmodel)
> names(DTmodel)
> summary(DTmodel)
```

This example assumes you want to use the default values for some of the parameters. The parameters shown here are for the formula and data parameters. For the formula parameter, you need to specify the target attribute and then list all the other attributes from the data set to include in the analysis. In our example, and in most cases, you want to feed all the attributes into the algorithm. This is illustrated using `~.` in the preceding example. The data parameter accepts the `ore.frame` object that contains the data set.

The output from `summary(DTmodel)` has not been shown because it would take up several pages. When you run the preceding code and examine the output generated by `summary(DTmodel)`, you will be able to see some of the Decision Tree properties, including the various nodes that form the Decision Tree.

The next step is to use this Decision Tree model on our Testing data set. We do this to see how the model performs on an unseen data set with known values for the target attribute. We can use the results from this step to measure the performance or accuracy of the model. The following example illustrates how the `DTmodel`, created in the previous example, can be applied to the Testing data set. The final part produces a confusion matrix to allow us to see how well the `DTmodel` performed at predicting the target values.

```
> # Test the Decision Tree model
> DTtest <- predict(DTmodel, Testing_Sample)
> # Generate the confusion Matrix
> with(DTtest, table(AFFINITY_CARD, PREDICTION))

                 PREDICTION
AFFINITY_CARD     0    1
              0 426   27
              1  81   66
```

The `predict` function takes the name of the model, the data set to be scored, and the name of the target attribute. In a similar way to using the `predict` function to score the Testing data set, you can use the `predict` function to score any new data sets or records to make a prediction for the target value. The following example illustrates this kind of scenario by taking a new data set called MINING_DATA_APPLY_V and predicting a value AFFINITY_CARD and a prediction probability value. The Apply data set and the results from the prediction are then combined into an integrated data set called DTapplyResults.

```
> # Apply the Decision Tree model to new data
> #  Add row indexing for the data frame
> row.names(MINING_DATA_APPLY_V) <- MINING_DATA_APPLY_V$CUST_ID
> # Score the new data with Decision Tree model
> DTapply <- predict(DTmodel, MINING_DATA_APPLY_V)
> # Combine the Apply data set with the Predicted values
> DTapplyResults <- cbind(MINING_DATA_APPLY_V, DTapply)
> head(DTapplyResults)
```

As an alternative to using the `cbind` function in this example, you could use the `supplemental.cols` parameter in the `predict` function. As your data sets increase in size, it will become advantageous to use this feature when producing a scored data set. The following example illustrates this alternative to using the `cbind()` function:

```
> # alternative approach using the supplemental.cols
> DTapply2 <- predict(DTmodel, newdata=MINING_DATA_APPLY_V,
                      supplemental.cols=c("CUST_ID", "CUST_GENDER", "AGE"))
> head(DTapply2,8)
```

Support Vector Machine

Support Vector Machine (SVM) is a popular machine learning technique that is typically used for classification (binary and multiclass) and regression. Oracle has implemented an in-database one-class SVM algorithm to allow you to perform anomaly detection. In this section, examples ARE given of how you can build and apply Support Vector Machines for classification, regression, and anomaly detection.

Support Vector Machines work by creating a hyperplane (or sets of hyperplanes) in a high-dimensional space. For classification, a hyperplane that provides the greatest separation of the data objects will be used. For regression, the Support Vector Machine will look to find a function such that the maximum number of data points lies within the epsilon-wide insensitivity type. For anomaly detection, the Support Vector Machine assumes a single class and will look to identify cases that are unusual or slightly different within the data set.

For Support Vector Machines, you can use the `ore.odmSVM` function. This function uses the in-database Support Vector Machine algorithm that is embedded in the Oracle Database. The `ore.odmSVM` function has the following syntax and default values:

```
> ore.odmSVM(formula,
             data,
             type,
             auto.data.prep = TRUE,
             class.priors = NULL,
             active.learning = TRUE,
             complexity.factor = "system.determined",
             conv.tolerance = 0.0001,
             epsilon = "system.determined",
             cache.size = 50000000,
             kernel.function = "system.determined",
             std.dev = "system.determined",
             outlier.rate = 0.1,
             na.action = na.pass)
```

The following subsections will illustrate how you can use the `ore.odmSVM` function to perform classification, regression, and anomaly detection. The data sets used in these subsections are sample data sets for Oracle Data Mining.

Classification Using `ore.odmSVM`

In this section, the `ore.odmSVM` function is used to build a Support Vector Machine model for classification using the in-database Support Vector Machine algorithm.

The sample code used to create the Training and Testing data sets in the following examples were created in the "Decision Tree" section of this chapter. The following example illustrates building a Support Vector Machine classification model (`type= "classification"`), testing the model, and creating the confusion matrix:

```
> # Support Vector Machine - Classification
> ?ore.odmSVM
> # Build the Support Vector Machine mode
> SVMmodel <- ore.odmSVM(AFFINITY_CARD ~., Training_Sample, type="classification")
> class(SVMmodel)
> names(SVMmodel)
 [1] "name"       "settings"   "attributes" "fit.values" "residuals"  "formula"
     "extRef"     "call"


> summary(SVMmodel)

Call:
ore.odmSVM(formula = AFFINITY_CARD ~ ., data = Training_Sample,
    type = "classification")
```

```
Settings:
                       value
prep.auto                 on
active.learning    al.enable
complexity.factor  1.099266
conv.tolerance        1e-04
kernel.cache.size  50000000
kernel.function    gaussian
std.dev            2.510129


Coefficients:  [1]
No coefficients with gaussian kernel

> # Test the Support Vector Machine model
> SVMtest <- predict(SVMmodel, Testing_Sample, "AFFINITY_CARD")
> # Generate the confusion Matrix
> with(SVMtest, table(AFFINITY_CARD, PREDICTION))

               PREDICTION
 AFFINITY_CARD   0    1
             0  411   42
             1   55   92
```

If you compare the results from the confusion matrix produced by the Decision Tree model and the Support Vector Machine model, you will notice some differences—particularly with one of the target attribute's values. You need to carefully evaluate these results, along with the results from other classification algorithms, to determine which model you should use on your new data.

The next step, after building and testing the SVM model, is to apply it to new data. Again, the code for this is very similar to what was shown previously.

```
> # Apply the Support Vector Machine model to new data
> #  Add row indexing to the data frame
> row.names(MINING_DATA_APPLY_V) <- MINING_DATA_APPLY_V$CUST_ID
> # Score the new data with Support Vector Machine model
> SVMapply <- predict(SVMmodel, newdata=MINING_DATA_APPLY_V,
                  supplemental.cols=c("CUST_ID", "CUST_GENDER", "AGE"))
> head(SVMapply)
```

Regression Using `ore.odmSVM`

For regression-type problems, the `ore.odmSVM` function allows you to specify the type of kernel to use for the algorithm. The default setting is `'system.determined'` and this allows the algorithm to determine the correct type of kernel setting to use. Alternatively, if you prefer to use a specific kernel type, you can specify `'linear'` or `'gaussian'`.

The following example illustrates the building and applying of a regression model using SVM and the INSUR_CUST_LTV_SAMPLE data set. With regression prediction, you are looking to predict a value of some continuous value attribute.

An example of this would be to calculate the lifetime value (LTV) of a customer. Just like our typical classification problems, with regression prediction you have a set of data where the LTV value is already determined. You can use a data set that contains many attributes about each customer and input this data set to the regression algorithms. The regression algorithm will then work out how each of these attributes and the values they contain contribute toward the value in the LTV attribute.

```
> # Support Vector Machines - Regression
> #  Build regression model using SVM - shows how to exclude an attribute
> SVMmodelReg <- ore.odmSVM(LTV ~. -LTV_BIN, INSUR_CUST_LTV_SAMPLE,
                            type="regression")
> class(SVMmodelReg)
> names(SVMmodelReg)
> summary(SVMmodelReg)
> SVMmodelReg$attributes

> # Apply the SVM Regression model to new data
> #  Add row indexing to the data frame
> row.names(INSUR_CUST_LTV_SAMPLE) <- INSUR_CUST_LTV_SAMPLE$CUSTOMER_ID
> # Score the data
> LTVapply <- predict(SVMmodelReg, newdata=INSUR_CUST_LTV_SAMPLE,
                      supplemental.cols=c("CUSTOMER_ID", "STATE", "SEX", "AGE"))
> head(LTVapply)
```

The LTV_BIN attribute was excluded from the input data set to the algorithm because this attribute is highly correlated to the LTV attribute, as LTV_BIN is created based on the values in LTV.

Anomaly Detection Using `ore.odmSVM`

You can use the `ore.odmSVM` function, and the underlying in-database SVM algorithm, for anomaly detection. Anomaly detection is implemented using a One-Class Support Vector Machine. For anomaly detection, you need to use a different approach to modeling your data. With this approach, the Anomaly Detection algorithm examines your data as one unit (that is, a single class). It then identifies the core characteristics and expected behavior of these case records. You need to apply the model to the same set of records that will label (or score) the data to indicate how similar or dissimilar each case record is from the core characteristics and expected behavior. You can then use this information to identify which case records (that is, the anomalous records) warrant further investigation.

The Anomaly Detection model, when applied to the data, will label that data with a prediction and a prediction probability score. If the prediction is 1, the case record is considered to be typical. If the prediction is 0 (zero), the case record is considered anomalous.

The following example uses a data set available on the Oracle Data Mining web pages and the Oracle Data Mining blog (http://tinyurl.com/j5adoeg), and it is used to demonstrate anomaly detection.

To get the SVM algorithm to perform anomaly detection, you need to set the `type` parameter to `"anomaly.detection"`. Another parameter you may want to adjust is the `outlier.rate`. The default value for this is 0.1 (or 10 percent). This value, in most cases, is too high, and it should be adjusted to an appropriate value that best fits with your particular scenario. In the following example, the outlier rate is changed to 0.02 (or 2 percent):

```
> # Anomaly Detection using 1-Class Support Vector Machines
> #   Add row indexing to the data frame
> row.names(CLAIMS) <- CLAIMS$POLICYNUMBER
> #   Build the 1-Class SVM model
> ADmodel <- ore.odmSVM(~. -POLICYNUMBER , CLAIMS, type="anomaly.detection"
                        , outlier.rate=0.02))
> class(ADmodel)
> names(ADmodel)
> summary(ADmodel)

> # Apply model to identify the anomalous records
> ADresults <- predict(ADmodel, CLAIMS, supplemental.cols="POLICYNUMBER")
> head(ADresults)

          '1'         '0' POLICYNUMBER PREDICTION
1   0.4054306 0.5945694            1          0
29  0.5208329 0.4791671           29          1
53  0.4906889 0.5093111           53          0
54  0.5529315 0.4470685           54          1
80  0.5162816 0.4837184           80          1
95  0.5433542 0.4566458           95          1
```

You can then use this resulting data set to focus on the anomalous records. The records labeled with a zero for the `PREDICTION` variable are considered anomalous. In addition, you get a prediction probability score. You use the value in this variable to rank the identified anomalous records based on the prediction probability value. The higher the prediction probability, the higher the likelihood of the record being anomalous. You can use these values to prioritize what records your analysts will look at first.

Naïve Bayes

For Naïve Bayes models, you can use the `ore.odmNB` function. This function uses the in-database Naïve Bayes algorithm that is embedded in the Oracle Database. The Naïve Bayes algorithm is based on conditional probabilities. It uses Bayes' Theorem, which is a formula that calculates a probability by counting the frequency of values and combinations of values in historical data. Bayes' Theorem finds the probability of an event occurring given the probability of another event that has already occurred.

The following example illustrates how to build and test a Naïve Bayes model. The sample code used to create the Training and Testing data sets, which are used in the following examples, was created in the "Decision Tree" section of this chapter.

```
> # Build the Naive Bayes model
> NBmodel <- ore.odmNB(AFFINITY_CARD ~., Training_Sample)
> class(NBmodel)
> names(NBmodel)
> summary(NBmodel)


> # Test the Naïve Bayes model
> NBtest <- predict(NBmodel, Testing_Sample, "AFFINITY_CARD")
> # Generate the confusion Matrix
> with(NBtest, table(AFFINITY_CARD, PREDICTION))

              PREDICTION
AFFINITY_CARD    0    1
            0  363   85
            1   33  119
```

The following sample code illustrates how you can use this Naïve Bayes model to score or label new data. The following code follows the same process for scoring data, and it use the same scoring data set used for the previous algorithms.

```
> # Apply the Naive Bayes model to new data
> #  Add row indexing to the data frame
> row.names(MINING_DATA_APPLY_V) <- MINING_DATA_APPLY_V$CUST_ID
> # Score the new data with Naive Bayes model
> NBapply <- predict(NBmodel, MINING_DATA_APPLY_V,
                    supplemental.cols=c("CUST_ID", "CUST_GENDER", "AGE"))
> head(NBapply)
```

Generalized Linear Model

For Generalized Linear Models (GLMs), you can use the `ore.odmGLM` function. This function uses the in-database GLM algorithm that is embedded in the Oracle Database. GLMs can be used for classification and for regression. For classification, binary logistic regression is supported by the GLM algorithm. For regression problems, (Gaussian) linear regression is used by the GLM algorithm, and it assumes there are no target transformations and constant variance over the range of target values.

The following example illustrates how to build a Generalized Linear Model for classification. This example also illustrates the listing of the individual attributes you want the algorithm to consider. The method can be used when you want to use a subset of the available attributes.

```
> # Generalized Linear Model (GLM) - Classification
> ?ore.odmGLM
> Training_Sample$AFFINITY_CARD <- as.factor(Training_Sample$AFFINITY_CARD)
> # Build the Generalized Linear Model
> GLMmodel <- ore.odmGLM(AFFINITY_CARD ~ CUST_GENDER+AGE+COUNTRY_NAME
                         +CUST_INCOME_LEVEL+EDUCATION+HOUSEHOLD_SIZE
                         +YRS_RESIDENCE+FLAT_PANEL_MONITOR+HOME_THEATER_PACKAGE
                         +Y_BOX_GAMES+OS_DOC_SET_KANJI,
                     data=Training_Sample, auto.data.prep=TRUE, type="logistic")
> class(GLMmodel)
> names(GLMmodel)
> summary(GLMmodel)
> GLMmodel
```

This example illustrates how you can use the GLM algorithm for classification. You can also use the GLM algorithm to perform regression. In the previous section on using the Support Vector Machine algorithm, an example was given on predicting the potential lifetime value (LTV) of customers. In the following example, the same LTV prediction is made using the GLM in-database algorithm.

```
> #  Build regression model using Generalized Linear Model
> GLMmodelReg <- ore.odmGLM(LTV ~ REGION+SEX+PROFESSION+AGE+HAS_CHILDREN+SALARY+
HOUSE_OWNERSHIP+MARITAL_STATUS,
                          data=INSUR_CUST_LTV_SAMPLE, type="normal")
> class(GLMmodelReg)
> names(GLMmodelReg)
> summary(GLMmodelReg)
> GLMmodelReg

> # Apply the Generalized Linear Model-Regression model to new data
> #  Add row indexing to the data frame
> row.names(INSUR_CUST_LTV_SAMPLE) <- INSUR_CUST_LTV_SAMPLE$CUSTOMER_ID
> # Score the data
> GLMapplyReg <- predict(GLMmodelReg, INSUR_CUST_LTV_SAMPLE, supplemental.
cols=c("CUSTOMER_ID", "STATE", "SEX", "AGE","LTV"))
> head(GLMapplyReg[,c("LTV", "PREDICTION")])
> # Calculate the difference between predicted and actual values
> GLMapplyReg$difference <- GLMapplyReg$PREDICTION - GLMapplyReg$LTV
> GLMapplyReg$percent_diff <- (GLMapplyReg$difference/GLMapplyReg$LTV)*100
> # Display subset of attributes and compare results
> head(GLMapplyReg[,c("LTV", "PREDICTION", "difference", "percent_diff")])

            LTV PREDICTION difference percent_diff
CU100    24891.25   22279.20 -2612.0488  -10.4938435
CU10006  23638.50   23874.16   235.6568    0.9969193
CU10011  35600.50   33320.06 -2280.4421   -6.4056462
CU10012  26070.00   28683.75  2613.7493   10.0258891
CU10020  25092.75   22525.37 -2567.3775  -10.2315511
CU10025  27149.00   29228.10  2079.1004    7.6581104
```

In this section, examples have been given that illustrate how you can use the in-database GLM algorithm, using the `ore.odmGLM` function, to perform classification and regression.

Clustering

Oracle R Enterprise exposes two of the ODM in-database clustering algorithms. These are the `ore.odmKMeans` clustering function for the in-database *k*-Means algorithm and the `ore.odmOC` function for the in-database orthogonal partitioning cluster (or O-Cluster) in-database algorithm. Cluster is one of the techniques used for unsupervised data mining.

Clustering is a process of dividing the data into smaller related subsets. Each of these subsets is called a *cluster*. Within each cluster, the data is similar to each other, and is dissimilar to the data in the other clusters. Clustering is a very useful method for exploring your data to find whether there are any clusters in it. Typically, clustering would be used in conjunction with other data mining algorithms as part of your data science projects.

The in-database *k*-Means algorithm runs an enhanced version of the typical *k*-Means algorithm. Oracle Data Mining builds models in a hierarchical manner, using a top-down approach with binary splits and refinements of all nodes at the end. The tree grows one node at a time. The node with the largest variance is split to increase the size of the tree until the desired number of clusters is reached. The algorithm evolves, producing the number of clusters specified. The number of clusters to be produced is set as part of the algorithm parameters. The O-Cluster algorithm uses a density-based distance measure, can handle data sets of any size but with a low number of attributes, and produces a user-defined number of clusters.

The following sample code illustrates how you can use the `ore.odmKMeans` function to build the *k*-Means model using the in-database algorithm. The example changes two of the default values for the algorithm. The first is the `num.centers` parameter. This defines how many clusters you want to create in the model. The default value is 10, but you will want to adjust this value to find the optimal number of clusters. The second parameter, whose default value is changed, is the `iterations` parameter. The default value is 3. The value set for this parameter determines the number of iterations you want the *k*-Means algorithm to perform. The higher the number, the longer the algorithm will take. The maximum number of iterations is 20.

```
> # Building a Cluster Model
> #   k-Means
> ?ore.odmKMeans()
> # Build a k-Means model for the INSUR_CUST_LTV_SAMPLE
> #   Default num.centers=10
> KMmodel <- ore.odmKMeans(~. -CUSTOMER_ID, data=INSUR_CUST_LTV_SAMPLE,
num.centers=5, iterations=5)
> KMmodel
> summary(KMmodel)
```

You can use the `summary` function, shown in the preceding example, to inspect the attributes and the values for these attributes that define the centroid of each cluster. You can then use this information along with your domain knowledge to work out and apply a business meaning or description for each of the clusters.

When you have built a *k*-Means cluster model that you are happy with, you can then use it to score or label your data. In the following example, we reuse the same data set for illustrative purposes:

```
> # Predict what cluster a record belongs too.
> KMapply <- predict(KMmodel, newdata=INSUR_CUST_LTV_SAMPLE,
                supplemental.cols=c("CUSTOMER_ID", "STATE", "SEX", "AGE","LTV"))
> head(KMapply)
```

Your data set (in this case, KMapply) will contain the cluster identifier that each record is most closely related to.

When you are using clustering as a precursor to classification, you can use the predicted cluster identifier as a way to partition the data set and then perform separate classification on each set of clustered records.

The second in-database clustering algorithm that is available in Oracle R Enterprise is the O-Cluster algorithm. This is available to you using the `ore.odmOC` function. O-Cluster is an Orthogonal Partitioning Clustering method that creates a hierarchical grid-based clustering model. The algorithm uses and axis-parallel uni-dimensional data projections to identify the areas of density. The algorithm looks to find cluster splitting points that result in distinct clusters that do not overlap and are balanced in size. The O-Cluster algorithm operates recursively, generating a hierarchical structure. The resulting clusters define dense areas. The algorithm will determine the number of clusters to produce automatically, up to a defined limit. The O-Cluster algorithm uses a grid-based approach, is suitable for data sets with more than 500 cases, has a high number of attributes, and automatically determines the number of clusters in the data set.

The following code example illustrates the O-Cluster algorithm applied to the same data set as was illustrated for *k*-Means. The example also asks for 5 clusters to be generated instead of the default 10.

```
> #  O-Cluster
> ?ore.odmOC()
> # Build an O-Cluster model for the INSUR_CUST_LTV_SAMPLE
> #  Default num.centers=10
> OCmodel <- ore.odmKMeans(~. -CUSTOMER_ID, data=INSUR_CUST_LTV_SAMPLE,
                        num.centers=5)
> OCmodel
> summary(OCmodel)


> # Predict what cluster a record belongs too.
> OCapply <- predict(OCmodel, newdata=INSUR_CUST_LTV_SAMPLE,
                supplemental.cols=c("CUSTOMER_ID", "STATE", "SEX", "AGE","LTV"))
> head(OCapply)
```

In this section, examples were given that illustrate how you can use the in-database clustering algorithms, using the `ore.odmKmeans` and `ore.odmOC` functions, to perform clustering.

Saving Your Data Mining Models

In this chapter, I have shown you how to use the various OREdm package functions to call and use the in-database data mining algorithms. The data sets and data mining models we create are temporary transient objects in the Oracle Database. When you disconnect your ORE session from the Oracle Database, these objects will no longer exist in your schema in the database. This means the next time you want to use these objects, you have to re-run the code to generate them. This is not something you will want to do repeatedly on your data science projects. Plus, you cannot share these temporary objects with other people on your team. What's more, if you have to re-run your code to regenerate these objects, it can take a lot of time if you have a large amount of data.

How do you overcome this issue? How can you save these objects to be used later?

For any ORE data frame, you can store these objects as tables in your schema in the Oracle Database using the `ore.create` function. This allows you to easily get access to the data at a later point, and it also allows you to share this data with other members of your data science team. However, it also means that your schema(s) can get cluttered with lots and lots of tables containing different data sets.

Back in Chapter 3, I gave examples of how you can store objects in an ORE datastore. This is perhaps a better option for saving our ORE data frames. Additionally we can use an ORE datastore to store the various data models created during our ORE session. By doing this it allows us to reload these objects from the ORE datastore, and we will no longer have to re-run our code to regenerate these objects.

I also mentioned back in Chapter 3, when demonstrating how to use ORE datastores, that you can create many ORE datastores. You can create hundreds of these within your schema. This allows you to group the objects for your project or subproject into one ORE datastore, which is a very useful way of organizing your work because you are only grouping objects for each project within its own ORE datastore.

Earlier in this chapter, I gave examples of how to create a Decision Tree model using the `ore.odmDT` function. I also showed you how to create a Training data set and a Testing data set. These data sets were reused with some of the other data mining algorithms. We could store these Training and Testing data sets in an ORE datastore, and these can be reused at a later time.

The following example illustrates creating an ORE datastore that contains the Training and Testing data sets (ORE data frames) and the Decision Tree model created by the `ore.odmDT` function:

```
> # Saving the Data Mining object to and ORE data store
> ore.save(list=c("Training_Sample", "Testing_Sample", "DTmodel"),
        name="ORE_DS_Decision_Tree", grantable=TRUE)
> # List the ORE data stores
> ore.datastore()
> # List the objects stored in the ORE data store
> ore.datastoreSummary("ORE_DS_Decision_Tree")

      object.name      class size length row.count col.count
1         DTmodel ore.odmDT 4462      9        NA        NA
2  Testing_Sample ore.frame 4486     18        NA        18
3 Training_Sample ore.frame 4486     18        NA        18
```

When you want to reuse or reload the objects in the ORE datastore, you can use the `ore.load` function, as shown next. This loads the objects into your R environment.

```
> # Load the ORE data store objects back into the R environment
> ore.load("ORE_DS_Decision_Tree")
> # Alternatively if you only want to reload the data sets
> ore.load("ORE_DS_Decision_Tree", c("Training_Sample", "Testing_Sample"))
```

Summary

Oracle Data Mining provides a suite of in-database data mining algorithms accessed using the Oracle Data Miner GUI or by using the SQL and PL/SQL interfaces. Oracle R Enterprise has a set of defined functions that allows you to use many of these Oracle Data Mining algorithms from an R interface using standard R conventions. These functions come as part of the OREdm package that comes with Oracle R Enterprise. Throughout this chapter, examples were given of how you can use these in-database algorithms using the ORE functions. This includes creating your Training and Testing sample data sets, creating a model using the available functions, testing the model, creating a confusion matrix, and applying the model to new data. The last section of this chapter demonstrated how you can save these data mining objects to an ORE datastore, thus allowing you to reuse these objects easily in your data science projects.

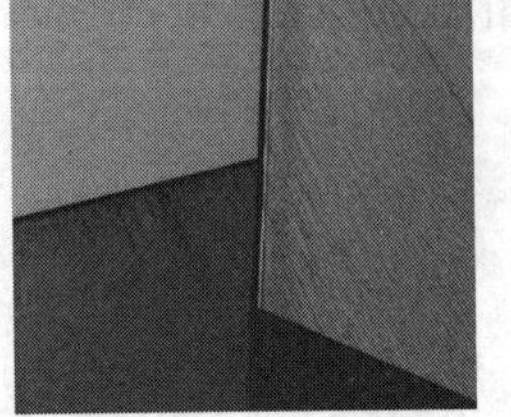

CHAPTER

8

Building Models Using ORE and Other Algorithms

Oracle R Enterprise comes with a suite of data mining algorithms that have been built specifically to work with the Oracle Database and on your Oracle Database server. In the previous chapter, I showed you how to use the Oracle Data Mining–specific data mining algorithms. In this chapter, I show you the additional data mining algorithms that Oracle has built and included in Oracle R Enterprise.

These Oracle R Enterprise–specific algorithms have been highly tuned to minimize memory usage and to work in a highly integrated way with the Oracle Database. The work that Oracle has put into creating these highly tuned algorithms allows you to work with greater volumes of data, possibility up to billions of records, and also to process this data at greater speed.

In addition to using the core algorithms available in Oracle R Enterprise, you can use the many algorithms available with the various R packages. In this chapter, I give some examples of how you can use these commonly available algorithms on the Oracle Database server.

The final part of this chapter looks at a special function in Oracle R Enterprise called `ore.predict`. The `ore.predict` function provides an efficient way to operationalize R-generated models for scoring in the Oracle Database.

What Algorithms Are Available?

Oracle R Enterprise offers the additional algorithms listed in Table 8-1. These algorithms are optimized to efficiently manage memory usage and to work with large volumes of data. These algorithms work with data that is defined using an ORE data frame.

ORE Algorithm	Description
`ore.glm`	Creates a generalized linear model (GLM) on the data associated with your ORE data frame
`ore.lm`	Creates a linear regression model on the data associated with your ORE data frame
`ore.neural`	Creates a neural networks model on the data associated with your ORE data frame
`ore.stepwise`	Creates a stepwise linear regression model on the data associated with your ORE data frame
`ore.randomForest`	Creates a random forest model on the data associated with your ORE data frame

TABLE 8-1.   *Data Mining Algorithms Available in the OREmodels Package*

Preparing Your Data to Build a Model

As you learned in the previous chapter, the Oracle Data Mining algorithms have a feature called Automatic Data Preparation (ADP). ADP has a defined set of rules on how to process and prepare data before it is input to the Oracle Data Mining algorithms. This feature is extremely useful and powerful and can save you a significant amount of time because you do not have to analyze or write all the data transformations that may be necessary.

When using the ORE algorithms listed in this chapter, or any of the many data mining algorithms that come with the R language, you will need to perform a detailed analysis of the data to determine what data transformations are required. Based on this analysis, you will need to write the R code necessary to perform these transformations.

The typical data transformations you will need to perform to prepare your data include the following:

- How to handle missing data at the attribute and record levels

- Data normalization

- Standardizing of variables

- Binning of data values

- Data value remapping

- Determining correlated variables

- Generating derived attributes

- Feature extraction

- Feature engineering

- Variable reduction techniques, including PCA, Attribute Importance, and so on

Sample Data Sets for This Chapter

In the previous chapter, when we used the Oracle Data Mining algorithms to build our data mining models, we used some of the sample data sets that come with the Oracle Database. This included a SQL script you can run in your Oracle schema to create various database views and to create some tables. An alternative approach is to use the Oracle Data Miner tool that comes as part of SQL Developer to create this sample data.

For this chapter, I use some alternative data sets to illustrate how to use the additional data mining algorithms that come with Oracle R Enterprise, how to use some of the other R data mining algorithms within the Oracle Database environment, and how to use the `ore.predict` function.

The first of these data sets is the USA Census data, which provides some demographic data and a variable that indicates whether a person earns above or below $50,000. This data set is commonly referred to by two names. The first is the Adults data set, and the second name is the AdultUCI data set (http://archive.ics .uci.edu/ml/datasets/Adult). This data set is also available as part of the arules package for the R language. This data set is also available on the UCI Machine Learning Repository Archive. The following code illustrates how you can read this data set from the archive website and load it into your local R environment as a data frame. The final part of this example uses the `ore.push` function, which takes the local data frame, moves it to the Oracle Database, and makes it available as an ORE data frame.

```
> # Load the Adult Census Data data set CensusIncome
> CensusIncome <- read.table("http://archive.ics.uci.edu/ml/machine-learning-
databases/adult/adult.data",
      sep=",",header=F,col.names=c("age", "type_employer", "fnlwgt", "education",
      "education_num","marital", "occupation", "relationship", "race","sex",
      "capital_gain", "capital_loss", "hr_per_week","country", "income"),
      fill=FALSE, strip.white=T, na.strings = "Unknown")
> census <- ore.push(CensusIncome)
```

For the examples shown in this chapter, you can use the data as it is in the data set. Alternatively, you may want to perform some data preparation by standardizing the values in some of the variables.

The second of the data sets is also available on the UCI Machine Learning Repository Archive website and is the Wine Quality data set (https://archive.ics.uci .edu/ml/datasets/Wine+Quality). There are two wine data sets provided: one for red wine and one for white wine. I use the white wine data set in this chapter. The following code illustrates how you can read this data set from the archive website, load it into your local R environment as a data frame, and then push the data frame to the Oracle Database using the `ore.push` function.

```
> # Load the (white) Wine Quality Data data set
> WhiteWine = read.table("http://archive.ics.uci.edu/ml/machine-learning-databases/
wine-quality/winequality-white.csv", sep=";", header=TRUE)
> wine <- ore.push(WhiteWine)
```

If you have followed these examples, you will now have the data sets used in this chapter. Alternatively, you could use your own data sets or the data sets I used to illustrate how to use the various in-database data mining algorithms in the previous chapter.

Building Models Using ORE Algorithms

Oracle R Enterprise comes with the set of algorithms listed in Table 8-1. These algorithms have been highly tuned to minimize the use of memory and process the data efficiently in an ORE data frame.

In this section, I show you how to use each of these algorithms to generate models and how to use these to score new data.

Generalized Linear Model

The first ORE algorithm we will look at is the `ore.glm` function. Generalized linear models (GLM) can be used to generate a regression model and can also generate a logistic regression model for a categorical response variable. The `ore.glm` function builds a GLM model using data in an ORE data frame using the Fisher scoring iteratively reweighted least squares (IRLS) algorithm. Check out the R help for more details on how the IRLS algorithm has been implemented.

The `ore.glm` function has the following syntax:

```
> ore.glm(formula,
         data,
         weights,
         family = gaussian(),
         start = NULL,
         control = list(...),
         contrasts = NULL,
         xlev = NULL,
         ylev = NULL,
         yprob = NULL, ...)
```

The `ore.glm` function has a similar signature and parameter list to the `glm` function that comes standard with the R language. When you use the `ore.glm()` function to build a model, the minimum set of parameters that need to be provided include the formula and the data set. With the formula, you can specify what attributes you want to include and/or exclude from the model build, as well as identify the target attribute. The data parameter is the ORE data frame that contains the data set to be used. The following example illustrates the creation of a GLM model using the Census Income data set (aka Adult or AdultUSI data set). The following example assumes that the Census Income data set has been moved to the Oracle Database using the `ore.push` function, and the ORE data frame called "census" points to the data in the Oracle Database. Alternatively, you could use the `ore.create` function to create a table in your Oracle schema.

```
> GLMmodel <- ore.glm(income ~., data=census, family=binomial())
> summary(GLMmodel)
```

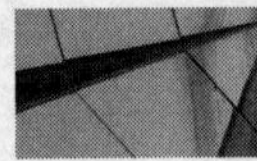

IMPORTANT
If you get an error message when you try to run the `ore.glm()` *function that says something like "Error in is.finite(reduceobj)," then you will need to apply a patch to your Oracle Database. The patch number and description is "20173897 WRONG RESULT OF GROUP BY FROM A TABLE RETURNED BY EXTPROC (Patch)."*

The `summary` function lists some of the details of the model generated, along with details of the coefficients. You can use the `names` function to get a list of all the various model details available.

```
> names(GLMmodel)
 [1] "coefficients"    "residuals"       "fitted.values"
 [4] "effects"         "R"               "rank"
 [7] "qr"              "family"          "linear.predictors"
[10] "deviance"        "aic"             "null.deviance"
[13] "iter"            "weights"         "prior.weights"
[16] "df.residual"     "df.null"         "y"
[19] "converged"       "boundary"        "model"
[22] "x"               "call"            "formula"
[25] "terms"           "data"            "offset"
[28] "control"         "method"          "contrasts"
[31] "xlevels"
```

In a similar way to all the other ORE algorithms, there is a specific `predict` function that allows you to score new data using the model. The following code illustrates how you can use the GLM model created previously to score or label a new data set. In this example, I use the data set that was used to build the model. If "response" is selected, the predictions are on the scale of the response.

```
> GLMscored <- predict(GLMmodel, newdata=census,
                       supplemental.cols=c("age", "income"),
                       type="response")
> head(GLMscored, 20)
```

In addition to the `summary` and `predict` functions, ORE comes with a number of overloaded functions that can be used with the ORE model generated using `ore.glm`. These include `vcov`, `residuals`, `coef`, `coefficients`, `deviance`, `effects`, `extractAIC`, `family`, `fitted`, `fitted.values`, `formula`, `logLik`, `model.frame`, `nobs`, and `weight`.

Linear and Stepwise Regression Models

Oracle R Enterprise comes with its own implementation of a regression linear model with a function called `ore.lm`. The `ore.lm` function performs least squares regression and is designed specifically to work with data represented by an ORE data frame. This implementation of the `ore.lm` function is optimized for memory usage, can be run in parallel, and has the ability to use the Oracle Database server, which allows it to process a greater volume of data than you would typically be able to process with the standard `lm` function that comes with the R language.

The `ore.lm` function has a similar API signature and parameter listing as the standard `lm` function in R. Therefore, in addition to the `ore.lm` function, Oracle has provided overloaded versions of the typical functions that you can use with the standard `lm` function in the R language. These functions are designed to work with the ORE model generated by the `ore.lm` function. They include `summary`, `logLik`, `hatvalues`, `vcov`, `predict`, `add1`, `drop1`, `anova`, `coef`, `coefficients`, `confint`, `deviance`, `effects`, `extracAIC`, `fitted`, `fitted.values`, `formula`, `model.frame`, `nobs`, `resid`, `residuals`, and `weights`.

To illustrate the use of the `ore.lm` function, I'm going to use the Wine Quality data set. Details of how to get access to this data set were provided earlier in this chapter. The Wine Quality data set was pushed to the Oracle Database and is now referenced by an ORE data frame called `wine`. The following example illustrates how you can use the `ore.lm` function to build a model that is focused on the alcohol level of the wine in the data set.

```
> wine <- ore.push(WhiteWine)
> LMmodel <- ore.lm(alcohol  ~., data=wine)
> LMmodel
> summary(LMmodel)


Call: lm(formula = alcohol ~ ., data = WhiteWine)
Residuals:      Min        1Q  Median        3Q       Max
-3.3343 -0.2553 -0.0255   0.2214 15.7789


Coefficients:
                        Estimate Std. Error   t value Pr(>|t|)
(Intercept)            6.719e+02  5.563e+00   120.790  < 2e-16 ***
fixed.acidity          5.099e-01  9.855e-03    51.745  < 2e-16 ***
volatile.acidity       9.636e-01  6.718e-02    14.342  < 2e-16 ***
citric.acid            3.658e-01  5.596e-02     6.538 6.88e-11 ***
residual.sugar         2.341e-01  2.960e-03    79.112  < 2e-16 ***
chlorides             -1.832e-01  3.207e-01    -0.571  0.56785
free.sulfur.dioxide   -3.665e-03  4.936e-04    -7.425 1.33e-13 ***
total.sulfur.dioxide   6.579e-04  2.217e-04     2.968  0.00301 **
density               -6.793e+02  5.696e+00  -119.259  < 2e-16 ***
```

```
pH                      2.383e+00  5.191e-02   45.916  < 2e-16 ***
sulphates               9.669e-01  5.751e-02   16.814  < 2e-16 ***
quality                 6.663e-02  8.341e-03    7.988 1.70e-15 ***
---
Signif. codes:  0 '***' 0.001 '**' 0.01 '*' 0.05 '.' 0.1 ' ' 1

Residual standard error: 0.4409 on 4886 degrees of freedom
Multiple R-squared:  0.8719,    Adjusted R-squared:  0.8716
F-statistic:  3024 on 11 and 4886 DF,  p-value: < 2.2e-16
```

The `summary(LMmodel)` in the preceding code listing displays the details of
the model that was created. It lists the coefficients and the various statistical
measures for the model, including R-squared and Adjusted R-squared.

You can explore many of the other properties of the model produced using the
variety of functions available to you, which have been listed earlier.

After generating the regression model, you can use the `predict` function to
apply the model to any new data that becomes available and conforms to the
original data format. The following example illustrates how you can use the
regression model produced to score the new data with a predicted value. The
following example selects the first 15 rows from our data set:

```
> data_score <- wine[1:15,]
> LMscored <- predict(LMmodel, newdata=data_score, supplemental.cols="alcohol")
> LMscored
    alcohol    output
1       8.8  8.709956
2       9.5  9.499076
3      10.1 10.687868
4       9.9  9.975722
5       9.9  9.975722
6      10.1 10.687868
7       9.6  9.693886
8       8.8  8.709956
9       9.5  9.499076
10     11.0 10.203548
11     12.0 11.783000
12      9.7 10.326858
13     10.8 11.214805
14     12.4 11.968924
15      9.7  9.931775
```

Stepwise regression is an automated process of building a model by successively
adding or removing variables based on the t-statistics of the estimated coefficients.
Stepwise regression is implemented in Oracle R Enterprise using stepwise least
squares regression. By default, `ore.stepwise` will perform the stepwise regression
in both directions, backward, forward, and alternate.

```
> wine <- ore.push(WhiteWine)
> SWmodel <- ore.stepwise(alcohol  ~. ^2, data=wine, add.p = 0.1, drop.p = 0.1)
> summary(SWmodel)
```

You can use the `step` function to output the details of each of the iterations from the stepwise regression model. As you can imagine, the output from this is very long, and I have not shown it here. However, in certain industries it is vital to produce this listing because it is required for various auditing and regulatory scenarios.

```
> SWsteps <- step(ore.lm(alcohol   ~ 1, data=wine),
              scope=terms(alcohol   ~. ^2, data=wine))
```

For the `step` function there is a parameter called `direction`. This is not listed in the preceding example because it will use the default setting of one of the following:

```
direction = c("both", "backward", "forward")
```

If you would prefer the steps to be performed in one direction, you can specify this, for example:

```
> SWsteps <- step(ore.lm(alcohol   ~ 1, data=wine),
              scope=terms(alcohol   ~. ^2, data=wine),
              direction="forward")
```

The output of the `steps` function is not shown here because it can be very long. Care needs to be taken when running this function because it can take a long time to run, depending on the number of attributes involved.

Neural Networks

Neural networks is a popular data mining technique used to model patterns and nonlinear relationships in noisy and complex data sets. Neural networks has been implemented in Oracle R Enterprise using a feed-forward network for regression and is specifically designed to work with data represented by an ORE data frame. Neural networks can have a number of hidden layers (with a default of zero hidden layers) and nodes. The `ore.neural` function comes with a wide range of parameters that allows you to fine-tune the neural networks model. Some of these parameters include the type of activations to use, tolerance levels, and upper and lower bounds for weight initializations.

For the simplest call of the `ore.neural` function, you can pass in the formula for the attributes and the name of the data set. In this case, we are going to use the Wine data set.

```
> wine <- ore.push(WhiteWine)
> NNmodel <- ore.neural(quality ~., data=wine)
> NNmodel
 Number of input units       11
 Number of output units      1
```

```
Number of hidden layers     0
Objective value             1.406247E+03
Solution status             Optimal (objMinProgress)
Output layer                number of neurons 1, activation 'linear'
Optimization solver         L-BFGS
Scale Hessian inverse       1
Number of L-BFGS updates    20
```

The example built a neural networks model with no hidden layer. If you would like to add a number of hidden layers, you can use the `hiddenSizes` parameter to specify the number of neurons at each level. For example, the following will use three hidden layers with five neurons at the first hidden layer, three neurons at the second hidden layer, and two neurons at the third hidden layer:

```
> NNmodel <- ore.neural(quality ~., data=wine, hiddenSizes=c(5, 3, 2))
```

With the `ore.neural` function, you can use a variety of activation methods for each of the hidden layers. By default, the `bSigmoid` activation method is used for the hidden layers and linear for the output layer. You can change these using the `activations` parameter. When listing the activations, you need to ensure that you list one activation for each layer as well as the output layer.

After you have created a neural network that gives you the degree of accuracy you require, you can then use this model to score or label new data. Just like with all our other data mining functions, you can use the `predict` function to score new data.

```
> NNscored <- predict(NNmodel, newdata=wine, supplemental.col="quality")
> head(NNscore)

  quality pred_quality
1       6     5.459094
2       5     5.608050
3       6     6.365405
4       5     5.629717
5       5     5.556396
6       6     5.554403
```

Random Forests

Random forests is an ensemble learning method that can be used for classification and regressions. With this method, multiple decision trees are constructed at training time by randomly selecting attributes for the split nodes. When used for prediction, the random forest of decision trees is scanned and each decision tree makes a prediction or votes. The final predicted value or outcome is determined by the mode value for classification problems and the mean value for regression-type problems. With the Oracle R Enterprise implementation of random forests, the trees can be grown in parallel, which is determined by the degree of parallel setting for ORE. The current implementation of random forests in Oracle R Enterprise supports classification. The degree of parallelism can be set using the `ore.parallel` function. When the degree of parallelism is set to more than the default of 1, the training data will be copied into memory for each parallel embedded R execution process. Care should be taken when deciding on the degree of parallelism to use, as well as careful management and setting of the amount of memory available, to each embedded R execution process.

Random forests is implemented in Oracle R Enterprise using the `ore.randomForest` function. By default, this function will create up to 500 trees during the build process, but you can change this value using the `ntree` parameter. The following example illustrates how to generate a random forests model using the Census data set:

```
> census <- ore.push(CensusIncome)
> RFmodel <- ore.randomForest(income ~., data=census, confusion.matrix=TRUE)
> RFmodel
> names(RFmodel)
```

In this example, I have included the parameter `confusion.matrix`. This parameter creates a confusion matrix for the model, which allows you to use this information as part of your evaluation of the random forest model that was produced. By default, this parameter is set to FALSE. The confusion matrix is calculated by applying the model to the entire training data set.

Each random forests data mining model (`ore.randomForest` object) produced comes with a large range of components you can examine. By using `names(RFmodel)`, as shown previously, you can list all these components. You can use these components to examine the various features of the random forests model that was produced. Care should be taken when examining the `forest` component because it will return the details of all the forests produced and that are part of the overall model.

Just like with the other Oracle R Enterprise data mining functions, there is a specific `predict` function that runs the in-database ORE random forests model on new data that is represented by an ORE data frame. The following example illustrates the use of this `predict` function and shows how to generate a scored data set that includes some of the attributes from the scoring data set:

```
> RFscored <- predict(RFmodel, newdata=census, type="response",
                      supplemental.cols="income")
> head(RFscored, 10)
```

Building Models Using R Packages and Algorithms

Throughout this chapter and Chapter 7, I have given examples of how you can build data mining models using the algorithms that are built into the Oracle Database, as well as other ORE algorithms that are tightly integrated with the Oracle Database and the Oracle Database server. By using these algorithms, you can use the computing capabilities of the Oracle Database server to process your data for building models and scoring data in the Oracle Database. This removes the need of having to extract data from the Oracle Database, thereby saving you a significant amount of time and allowing your data mining to be used in production environments.

The R language comes with a vast array of packages that allows you to perform almost any type of analytics you may want. In addition to the algorithms that come with Oracle R Enterprise, you have the ability to use many of these other algorithms available with the R language.

In Chapter 14, I give some examples of how you can install some of these R packages within your Oracle R Enterprise environment on the Oracle Database server. Doing this allows you to access these algorithms and use the Oracle Database server as a powerful compute engine.

After installing the new algorithms via their R package, you have a number of ways to use them. The first of these is to run your R scripts on the Oracle Database server. The following example illustrates how you can use the `rpart` package to create a recursive partitioning tree using the Census data set:

```
> library(rpart)
> rpartModel <- rpart(income ~., method="class", data=CensusIncome)
> rpartModel
```

Although this R code will be run on the Oracle Database server in an R engine, the `rpart` algorithm and package are not part of the core Oracle R Enterprise environment. In this case, you will need to extract the data that is in the Oracle Database to the local R environment. Because this will be happening in an R engine on the Oracle Database server, you will not have any transportation issues due to moving the data across the network.

An alternative approach to this is to use the Oracle R Enterprise embedded R execution feature. This feature allows you to package up a set of R statements and send these to the Oracle Database. The Oracle Database will then execute this code in an Oracle Database–controlled server-side R engine. The following example illustrates how you can take the Census data set, which is located in the R environment, push it to the Oracle Database, load the `rpart` R library, create an `rpart` model, use the model to score the data set, and then return the scored data set:

```
> rp <- ore.tableApply (
    ore.push(CensusIncome),
```

```
  function(dat) {
    library(rpart)
    Rmodel <- rpart(income ~., method="class", data=dat)
    pred_Income <- predict(Rmodel, dat, type="class")
    pred_Income2 <- cbind(dat, pred_Income)
    pred_Income2
  }
)
```

All of the work of creating the model and scoring the data will be performed on the Oracle Database server using the embedded R execution feature. The preceding example still involves the moving of data. But what if the data already exists in the Oracle Database? The scored data set remains in the Oracle Database as an ORE data frame. You can use this object in the Oracle Database, or you can pull the scored data set to your R environment using `ore.pull` for further analytics.

The following example illustrates the creation of a table in your Oracle schema for storing the data set. This is a typical scenario when the data set you want to process resides in the Oracle Database. It is this table in your schema that will be used in the following example.

```
> census_data <- ore.create(CensusIncome, "CENSUS_INCOME")
> rp <- ore.tableApply (
    CENSUS_INCOME,
    function(dat) {
      library(rpart)
      Rmodel <- rpart(income ~., method="class", data=dat)
      pred_Income <- predict(Rmodel, dat, type="class")
      pred_Income2 <- cbind(dat, pred_Income)
      pred_Income2
    }
)
```

Based on the preceding examples, you can see how easy it is to start using the vast collection of algorithms available for the R language. The following example illustrates how you can use the `glm` functions that come with R. This example has two parts. The first part illustrates how you can create a GLM model on the Oracle Database server, and the second part illustrates using the embedded R execution method.

```
> # Example using the standard glm function that comes with R
> data <- ore.pull(wine)
> gm <- glm(quality ~., data=data)
> pred_Quality <- predict(gm, data)
> pred_Quality2 <- cbind(data, pred_Quality)
> head(pred_Quality2)

> # now the embedded R execution method
> GLMresult <- ore.tableApply (
```

```
      ore.push(WhiteWine),
      function(dat) {
        gm <- glm(quality ~., data=dat)
        pred_Quality <- predict(gm, dat)
        pred_Quality2 <- cbind(dat, pred_Quality)
        pred_Quality2
      }
  )
> GLMresult_scored <- ore.pull(GLMresult)
> head(GLMresult_scored)
```

Similarly, you can use the kmeans function that comes with the R language:

```
> # Use embedded R execution to generate a kMean model
> KMmodel <- ore.tableApply (
      ore.push(WhiteWine),
      function(dat) {
        km <- kmeans(dat, 5)
        km
      }
  )
> class(KMmodel)
> km <- ore.pull(KMmodel)
> class(km)
> summary(km)
> km
```

In this section, I have demonstrated two different ways you can use some of the vast array of algorithms available with the R language. You can install and run these algorithms and their packages on the Oracle Database server, or you can use the ORE embedded R execution functions to run the code in the Oracle Database–controlled server-side R engine.

In the next section of this chapter, I demonstrate how you can use the `ore.predict` function. You will see how the examples and models created in this section can be used with this function.

Using `ore.predict` for Optimizing In-database Scoring

With many data science projects, you will have a variety of models created for scoring your data. These models may have been created using the wide range of algorithms available with the R language. In the previous section, I illustrated how you can use some of the algorithms by running them on the Oracle Database server or by running them using the embedded R execution feature of Oracle R Enterprise.

Type of Model	Description	Signatures for `ore.predict`
`glm`	Generalized Linear Model	`ore.predict-glm`
`kmeans`	*k*-Means Clustering Model	`ore.predict-kmeans`
`lm`	Linear Regression Model	`ore.predict-lm`
`matrix`	A `matrix` with no more than 1000 rows for use in an `hclust` hierarchical clustering model	`ore.predict-matrix`
`multinom`	Multinomial Log-linear Model	`ore.predict-multinom`
`nnet`	Neural Network Model	`ore.predict-nnet`
`ore.model`	An Oracle R Enterprise Model	`ore.predict-ore.model`
`prcomp`	Principal Components Analysis on a matrix	`ore.predict-prcomp`
`princomp`	Principal Components Analysis on a numeric matrix	`ore.predict.princomp`
`rpart`	Recursive Partitioning and Regress Tree Model	`ore.predict.rpart`

TABLE 8-2.   *Models Supported by the `ore.predict` Function*

Rather than having to rewrite your R scripts to re-create the models using the algorithms and functions supplied as part of Oracle R Enterprise, you now have the option to use these existing models and allow Oracle R Enterprise to run them on an ORE data frame that points to data in the Oracle Database. This way, you don't have to extract and process the data in a data frame in the local R environment.

Oracle R Enterprise supports the ability for a non-Oracle R Enterprise model to score and label data that resides in the Oracle Database. The `ore.predict` function is provided to allow you to perform this functionality. By using `ore.predict`, you can maximize the use of the Oracle Database as a compute engine. It simplifies the application workflow and logic, simplifies the technical architecture, and allows for easier integration and usage within your applications and analytic environments.

Although the R language comes with a large number of algorithms, not all of these are supported by the `ore.predict` function. Table 8-2 lists the various algorithms supported by `ore.predict`.

Although you can use the `ore.predict` function for models produced using the ORE algorithms (see Chapter 7 and earlier in this chapter), I would recommend using the `predict` function as the way you remove an extra layer of translation instead.

In the previous section, I gave examples of using some of the data mining functions that come with the R language on your data. There were two main approaches to doing this. The first was to run your script on the Oracle Database server, extracting the data and generating or using the data mining model. The second approach was to use the embedded R execution feature of Oracle R Enterprise. This allows you to write the R code in your local R environment but execute the code at the database server using the embedded R execution feature.

Another alternative is to score your data in the Oracle Database using the `ore.predict` function that uses the model details defined by the R model. The R model developed by one of the algorithms, and supported by the `ore.predict` function (see Table 8-2), will have its various model information extracted from the R model and translated and run within the Oracle Database. This allows you to utilize the computing and performance capabilities of Oracle R Enterprise and the Oracle Database for extremely fast and efficient scoring of your data in the Oracle Database. Additionally, it allows for easy integration into your existing applications, workflows, dashboards, and architecture.

The following examples are based on the data mining models created in the previous section. The first of these examples uses the `rpart` package and algorithm to create a recursive partitioning model for the census data. The following code illustrates a full example of building a model using the `rpart` algorithm on data that is stored in the local R environment (in a data frame called `WhiteWine`) and then uses the `ore.predict()` function to score data in the Oracle Database using an ORE data frame:

```
> library(rpart)
> rpartModel <- rpart(income ~., method="class", data=CensusIncome)
> rpartModel
> # Score the data in the CENSUS_INCOME table
> pred_Income <- ore.predict(rpartModel, CENSUS_INCOME, type="class")
> pred_Income2 <- cbind(CENSUS_INCOME, pred_Income)
> head(pred_Income2)
> table(pred_Income2$income, pred_Income2$pred_Income)
```

Similarly, you can use the `glm` model created in the previous section to score data in your Oracle Database using the `ore.predict` function:

```
> gm <- glm(quality ~., data=WhiteWine)
> ore.create(WhiteWine, "WHITE_WINE")
> pred_Quality <- ore.predict(gm, newdata=WHITE_WINE)
> pred_Quality2 <- cbind(WHITE_WINE, pred_Quality)
> head(pred_Quality2)
```

You can also use the `ore.predict` function to label a data set with a predicted cluster based on the kMeans model that was created:

```
> KMmodel <- kmeans(WhiteWine, centers=5)
> KMmodel pred_Cluster <- ore.predict(KMmodel, newdata=WHITE_WINE)
> head(pred_Cluster)
> pred_Cluster2 <- cbind(WHITE_WINE, pred_Cluster)
> head(pred_Cluster2)
```

Summary

Oracle R Enterprise comes with a wide range of advanced analytics algorithms. These algorithms have been covered in Chapter 7 and in this chapter. These algorithms consist of the in-database data mining algorithms and additional algorithms specifically built to be more efficient, to have better memory usage, and to work in a very integrated way with the Oracle Database. These algorithms allow you to work with data that is located in the Oracle Database, thus enabling you to utilize the database server as a powerful compute engine. In addition to the algorithms supplied as part of Oracle Advanced Analytics, and specifically with Oracle R Enterprise, you have a number of ways of incorporating and using the vast array of algorithms available with the R language. In this chapter, a number of examples were given to illustrate how you can use these algorithms to build models and score data in the database.

CHAPTER 9

Creating R Scripts in the User-defined R Script Repository

When working with your ORE code, you will start to build up many pieces of repeated code. One way to consolidate them is to create R functions that contain your code. When it comes to using the embedded R execution features of Oracle R Enterprise, you will be required to store these R functions as user-defined R scripts. Additionally, if you want to be able to use your R analytics within SQL, you will need to create these as user-defined R scripts in the R Script Repository in the Oracle Database. These user-defined R scripts are stored in the Oracle Database and can be called using some of the ORE embedded R execution functions or the equivalent SQL functions. Enabling these user-defined R scripts to be called using SQL allows your R analytics to be included in any application that uses SQL to access the data in the database. These ORE functions and SQL functions are discussed in Chapter 10.

In this chapter we will look at how you can store your R functions as user-defined R scripts. There are two different ways of creating and managing these user-defined R scripts. Which one you use kind of depends on whether your role is in a data analytics team or an application development team. If you are in a data analytics team, you will probably work with the ORE functions to create and manage scripts in the R Script Repository in the Oracle Database. On the other hand, as an application developer you will use these exact same R scripts and include them in your code using SQL. There is also a set of SQL functions that allows you to create and manage user-defined R scripts.

Using the R Script Repository

In this section we look at the set of ORE functions available to you to create and manage your user-defined R scripts. These R scripts are stored in the R Script Repository. You do not need to create an R Script Repository because it is created for you when you install ORE for your Oracle Database. Table 9-1 lists the ORE functions that are used to create and manage R scripts in the R Script Repository in the Oracle Database.

The following sections explore examples of how you can use each of these ORE functions for creating and managing user-defined R scripts.

When you create a user-defined R script, you are creating an object in the Oracle Database. Because of this, you need an additional database system privilege in order to create and store user-defined R scripts in the R Script Repository. During the installation of ORE, a new database role was created called RQADMIN. All Oracle schemas that will be creating user-defined R scripts in the R Script Repository will need to have this role granted to them. To do this, you or your DBA will need to connect to the Oracle Database as SYSDBA and run the following command, where *<ORE_USER>* is the name of the Oracle schema that will be creating the user-defined R scripts:

```
SQL> grant rqadmin to <ORE_USER>;
```

R Function	Description
`ore.scriptCreate`	Adds an R script to the R Script Repository.
`ore.scriptDrop`	Deletes an R script from the R Script Repository.
`ore.scriptList`	Lists the details of the R scripts that are stored in the R Script Repository.
`ore.scriptLoad`	Loads the named R function from the R Script Repository into the R environment.
`ore.grant`	Grants an Oracle schema access to run a user-defined R script. The `ore.grant` is performed by the Oracle schema that created and owns the user-defined R script.
`ore.revoke`	This command removes the execute privilege on a user-defined R script from another Oracle schema. This command will be performed by the owner of the user -R script.

TABLE 9-1.   *ORE Functions for Creating and Managing R Scripts in the R Script Repository*

Creating and Dropping R Scripts

User-defined R scripts allow for the repeated use of these functions within your ORE code and provide ease of deployment in your applications using the ORE SQL API functions. When you create a user-defined R script, it is stored in the R Script Repository in the Oracle Database.

Here is the syntax of the ORE function to create and store a user-defined R script:

```
ore.scriptCreate(name, FUN, global = FALSE, overwrite = FALSE)
```

The `ore.scriptCreate` function requires two main parameter values. The first of these parameters is the unique name for the R script. The name needs to be unique for the user creating it. The second parameter is the specification of the function.

The following example illustrates the creation of an R script called `CustomerAge`. The R function calculates the approximate age based on the year the customer was born, which is supplied as a parameter to the function.

```
> ore.scriptCreate("CustomerAge", function (YearBorn) {
     CustAge <- as.numeric(format(Sys.time(), "%Y")) - YearBorn
     data.frame(CustAge)
  } )
```

To call this function, you can use one of the ORE embedded R execution functions, such as `ore.doEval`:

```
> #Example of calling an User defined R script using the ore.doEval function
> # Call the script to calculate the age. Returns an ore.object
> res <- ore.doEval(FUN.NAME="CustomerAge", YearBorn=2010)
> res
> 6
    CustAge
1       6
```

The `ore.doEval` function, in this example, calls the user-defined R script `CustomerAge` and passes in the year to be used by the function contained in our user-defined R script.

It is advisable that you create and test the function as an independent R function before storing it as a user-defined R script. By doing this, you ensure that the function performs as required and produces any results in the format needed for later use.

As mentioned earlier, the user-defined R script is saved to the local Oracle schema, and only the user of the schema will have access to that R script. If you have an R function, and hence a user-defined R script, that you would like to share with all schemas in the Oracle Database, you can set the `global` parameter to `TRUE`. By default, the `global` parameter is `FALSE`. Using our previous example, the following shows the `ore.createScript` with the `global` parameter:

```
> ore.scriptCreate("CustomerAge", function (YearBorn) {
       CustAge <- as.numeric(format(Sys.time(), "%Y")) - YearBorn
       data.frame(CustAge)
   }, global=TRUE )
```

You can use the `ore.grant` and `ore.revoke` functions to control who can invoke your user-defined R scripts. The next section looks at these commands.

The final parameter for the `ore.createScript` function is the `overwrite` parameter. By default, this is set to `FALSE` to prevent you from replacing the currently stored user-defined R script with another version that has the same name, or replacing it with completely different content. But when you are going through the development and testing of your R script, you may need to store the script again. In order to do this efficiently, you can set the `overwrite` parameter to `TRUE`, as illustrated here:

```
> ore.scriptCreate("CustomerAge", function (YearBorn) {
       CustAge <- as.numeric(format(Sys.time(), "%Y")) - YearBorn
       data.frame(CustAge)
   }, overwrite=TRUE)
```

In this example, no value is specified for the `global` parameter. This was set to `TRUE` in the previous example, making it globally available in the Oracle Database.

But in this example, the `global` parameter will revert to the default value and will now convert the previously defined global R script back to being a private R script for the current schema.

When you want to remove an R script from the R Script Repository, you can use the `ore.scriptDrop` function. If you want to use the `ore.scriptDrop` function to drop the previously created `CustomerAge` script, you can do so as follows:

```
> ore.scriptDrop("CustomerAge")
```

The `ore.scriptDrop` function also has a `global` parameter. If the user-defined R script was created as a global user-defined R script, you need to use `global=TRUE` in the `ore.scriptDrop` function, like so:

```
> ore.scriptDrop("CustomerAge", global=TRUE)
```

Take care when dropping user-defined R scripts because they may be used by other users and in many of your processes and applications.

Granting and Revoking Privileges to User-defined R Scripts

To control who has access to run your R scripts, you can use the `ore.grant` function to grant read access for an R script to only the people who require it. Similarly, when you want to remove this privilege from a specific user and without affecting any other users of the R script, you can use the `ore.revoke` function.

Here is the syntax of the `ore.grant` and `ore.revoke` functions when used with user-defined R scripts:

```
ore.grant(name, type = "rqscript", user)

ore.revoke(name, type = "rqscript", user)
```

The `name` parameter is the name of the user-defined R script (that is, the function name), and the `user` parameter is the name or list of Oracle schemas to which you want to grant read access or from which you want to revoke read access for the R script. The following example illustrates how you can grant read access for the `CustomerAge` R script to the DMUSER schema and then revoke that access:

```
> ore.grant("CustomerAge", type = "rqscript", "DMUSER")

> ore.revoke("CustomerAge", type = "rqscript", "DMUSER")
```

Using the R script in another schema, the user can reference the name of the R script as if it was a local R script. In the preceding `ore.grant` function, the DMUSER is granted read access to the `CustomerAge` user-defined R script. When you connect to the DMUSER schema, you can now call this user-defined R script, just like earlier in this chapter:

```
> ore.connect(user="dmuser", service_name="pdb12c", host="localhost",
              password="dmuser", port=1521, all=TRUE)
> # Call the script to calculate the age. Returns an ore.object
> res <- ore.doEval(FUN.NAME="CustomerAge", YearBorn=2010)
> res
    CustAge
1        11
```

Managing the R Script Repository

After you have created your user-defined R scripts, you may from time to time need to check what scripts exist for your Oracle schema or to which scripts you have been given privileges. The `ore.scriptList` function allows you to list the R scripts that are available to you. When you use the `ore.scriptList` function, you get a list of all the scripts, but you can also search for scripts that have a particular type (for example, user, global, grant, and granted). Additionally, when your list of R scripts is large, you can enter a subset of an R script name. In this case, all R scripts containing the search term will be returned by the function. The following example illustrates some of the ways you can use the `ore.scriptList` function to search the ORE Script Repository:

```
> # list all the scripts available for the user
> ore.scriptList()
> # list the scripts based on the different types
> ore.scriptList(type="all")
> ore.scriptList(type="user")
> ore.scriptList(type="global")
> ore.scriptList(type="grant")
> ore.scriptList(type="granted")
> ore.scriptList(name="CustomerAge")
> # search for user defined R scripts that contain a string pattern as part
> # of their name
> ore.scriptList(pattern="Cust")
```

Another ORE function available to you is the `ore.scriptLoad` function. This allows you to load the function, contained within the user-defined R script, into your local R environment and give it a local function name. This way, you can reuse the code without having to use one of the embedded R execution functions, as illustrated earlier. The following example takes the `CustomerAge` R script we created earlier and loads it to the current R environment and gives this function the name CUSTAGE:

```
> ore.scriptLoad(name="CustomerAge", newname="CUSTAGE")
```

CUSTAGE now exists in the local R environment and can simplify calling of the function, as shown next, where we pass in a year as a parameter to the function and get the returned result displayed:

```
> CUSTAGE(2003)

    CustAge
1       13
```

Creating Scripts Using the SQL API

Oracle R Enterprise comes with a set of SQL functions that allows you to create and manage scripts in R Script Repository in the Oracle Database. With the SQL interfaces for Oracle R Enterprise, you can now make available the vast array of analytic and graphing features available with the R language by using just SQL. Any application that can use SQL and the Oracle Database can now include this expanded set of analytics and graphics.

In the previous section of the chapter, we worked through the various ORE functions that allow you to create and manage user-defined R scripts. These scripts are stored in the Oracle Database in the R Script Repository. There is a similar set of SQL functions that allows you to create and manage R functions in the R Script Repository in the Oracle Database. These functions are listed in Table 9-2.

PL/SQL Procedure	Description
sys.rqScriptCreate	Creates the supplied R function in the R Script Repository
sys.rqScriptDrop	Removes the R function/script from the R Script Repository
rqGrant	Grants read privileges on an ORE datastore or stored R function/script in the R Script Repository
rqRevoke	Revokes read privileges on an ORE datastore or stored R function/script in the R Script Repository

TABLE 9-2.   *PL/SQL Procedures for Managing User-defined R Scripts*

The following sections show you how to use these SQL functions to create and manage your R scripts in the R Script Repository. We will look at the various SQL functions that are available to run your R scripts in Chapter 10.

Creating an R Script

Earlier in this chapter you saw how to use the ORE R functions to create and store your R scripts in R Script Repository in the Oracle Database. The first of the ORE SQL functions we will look at is the `sys.rqScriptCreate` function. This function allows you to create an R script in R Script Repository in the Oracle Database using SQL.

The syntax of the `sys.rqScriptCreate` function is as follows:

```
sys.rqScriptCreate (
    V_NAME VARCHAR2 IN
    V_SCRIPT CLOB IN
    V_GLOBAL BOOLEAN IN DEFAULT
    V_OVERWRITE BOOLEAN IN DEFAULT)
```

The structure of the `sys.rqScriptCreate` function is very similar to the `ore.scriptCreate` function you saw earlier in the chapter. The script accepts four parameters: the first parameter is the name of the user-defined R script, the second parameter is the R function, the third parameter defines whether the user-defined R script will be local or global, and the fourth parameter details whether the existing user-defined R script should be overwritten. The third parameter (`V_GLOBAL`) and fourth parameter (`V_OVERWITE`) are optional, and both have a default value of `FALSE`. The following code gives an example of creating a user-defined R script that loads a model from an ORE datastore and then uses it to create a predicted value. The R script then returns the actual value along with the predicted value.

```
BEGIN
    sys.rqScriptCreate('DEMO_LM_APPLY', 'function(dat, ds_name) {
        ore.load(ds_name)
        pre <- predict(mod, newdata=dat, supplemental.cols="alcohol")
        res <- cbind(dat, PRED=pre)
        res <- res[,c("alcohol", "PRED")]
    } ');
END;
```

You will notice that we need to call this ORE SQL function as part of a PL/SQL block, hence the `BEGIN` and `END` statements in the example. The example creates a user-defined R script called `DEMO_LM_APPLY` in the R Script Repository for the current schema. The R function accepts two parameters. The first parameter is the data set to be used by the code within the R function, and the second is the name of an ORE datastore that contains the linear regression model used to calculate the predicted value (this example assumes that the model was previously created and stored in the ORE datastore; see Chapter 10 for more details). As you can see, no values are defined for the third and fourth parameters of the `sys.rqScriptCreate` function. This means it will only be usable by the schema running this code, and if an R script already exists, it will not be overwritten.

When the R script is created, we can use one of the ORE SQL API functions (see Chapter 10 for more details on these functions) to run it. For this particular example, we can use the `rqTableEval` function:

```
select *
from table(rqTableEval(cursor(select * from white_wine),
          cursor(select 1 as "ore.connect", 'DEMO_LM_DS' as "ds_name" from dual),
          'select 1 as "alcohol", 1 as "PRED" from dual',
          'DEMO_LM_APPLY') );

   alcohol       PRED
---------- ----------
        10 9.58434071
      10.6 8.83113972
      10.7  10.378701
        10 9.58434071
      12.5  12.146045
      10.6 8.83113972
      12.8  12.668966
...
```

If you want your R script to be made available for others to use in their SQL queries and their applications, you need to create the script with the `V_GLOBAL` parameter set to `TRUE`, as illustrated here:

```
BEGIN
    sys.rqScriptCreate('DEMO_LM_APPLY', 'function(dat, ds_name) {
        ore.load(ds_name)
        pre <- predict(mod, newdata=dat, supplemental.cols="alcohol")
        res <- cbind(dat, PRED=pre)
        res <- res[,c("alcohol", "PRED")]
    } ', TRUE);
END;
```

Care needs to be taken with what R scripts you create as global. If this is not something you want to happen, then create your R scripts as private (the default) and then use `rqGrant` and `rqRevoke` to mange who has access to each user-defined R script.

As you go through the development and testing of your R scripts, you may need to re-create them. You can either precede the `sys.rqScriptCreate` with a `sys.rqScriptDrop` function or use the fourth parameter to the `sys.rqScriptCreate` function to overwrite the existing R script. The following example illustrates this, as well as makes the user-defined R script private:

```
BEGIN
    sys.rqScriptCreate('DEMO_LM_APPLY', 'function(dat, ds_name) {
```

```
        ore.load(ds_name)
        pre <- predict(mod, newdata=dat, supplemental.cols="alcohol")
        res <- cbind(dat, PRED=pre)
        res <- res[,c("alcohol", "PRED")]
    } ', FALSE, TRUE);
END;
```

We could have used the named parameters and replaced the third and fourth parameters with the following line. Although a value is not given for the V_GLOBAL parameter, when the code is run, the R script will be re-created and the default value for V_GLOBAL will be used (FALSE):

```
    } ', overwrite => TRUE);
```

Dropping a Script

When the time comes for you to remove a user-defined R script from the R Script Repository, you can use the sys.rqScriptDrop function. The following example illustrates how to drop the DEMO_LM_APPLY script that was previously created:

```
-- Using the sys.rqScriptDrop function to remove an user defined R script
BEGIN
    sys.rqScriptDrop('DEMO_LM_APPLY');
END;
```

Granting and Revoking Access

You have seen that when you create a user-defined R script, you have the option to make the script private (the default) or to make the script global. To allow you to control who can access and use your R scripts, you can use the rqGrant function to grant individual users access to the script.

The rqGrant function can also be used for granting access to an ORE datastore. To define that the grant is for a user-defined R script, use the second parameter for this function, which is rqscript. The first parameter is the name of the R script, and the third parameter is the name of the Oracle schema to which you are granting the access. The following example illustrates the granting of access to the DEMO_LM_APPLY R script to the DMUSER schema:

```
-- Grant the DMUSER user access to the DEMO_LM_APPLY user defined R script
BEGIN
    rqGrant('DEMO_LM_APPLY', 'rqscript', 'DMUSER');
END;
```

If the script was already created as a global and you then tried to grant access to an individual user, you would receive an Oracle error message informing you of this.

When another Oracle schema no longer needs access to the R script, you can revoke the access privilege from that schema. The ORE function `rqRevoke` can be used for this purpose, and it has the same syntax and structure as the `rqGrant` function, where the first parameter is the name of the R script, the second parameter defines that we are processing an R script, and the third parameter is the name of the Oracle schema from which the privilege is being revoked. The following example illustrates the revoking of access to the DEMO_LM_APPLY function from the DMUSER schema:

```
-- Grant the DMUSER user access to the DEMO_LM_APPLY user defined R script
BEGIN
    rqRevoke('DEMO_LM_APPLY', 'rqscript', 'DMUSER');
END;
```

Data Dictionary Views for User-defined R Scripts

When you want to view what user-defined R scripts you have in your R Script Repository, you can use one of the data dictionary views listed in Table 9-3. These allow you to view all the R scripts you have created or have been granted access to use, either by an `ore.grant` R function or by an `rqGrant` SQL function.

```
-- Viewing the scripts in the R Script Repository
select * from all_rq_scripts;
select * from user_rq_scripts;
select * from user_rq_script_privs;
select * from sys.rq_scripts;
select * from sys.rq_scripts where owner='RQSYS';
```

Data Dictionary View	Description
ALL_RQ_SCRIPTS	Contains details of the scripts in the R Script Repository that are available to the current user
USER_RQ_SCRIPTS	Contains details of the scripts in the R Script Repository that are owned by the current user
USER_RQ_SCRIPT_PRIVS	Contains details of the scripts in the R Script Repository that the current user has granted read access to and the user to whom access has been granted
SYS.RQ_SCRIPTS	Contains details of the system scripts in the R Script Repository

TABLE 9-3.   *Oracle Data Dictionary Views for User-defined R Scripts*

Summary

When you're writing your R code, it is useful to group certain parts of your code together into defined units. Typically in R you can do this by creating R functions. Oracle R Enterprise allows you to store these functions in the Oracle Database and share them with other users. This can be achieved by creating user-defined R scripts that contains the R function code. With ORE, you can create user-defined R scripts by using the R functions or by using the SQL functions shown in this chapter. Once a user-defined R script is stored in the R Script Repository in the Oracle Database, it can be used in a variety of ways, including being used with the embedded R execution functions that can be called using the ORE R API functions or the ORE SQL API functions. You can now expose the vast analytic capabilities of the R language using SQL. This allows you to include R analytics within your custom-developed application and analytic dashboards. The next chapter provides examples of how you can use the embedded R execution functions that call user-defined R scripts, including the R scripts created in this chapter.

CHAPTER 10

Embedded R Execution

The embedded R execution feature of Oracle R Enterprise allows you to run R scripts on the Oracle Database server, which in turn allows you to use the vast array of analytic features of the R language to analyze and process your data. With embedded R execution, the Oracle Database will spawn one or more R processes. The number of R processes spawned depends on the type of ORE function you use and the parameter settings. These ORE functions allow you to process significantly greater volumes of data, in a shorter period of time and in parallel, compared to the traditional method of using R on your client machine.

The embedded R execution feature of Oracle R Enterprise comes with a set of ORE R functions and a set of ORE SQL functions. This chapter provides examples to illustrate how you can use each of these functions.

Embedded R Execution Using the R Interface

Oracle R Enterprise comes with a set of R features that allows you to call an R function and have the Oracle Database execute it as an R process on the server. With embedded R execution, some of these R functions allow you to create multiple parallel R processes on the database server that are dynamically started and managed by the database.

Table 10-1 lists the embedded R execution functions available in Oracle R Enterprise.

R Function	Description
`ore.doEval`	Executes a user-defined R script that is passed to it and returns any result generated.
`ore.tableApply`	Executes a user-defined R script on all rows on a supplied data set.
`ore.groupApply`	Executes a user-defined R script on partitions of the supplied data set. The partitions are defined on one or more attributes of the data set. Parallel execution is supported for each partition.
`ore.rowApply`	Executes a user-defined R script on a defined set of rows (chunks) from the supplied data set. Parallel execution is supported for each set of rows (chunks).
`ore.indexApply`	Executes the user-defined R script with no automatic transfer of data but provides the index of the invocation, 1 to n, where n is the number of times to invoke the function. Parallel execution is supported for each invocation.

TABLE 10-1. *Embedded R Execution Functions in Oracle R Enterprise*

Each of the functions listed in Table 10-1 has an equivalent SQL function. These are covered in the "Embedded R Execution Using the SQL Interface" section later in this chapter.

How to Use the ore.doEval Function

The `ore.doEval` function is a good general-purpose function that allows you to run a user-defined R script in a database-side R engine. The specific R code can be passed as a parameter or can be wrapped in a user-defined R script, as was described in Chapter 9.

Here is the syntax of the `ore.doEval` function:

```
ore.doEval(FUN, ..., FUN.VALUE = NULL, FUN.NAME = NULL, FUN.OWNER = NULL)
```

The `ore.doEval` function has been used in various chapters in this book to perform specific tests on the Oracle Database server and the Oracle R Enterprise installation. To illustrate the various aspects of the `ore.doEval` function, the following examples show you a number of ways you can use it.

The first example illustrates using the `ore.doEval` function in its most basic form. We pass some simple R code to this function, and the function then runs this R code using the embedded R execution feature of Oracle R Enterprise. The example consists of two calls of the `ore.doEval` function. The first gets the current version of R installed on the Oracle Database server, and the second tests for the version number of one of the installed R packages (see Chapter 14 for details of how to install this R package).

```
> # Check the version of R install on the Oracle Database server for ORE
> ore.doEval(function() R.Version())
> # Check R package version number. This packages is installed in ORE in Ch14
> ore.doEval(function() packageVersion("e1071"))
```

In this example, the results from the call to `ore.doEval` are returned and displayed to the user. In the next example, we look at how you can manage the values returned from the `ore.doEval` function. The `ore.doEval` function returns an ORE object (`ore.object`). In the following example, a string is created and returned. When you examine the returned object, you will see that it is an `ore.object`, which means that the results generated are still in the Oracle Database and have been displayed via the ORE Transparency layer to you.

```
> # Managing the format of the returned object
> res <- ore.doEval(function() paste("Hello Brendan", "the time is",
                    format(Sys.time(),"%X")))
> # Display the result
> res
 [1] "Hello Brendan the time is 10:58:46"
> # Check the class of the object
> class(res)
 [1] "ore.object" attr(,"package")
 [1] "OREembed"
```

To be able to use the data in the retuned object, you need to change the format of the results from an ORE object (`ore.object`) to an ORE data frame (`ore.frame`). To do this, you need to define the format of the ORE data frame using the `FUN.VALUE` parameter. This is illustrated in the following example, where we define the format of the data frame for the returned results:

```
> # Return a ore.frame for the result of the function
> res <- ore.doEval(function() data.frame(paste("Hello Brendan", "the time is",
                  format(Sys.time(),"%X"))),
  FUN.VALUE = data.frame(text_string = character(), stringsAsFactors = FALSE))
> # Display the result
> res
                          text_string
1  Hello Brendan the time is 11:03:48

> class(res)
 [1] "ore.frame" attr(,"package")
 [1] "OREbase"
```

You can also use `ore.doEval` to call an R script that is stored in the R Script Repository. Creating R scripts was covered in Chapter 9, and one of the R scripts we created was `CustomerAge`. This function calculates the approximate age of a customer based on the year of birth, which is passed as a parameter to the function. Again, you need to be careful with what type of object you would like returned from the call to the `ore.doEval` function. The following example illustrates the two scenarios you can have. The first part of this example returns an `ore.object`, and the second returns an `ore.frame` because the return format has been defined using the `FUN.VALUE` parameter.

```
> # Call the script to calculate the age. Returns an ore.object
> ore.doEval(FUN.NAME="CustomerAge", YearBorn=2010)
> res <- ore.doEval(FUN.NAME="CustomerAge", YearBorn=BirthYear)
> class(res)
> res

> # Call the script to calculate the age. Returns an ore.frame
> res2 <- ore.doEval(FUN.NAME="CustomerAge", YearBorn=2010,
                  FUN.VALUE=data.frame(Age=1))
> class(res2)
> res2
```

The final feature of the `ore.doEval` function is the `ore.connect` parameter, which allows you to connect to the Oracle Database and access the data and objects that exist in an ORE datastore. In the following example, we have a new version of our `CustomerAge` function called `CustomerAge2` that calculates the difference between the customer age and some reference age. The reference age (`refAge`) is a variable that is stored in an ORE datastore called `ORE_DS`.

```
> # Create a script to calculate the age difference to a reference value
> ore.scriptDrop("CustomerAge2")
> ore.scriptCreate("CustomerAge2", function (YearBorn) {
     ore.load("ORE_DS", refAge)
     CustAge <- as.numeric(format(Sys.time(), "%Y")) - YearBorn
     data.frame(CustAge-refAge)
  } )
```

When calling the ore.doEval function, you can add the ore.connect parameter to it. The ore.connect parameter allows the function to connect to the current schema and access the ORE datastore that is housed in it.

```
> # Call the script to calculate the age. Returns an ore.frame
> res3 <- ore.doEval(FUN.NAME="CustomerAge2", YearBorn=BirthYear,
                   FUN.VALUE=data.frame(Age=1), ore.connect=TRUE)
> class(res3)
> res3
```

When using ore.doEval with the ore.connect=TRUE parameter setting, you can also get access to the data in your schema. For example, if data existed in a table or view in your schema that you wanted to analyze, you can use the ore.sync and ore.pull functions, within the ore.doEval function, to make the data available for analysis, like so:

```
> # Use data in your schema
# connect to the DMUSER schema
> ore.connect(user="dmuser", service_name="pdb12c", host="localhost",
            password="dmuser", port=1521, all=TRUE)
> # aggregate the data based on AGE attribute
> res4 <- ore.doEval(function(){
           ore.sync(table="MINING_DATA_BUILD_V")
           dat <- ore.pull(ore.get("MINING_DATA_BUILD_V"))
           aggdata <- aggregate(dat$AFFINITY_CARD,
                    by = list(Age = dat$AGE),
                    FUN = length) },
        FUN.VALUE=data.frame(AGE=1, AGE_NUM=1), ore.connect=TRUE)
> res4
```

How to Use the ore.tableApply Function

The ore.tableApply function extends the capabilities of the ore.doEval function, shown in the previous section, by allowing your R code to run on the data that is contained in a table in your schema in the Oracle Database or that is available via an ORE data frame.

Here is the syntax of the ore.tableApply function:

```
ore.tableApply(X, FUN, ..., FUN.VALUE = NULL, FUN.NAME = NULL, FUN.OWNER = NULL)
```

In the previous section, examples were given showing you how to use the `ore.doEval` function to process data from an ORE data frame or data in your schema. Although this is useful, the `ore.doEval` function is not optimized to process the data in your schema in this way. The `ore.tableEval` function, however, *is* optimized to process this kind of data. Here's an example:

```
> # connect to the DMUSER schema
> ore.connect(user="dmuser", service_name="pdb12c", host="localhost",
             password="dmuser", port=1521, all=TRUE)
> # count the number of customers for each AGE
> ageProfile <- ore.tableApply(MINING_DATA_BUILD_V,
                 function(dat) {
                       aggdata <- aggregate(dat$AFFINITY_CARD,
                                      by = list(Age = dat$AGE),
                                      FUN = length)
                 },
                 FUN.VALUE=data.frame(AGE=1, AGE_NUM=1) )
> ageProfile
    AGE AGE_NUM
  1  17      18
  2  18      21
  3  19      32
  4  20      32
  5  21      26
  6  22      42
...
> class(ageProfile)
```

This example illustrates using the `ore.tableApply` function to count the number of customers for each value of `AGE` for the records contained in the `MINING_DATA_BUILD_V` view. The `ore.tableApply` loads the data from the specified `ore.frame` into the R engine and passes it to the user function as the first argument. It then aggregates the data and finally returns the results in an ORE data frame that is defined by the `FUN.VALUE`.

You can also call an R script using the `ore.tableApply` function. For example, you can write your R code and have it stored as a script in the Oracle Database. This ORE script can be reused in other parts of your analytics without you having to copy or rewrite the code you defined in the `ore.tableApply` function, as shown in the preceding example. Your R scripts can also be incorporated into and used in your applications for easy deployment. The following example illustrates how you can take the R function code shown in the previous example and store it as an ORE script:

```
> # Create a script to aggregate the data based on AGE attribute
> ore.scriptDrop("CustomerAge3")
> ore.scriptCreate("CustomerAge3", function (dat) {
     aggdata <- aggregate(dat$AFFINITY_CARD,
                    by = list(Age = dat$AGE),
                    FUN = length) } )
```

You can now use the script in the `ore.tableApply` function, as shown next. The table or view that is defined as the first parameter is passed to the function call. Just like in our previous example, the output is formatted to return an ORE data frame by using `FUN.VALUE`.

```
> # using ore.tableApply to call a script age
> Profile2 <- ore.tableApply(MINING_DATA_BUILD_V,
                      FUN.NAME="CustomerAge3",
                      FUN.VALUE=data.frame(Age=1, x=1) )
> class(ageProfile2)
> head(ageProfile2)
```

The `ore.tableApply` function is efficient at processing a function consisting of a number of R commands on the data that exists in a table or view in your Oracle schema. The ORE functions `ore.doEval` and `ore.tableApply` run serially by executing a single R process with the entire data in memory; therefore, care needs to be taken to ensure that the R process does not consume most of the available memory on the Oracle Database server. The other embedded R functions covered in the following sections are enabled for parallel execution.

How to Use the ore.groupApply Function

The `ore.groupApply` function allows you to process a data set by partitioning the data on one or more of the attributes in the data set. The supplied R function code will be applied to each partition of the data set that corresponds with values of attributes used to partition the data set. For example, suppose we have STATE as the attribute to partition the data set. If values contained in this attribute are for USA, we would have 50 distinct values. This means that the supplied R function code would be applied to the records for each value of STATE. The attribute (or attributes) used to partition the data set is indicated by the INDEX parameter.

Here is the syntax of the `ore.groupApply` function:

```
ore.groupApply(X, INDEX, FUN, ..., FUN.VALUE = NULL,
            FUN.NAME = NULL, FUN.OWNER = NULL,
            parallel = getOption("ore.parallel", NULL))
```

The `ore.groupApply` function is one of a set of ORE functions, also including `ore.rowApply` and `ore.indexApply`, that has the ability to spawn multiple parallel embedded R processes on the database server. This allows for data sets to be divided into smaller parts, and each of the embedded R processes will process each of these smaller parts. This allows the data set to be processed more quickly than sequentially processing the entire data set.

The following example illustrates the use of `ore.groupApply`. This example uses the wine data set that has been used in other chapters, and it illustrates how you can calculate the mean value of one of the data set attributes (`residual.sugar`) grouped by or partitioned by another attribute (`quality`). The partitioned attribute is passed as the second parameter of the `ore.groupApply` function.

```
> # calculate the mean Residual Sugar for each category of Wine Quality
> avgAge <- ore.groupApply(WHITE_WINE, WHITE_WINE$quality, function(dat){
                avgSugar <- mean(dat$residual.sugar)
                data.frame(unique(dat$quality), avgSugar) },
                FUN.VALUE=data.frame(QUALITY=1, AVG_SUGAR=1))
> class(avgAge)
> avgAge
    QUALITY AVG_SUGAR
  1       3  6.392500
  2       4  4.628221
  3       5  7.334969
  4       6  6.441606
  5       7  5.186477
  6       8  5.671429
  7       9  4.120000
```

This example illustrates the partitioning of the data based on one of the other attributes in the data set. When you're working with more advanced analytics techniques and with the various machine learning algorithms, it is useful to build and apply these models based on smaller partitions. These smaller partitions can be based on multiple attributes. The following example illustrates how you can partition on two attributes, and you can see how easy it is to expand the list to more:

```
> # calculate the mean Residual Sugar for each category of Wine Quality
> avgAge2 <- ore.groupApply(WHITE_WINE, WHITE_WINE[,c("quality", "alcohol")],
          function(dat){
              avgSugar <- mean(dat$residual.sugar)
              data.frame(unique(dat$quality), unique(dat$alcohol), avgSugar) },
              FUN.VALUE=data.frame(QUALITY=1, ALCOHOL=1, AVG_SUGAR=1))
> avgAge2
    QUALITY   ALCOHOL AVG_SUGAR
  1       3  8.000000  5.100000
  2       3  8.500000  1.600000
  3       3  9.100000  7.600000
  4       3  9.400000  1.550000
  5       3  9.600000  1.400000
  6       3  9.700000 11.100000
...
```

Care needs to be taken with all these ORE functions that spawn multiple embedded R processes on the database server so as to limit the number of R processes that will be spawned.

How to Use the ore.rowApply Function

The `ore.rowApply` function allows you to process a data set by dividing the data into chunks of a defined size. By doing this, you are creating smaller chunks of data, and each of these chunks will be processed based on R code supplied in the function.

The `ore.rowApply` function is another of the ORE embedded functions that can process the data in parallel. See the section later in this chapter, "Parallel Execution of Embedded R Functions," on this parallel feature. When parallel processing is enabled, the `ore.rowApply` function will spawn multiple embedded R processes on the Oracle server, and each one will process the data for each of the chunks that has been created, thus allowing for large-scale processing of data in parallel.

Here is the syntax of the `ore.rowApply` function:

```
ore.rowApply(X, FUN, ..., FUN.VALUE = NULL,
             FUN.NAME = NULL, FUN.OWNER = NULL, rows = 1,
             parallel = getOption("ore.parallel", NULL))
```

The following example illustrates how you can use the `ore.rowApply` function. This example uses a linear regression model developed in Chapter 8. This model is stored in an ORE datastore. The following code was shown in Chapter 8, with an additional statement that stores the linear regression model in an ORE datastore. This is to allow this model to be reused at a later stage.

```
> # ore.lm model created in chapter 8
> LMmodel <- ore.lm(alcohol  ~., data=WHITE_WINE)
> LMmodel
> summary(LMmodel)
> # save the model to an ORE data store
> ore.save(LMmodel, name="MODELS_DS")
```

You can now use this linear regression model in an `ore.rowApply` function to score the data set. To apply for the multiple embedded R processes to be created, we can divide the data set to be processed into a number of chunks. These partitions are based on a defined number of records specified using the `rows` parameter. In the following example, the `rows` parameter is set at 500 records:

```
> amtAlcohol <- ore.rowApply(WHITE_WINE, function(dat){
          ore.load("MODELS_DS", list="LMmodel")
          LMscored <- predict(LMmodel, newdata=dat)
          lmRes <- cbind(dat, LMscored)
          res<- data.frame(alcohol=lmRes$alcohol, lmRes$LMscored)
          res },
       FUN.VALUE=data.frame(alcohol=1, LMscored=1),
       ore.connect=TRUE,
       rows=500)
```

The `ore.rowApply` function takes the name of the data set to be processed as the first parameter. The first step the function performs is to load the saved model from the ORE datastore called `MODELS_DS`. To enable this to happen, we need to have the parameter `ore.connect=TRUE`. The linear regression model, `LMmodel`, is then used to score the data set. It then combines the original data set with the scored value and finally selects the variables to return as the result of the function.

The `FUN.VALUE` parameter is used to define the format of the returned ORE data frame. In this case, it is an ORE data frame that consists of two variables called `alcohol` and `LMscored`. If you do not define a value for the `FUN.VALUE` parameter, the results will be returned as an ORE list, and additional processing is needed to convert this to a data frame.

An interesting experiment you can perform to see the results from each of the embedded R processes is to remove the `FUN.VALUE` parameter. When you run the `ore.rowApply` function, you will be able to see that the returned results are a list of values for each of the embedded R processes.

How to Use the ore.indexApply Function

The `ore.indexApply` function allows you to process a data set a defined number of times based on an index value. The number of times the function will be executed is defined by the index parameter for the `ore.indexApply` function. The R code contained within the function will then be performed on each of these partitions.

Here is the syntax of the `ore.indexApply` function:

```
ore.indexApply(times, FUN, ..., FUN.VALUE = NULL,
            FUN.NAME = NULL, FUN.OWNER = NULL,
            parallel = getOption("ore.parallel", NULL))
```

The following example illustrates how you can use the `ore.indexApply` function. This example takes a random sample of records from the supplied data set. The data set, `CUSTOMERS_USA`, was created back in Chapter 3. The first parameter is the `index` value. This `index` parameter is set to 5. The parameter `dat` defines the data set to be used, and the parameter `samplePercent` defines the percentage of records to be randomly sampled during each indexed execution. A different sample will be generated for each index execution. The output from this example is an ORE list containing the randomly sampled data from each of the five executions.

```
> idxSample <- ore.indexApply(5, function(index, dat, samplePercent){
                set.seed(index)
                # calculate the sample size
                SampleSize <- nrow(dat)*(samplePercent/100)
                # Create an index of records for the Sample
                Index_Sample <- sample(1:nrow(dat), SampleSize)
                group <- as.integer(1:nrow(dat) %in% Index_Sample)
                # Create a sample data set
                sampleData <- dat[group==TRUE,]
                res <- data.frame(sampleData[,1:4])
            },
            dat=CUSTOMERS_USA,
            samplePercent=20)
> idxSample
```

The output from this example is an ORE list, and you may want to convert it to a data frame. This can be done using the `FUN.VALUE` parameter to convert the returned ORE list (referred to by `idxSample` in the preceding example) to a data frame.

Parallel Execution of Embedded R Functions

In the preceding sections, it was mentioned that the `ore.groupApply`, `ore.rowApply`, and `ore.indexApply` functions can spawn multiple embedded R processes on the Oracle Database server to allow the data to be processed in parallel. When you look at the syntax for these functions, you will see that they have a `parallel` parameter with the following format:

```
parallel = getOption("ore.parallel", NULL)
```

This default parameter setting checks the current R environment for the current setting for the environment `ore.parallel` value. By default, when you connect to ORE, this environment variable will be set to `FALSE` or `NULL`, depending on your environment. This means that parallel processes will not be spawned and instead the `ore.groupApply`, `ore.rowApply`, and `ore.indexApply` functions will be run sequentially, using a single R engine. To enable the parallel execution of these functions, you need to turn this parallel feature on. You can do so by setting the R environment variable to a number greater than 1. For example, the following R command sets `ore.parallel` to 8:

```
> options("ore.parallel" = 8)
```

Alternatively, instead of specifying a value, you can assign a value of `TRUE`, in which case the Oracle Database default degree of parallelism will be used:

```
> options("ore.parallel" = TRUE)
```

The next thing you need to do is to enable the `ore.groupApply`, `ore.rowApply`, or `ore.indexApply` function to use. Based on the syntax of the `parallel` parameter, it will automatically pick up the `ore.parallel` setting. If `ore.parallel` has been set to `TRUE` or to a number, then this is what the function will use. Alternatively, to enable the parallel execution of the function, you can set the `parallel` parameter to a value, or you can set it to `TRUE` to use the database default degree of parallelism. The following example shows the `ore.indexApply` function from the previous section, which now includes the `parallel` parameter:

```
> idxSample <- ore.indexApply(5, function(index, dat, samplePercent){
                set.seed(index)
                # calculate the sample size
                SampleSize <- nrow(dat)*(samplePercent/100)
                # Create an index of records for the Sample
                Index_Sample <- sample(1:nrow(dat), SampleSize)
```

```
            group <- as.integer(1:nrow(dat) %in% Index_Sample)
            # Create a sample data set
            sampleData <- dat[group==TRUE,]
            res <- data.frame(sampleData[,1:4])
         },
      dat=CUSTOMERS_USA,
      samplePercent=20,
      parallel=TRUE)
```

Embedded R Execution Using the SQL Interface

Oracle R Enterprise comes with a set of SQL features that allows you to call R code from SQL and PL/SQL code. These SQL features consist of a number of APIs that allow you to access and run R code using the embedded R execution feature of Oracle R Enterprise. In the first half of this chapter, we looked at the ORE embedded R execution functions using the R API. Table 10-2 lists the ORE SQL API functions. You will see that there is an equivalent SQL API function for each of the ORE R functions, except for the `ore.indexApply` function. In this section we look at each of the ORE SQL API functions and how you can use them to run your R code.

For me, this is one of the most powerful features of Oracle R Enterprise. By using the ORE SQL API functions, you can now access the vast array of the analytical capabilities of the R language to any application that can run SQL on the Oracle Database. In addition to the vast array of analytics available in R, the ORE SQL API functions allow you to expose graphics, created in R, to your applications.

Again, note that there is no SQL API function that is equivalent to the `ore.indexApply` function.

When using these ORE SQL API functions, you need to follow a two-step process. The first step is to create an ORE script that contains the R function code you want to run. The second step is to write a SQL `SELECT` statement that uses one of the ORE SQL API functions to run the ORE script and to return the results.

How to Use the rqEval SQL Function

The first of the SQL API functions we will look at is the `rqEval` function. This is the equivalent of the `ore.doEval` R function. This function executes an R script, passing any parameters that are necessary.

The `rqEval` function has the following syntax:

```
rqEval (
    PAR_CUR REF CURSOR IN
    OUT_QRY VARCHAR2 IN)
    EXP_NAM VARCHAR2 IN)
```

SQL API	Equivalent ORE function	Description
rqEval	ore.doEval	Executes a user-defined R script that is passed to it and returns any result generated.
rqTableEval	ore.tableApply	Executes a function or script on all rows on a supplied data set.
"rqGroupEval"	ore.groupApply	Executes a function or script on partitions of the supplied data set. The partitions are defined on one or more attributes of the data set. Parallel execution is supported for each partition. Note: There is no specific function called "rqGroupEval." Instead you have to define this function, in a specific way, for your data.
rqRowEval	ore.rowApply	Executes a function or script on a defined set of rows (chunks) from the supplied data set. Parallel execution is supported for each set of rows (chunks).

TABLE 10-2.   *SQL API Functions for Embedded R Execution*

Table 10-3 describes the parameters for the rqEval SQL API function.

To illustrate how to use the rqEval SQL API function, we'll use the same examples that were used to illustrate the ore.doEval function. The first of these examples is a function that was created to calculate the approximate age of a customer. The current year of birth is passed as a parameter to this function. In the section for ore.doEval, a script called CustomerAge was created and stored in the Oracle Database. Although this script was created using the ORE R interfaces, it can also be accessed using the SQL API functions. For example, the following SQL query calls the CustomerAge function and passes in the year of birth as 2005. Our SELECT statement defines the parameter to pass to the R script, defines the format of the returned data set, and the name of the R script.

```
select *
from table(rqEval(cursor(select 2005 "YearBorn" from dual),
                  'select 1 CustAge from dual',
                  'CustomerAge') );
   CUSTAGE
----------
        11
```

Parameter Name	Description
PRA_CUR	This is a cursor that contains the additional parameter values to pass to the R script that is named by the EXP_NAM parameter.
OUT_QRY	This specifies the format of the returned results. These formats and their values include the following:

OUT_QRY (continued):

- **NULL:** This returns the data and any image objects.

- **A SQL SELECT statement:** This will list the column names (and data types) of the table returned by the rqEval function. If an image has been created, it will be ignored and not returned in this particular scenario. The table format can be based on an existing table structure, or you can create a structure of the results based on using the DUAL table.

- **XML:** Used to specify that the results should be returned in XML format for both the table results and any images created. You will need to use the XML format if your query results contain a CLOB.

- **PNG:** Can be used when the results contain a BLOB that contains an image that was created in the R script.

| EXP_NAM | This is the name of the ORE script. |

TABLE 10-3. *Parameters for the* rqEval *SQL API Function*

The next sample rqEval function uses the earlier example that prints the "Hello Brendan" statement. When we wrote the code for this when using the ore.doEval function, we did not write an R script for it. We were able to include the function code in the call to the ore.doEval function. When we want to do something similar using the SQL API functions, we need to create an R script that runs the required code and then save it to the R Script Repository. The following code illustrates how you can create the ORE script for this example:

```
BEGIN
    --sys.rqScriptDrop('HelloBrendan');
    sys.rqScriptCreate('HelloBrendan',
        'function() {
            res<-data.frame(paste("Hello Brendan", "the time is",
format(Sys.time(),"%X")))
            res
        } ');
END;
```

Because this R script does not have any parameters, you can use `NULL` as the first parameter in the `rqEval` function call. The second parameter defines the output format. In this example, it is a character string whose length can be defined. The third parameter is the name of the ORE script.

```
-- Call the HelloBrendan ORE script
select * from table(rqEval(NULL,
                   'select cast(''a'' as varchar2(35)) "Ans" from dual',
                   'HelloBrendan') );
Ans
-----------------------------------
Hello Brendan the time is 15:19:32
```

How to Use the rqTableEval SQL Function

When you want your R script to process more than one row of data, you will have to use the `rqTableEval` SQL API function. This function allows you to pass multiple records or the rows from a `SELECT` statement to the ORE script as a parameter (`INP_CUR`). Additional parameters for the R script can also be passed as a cursor.

The `rqTableEval` SQL API function has the following syntax:

```
rqTableEval (
    INP_CUR REF CURSOR IN
    PAR_CUR REF CURSOR IN
    OUT_QRY VARCHAR2 IN
    EXP_NAM VARCHAR2 IN)
```

Table 10-4 describes the parameters for the `rqTableEval` SQL API function.

The first of our examples to illustrate the use of the `rqTableEval` function will perform an aggregation of the data that is contained the MINING_DATA_BUILD_V table in the DMUSER schema. This data set was used in Chapter 7, so refer to that chapter for how to set up this data. The first step is to create and define the R script to perform the aggregation:

```
BEGIN
    --sys.rqScriptDrop('AgeProfile1');
    sys.rqScriptCreate('AgeProfile1',
       'function(dat) {
           aggdata <- aggregate(dat$AFFINITY_CARD,
                              by = list(Age = dat$AGE),
                              FUN = length)
       } ');
END;
```

Parameter Name	Description
INP_CUR	This is the cursor that defines the data to be passed to and used by the R script. It is passed as a `data.frame` in the first argument of the R script.
PAR_CUR	This is a cursor that contains the additional parameter values to pass to the R script that is named by the EXP_NAM parameter.
OUT_QRY	This specifies the format of the returned results. These formats and their values include the following: ■ **NULL**: This returns the data and any image objects. ■ **A SQL SELECT statement**: This will list the column names (and data types) of the table returned by the `rqTableEval` function. If an image has been created, it will be ignored and not returned in this particular scenario. The table format can be based on an existing table structure, or you can create a structure of the results based on using the DUAL table. ■ **XML**: Used to specify that the results will be returned in XML format for both table results and for any images created. You will need to use the XML format if your query results contain a CLOB. ■ **PNG**: Can be used when the results contain a BLOB that contains an image created in the R script.
EXP_NAM	This is the name of the R script.

TABLE 10-4.   *Parameters for the* `rqTableEval` *SQL API Function*

You can now call this R script using the `oreTableEval` function. The first parameter defines the input data set. This can be defined as a SELECT statement on a table or view. Because the `AgeProfle1` script does not have any additional parameters apart from input data set, the second parameter (PAR_CUR) is set to NULL. The third parameter (OUT_QRY) is defined by a SELECT statement that defines the headings for the columns in the output. The final parameter is the name of the R script.

```
select
*
from table(rqTableEval(cursor(select * from MINING_DATA_BUILD_V),
                 NULL,
                 'select 1 AGE, 1 AGE_NUM from dual',
                 'AgeProfile1') );
```

```
       AGE     AGE_NUM
---------- ----------
        17         18
        18         21
        19         32
        20         32
        21         26
        22         42
        23         41
...
```

In addition to using the analytical capabilities of the R language, you can produce charts using the R graphics features. You can then expose these charts and graphics to your applications using the SQL API functions that return these objects in an XML or PNG format. To illustrate this capability, we can extend our `AgeProfile1` function to produce a chart that plots the number of people at each age. This extended function is called `AgeProfile2`. The first step is to create the ORE script:

```
BEGIN
    --sys.rqScriptDrop('AgeProfile2');
    sys.rqScriptCreate('AgeProfile2',
       'function(dat) {
            aggdata <- aggregate(dat$AFFINITY_CARD,
                                  by = list(Age = dat$AGE),
                                  FUN = length)
            res <- plot(aggdata$Age, aggdata$x, type = "l")
        } ');
END;
```

When you call this R script using the `rqTableEval` function, you can specify the format of the result from the R script. Because the result will be a chart, you can specify this as PNG, as shown in the following `SELECT` statement:

```
select * from table(rqTableEval(cursor(select * from MINING_DATA_BUILD_V),
                NULL,
                'PNG',
                'AgeProfile2') );
NAME
-------------------------------------------------------------------------------- ID
----------
IMAGE
--------------------------------------------------------------------------------

         1
89504E470D0A1A0A0000000D49484452000001E0000001E008060000007DD4BE9500002000494441
54789CEDDD797494F5BD3FF0F79305421632210B181609C90448D15A542C138522B46CB5B66CAD5A
```

The `rqTableEval` function returns the PNG-formatted chart as a BLOB data type. You can easily include this chart in your applications. Figure 10-1 shows the chart created by the ORE script. You can easily view this BLOB object when examining the returned results in SQL Developer.

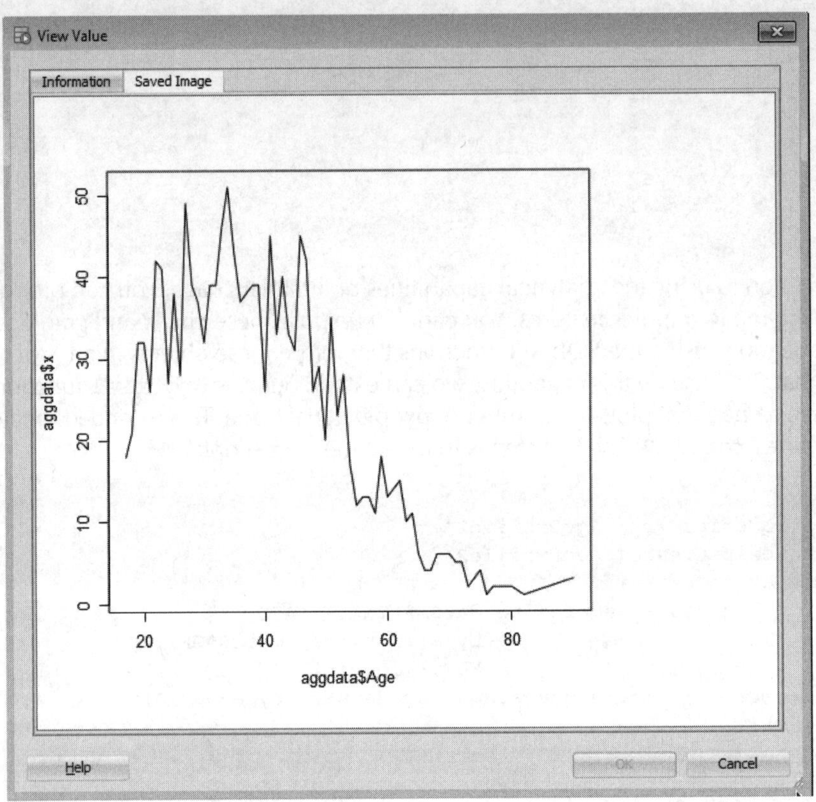

FIGURE 10-1. *AgeProfile2 chart returned as a BLOB data type (viewed using SQL Developer)*

One of the most common ways I use the `rqTableEval` function within SQL is to build and apply data mining models on my data. In Chapter 7, I showed you how to build and use data mining models using the in-database Oracle Data Mining algorithms; in Chapter 8, I showed you how to use the ORE data mining algorithms. The example covered in these two chapters uses the R language. Depending on your technical infrastructure, you might want to build and apply data mining models, created using the functionality in R, using the ORE SQL API functions. To illustrate this, the following example builds and applies a linear regression model on the `WHITE_WINE` data set.

The first phase of this process is to build the linear regression model. Just like in the previous examples, there are two steps. The first of these steps is to create an R script that contains the R code to create the model. Because this R script produces a model that we will want to use at a later time, we need to save this model. We do this by saving the model to an ORE datastore called `DMEMO_LM_DS`. The following

code is the R script to create and store a linear regression model for the WHITE_
WINE data set. The SELECT query is then used to run the script, which in turn
creates the model and stores it.

```
--Phase 1: Creating the Data Mining model
-- Create a Linear Regression model and store in an ORE data store
BEGIN
    --sys.rqScriptDrop('DEMO_LM');
    sys.rqScriptCreate('DEMO_LM',
        'function(dat, ds_name) {
            mod <- lm(alcohol  ~., data=dat)
            ore.save(mod, name=ds_name, overwrite=TRUE)
        } ');
END;


-- Now you need to run the DEMO_LM ORE script to create the model
select *
from table(rqTableEval(cursor(select * from white_wine),
        cursor(select 1 as "ore.connect", 'DEMO_LM_DS' as "ds_name" from dual),
        'XML',
        'DEMO_LM') );
```

The second phase is to use the linear regression model we just created and
apply it to new data. In the following example, we reuse the WHITE_WINE data set.
Again, we have a two-step process. The first step is to create a script that retrieves
the linear regression model from an ORE datastore and then applies this model to
the input data set. The second step is to use a SELECT query to call the R script and
perform the commands specified in the R script. The outputs from this script are then
displayed to the user. The outputs in this example include the original alcohol
amount and the predicted alcohol amount.

```
-- Phase 2: Applying the Data Mining model
-- Create the script that applies the stored model to new data
--   Return the actual value and the predicted value
BEGIN
    sys.rqScriptDrop('DEMO_LM_APPLY');
    sys.rqScriptCreate('DEMO_LM_APPLY',
        'function(dat, ds_name) {
            ore.load(ds_name)
            pre <- predict(mod, newdata=dat, supplemental.cols="alcohol")
            res <- cbind(dat, PRED=pre)
            res <- res[,c("alcohol", "PRED")]
        } ');
END;


-- Run the apply script on the new data
select *
from table(rqTableEval(cursor(select * from white_wine),
        cursor(select 1 as "ore.connect", 'DEMO_LM_DS' as "ds_name" from dual),
        'select 1 as "alcohol", 1 as "PRED" from dual',
        'DEMO_LM_APPLY') );
```

```
   alcohol        PRED
---------- ----------
        10 9.58434071
      10.6 8.83113972
      10.7  10.378701
        10 9.58434071
      12.5  12.146045
      10.6 8.83113972
      12.8  12.668966
...
```

How to Use the "rqGroupEval" SQL Function

Technically we have no *"rqGroupEval"* function in the way that we have the other SQL API functions. Although you will see references to this function in various documents and websites, they are referring to the *concept* of the *"rqGroupEval"* function, and this can lead to lots of confusion.

Instead of providing a *"rqGroupEval"* function, what Oracle has done is provide a framework and a SQL object to allow you to define and create your own *"rqGroupEval"* function. Here are the steps you need to complete to create your *"rqGroupEval"* function:

- Create your user-defined R script that contains the R code you want to execute.

- Define a data type structure for the input data set.

- Define a PL/SQL function (that is, the equivalent of the *"rqGroupEval"* function), the parameters (as outlined in Table 10-5), and the attribute to use to cluster or group the data. You can also specify whether the function is to be used in parallel.

- Write your SQL statement to call the *"rqGroupEval"* function you have just created.

Following these steps, we first need to create our user-defined R script. A number of examples have been given on how to use the `sys.rqScriptCreate` function to create an R script. The following example is based on the same scenario that was shown when using the `ore.groupApply` function earlier in the chapter. This example calculates the mean residual sugar value based on each grouping of attributes. The following is the PL/SQL code to create our R script:

```
BEGIN
    --sys.rqScriptDrop('DEMO_GROUP_EVAL');
    sys.rqScriptCreate('DEMO_GROUP_EVAL',
        'function(dat) {
```

```
        dat$AVG_SUGAR <- mean(dat$residual.sugar)
        res <- dat[,c("alcohol", "residual.sugar", "AVG_SUGAR")]
    } ');
END;
```

For the second step, we need to create a data structure for the input data set. In this example, the input data set will be all the data from the `WHITE_WINE` table in our schema, and we will use the `%ROWTYPE` to define the record structure:

```
CREATE OR REPLACE PACKAGE WhiteWinePkg AS
    TYPE cur IS REF CURSOR RETURN WHITE_WINE%ROWTYPE;
END WhiteWinePkg;
```

The third step is to define your equivalent of the *"rqGroupEval"* function. In the following code we create a function called `My_GroupEval`. This function is based on a SQL object called `rqGroupEvalImpl`, and this SQL object is defined within SQL.

```
CREATE OR REPLACE FUNCTION My_GroupEval(
    inp_cur WhiteWinePkg.cur,
    par_cur SYS_REFCURSOR,
    out_qry VARCHAR2,
    grp_col VARCHAR2,
    exp_txt CLOB)
RETURN SYS.AnyDataSet
PIPELINED PARALLEL_ENABLE (PARTITION inp_cur BY HASH ("alcohol"))
CLUSTER inp_cur BY ("alcohol")
USING rqGroupEvalImpl;
```

When defining our function, we need to allow for the input parameters described in Table 10-5 and follow a similar format and description as the other SQL API functions.

In addition to defining the structure of our `GroupEval` function, we can specify whether the function is to be run in parallel (see the line beginning with `PIPELINED`). Plus, we need to define the column that will be used to cluster the data.

HINT
If you would like to group on multiple attributes, you cannot list each of these attributes. Instead, you should merge or combine the attributes into one attribute.

The final step of the process is to write the `SELECT` statement that will be used to call our *"rqGroupEval"* function, passing all the parameters and defining the

Parameter Name	Description
INP_CUR	This is the cursor that defines the data to be passed to and used by the R script. It is passed as a `data.frame` in the first argument of the R script.
PAR_CUR	This is a cursor that contains the additional parameter values to pass to the ORE script that is named by the EXP_NAM parameter.
OUT_QRY	This specifies the format of the returned results. These formats and their values include the following: ■ **NULL**: This returns the data and any image objects. ■ **A SQL SELECT statement**: This will list the column names (and data types) of the table returned by the function. If an image has been created, it will be ignored and not returned in this particular scenario. The table format can be based on an existing table structure, or you can create a structure of the results based on using the DUAL table. ■ **XML**: Used to specify that the results will be returned in XML format for both table results and any images created. You will need to use the XML format if your query results contain a CLOB. ■ **PNG**: Can be used when the results contain a BLOG that contains an image created in the ORE script.
GRP_COL	The name of the columns to be used to group the partitions of the data.
EXP_NAM	This is the name of the R script.

TABLE 10-5. *Parameters for the "rqGroupEval" SQL API Function*

format of the returned results and/or data set. The following SELECT illustrates how to call the My_GroupEval function that was just created:

```
SELECT *
FROM table(MY_GroupEval(
        cursor(SELECT * FROM WHITE_WINE),
        NULL,
        'select 1 as "alcohol", 1 as "residual_sugar", 1 as "Avg_Sugar"
    from dual',
        'alcohol',
        'DEMO_GROUP_EVAL'));
```

How to Use the rqRowEval SQL Function

The `rqRowEval` function is designed to allow you to process different chunks of your data set and apply a defined R script to each of these partitions. The data set chunks are defined by the number of records to be included in each partition. The size of the partitions is determined by the value for the `ROW_NUM` parameter to the `rqRowEval` function. The `rqRowEval` SQL function is equivalent to the `ore.rowApply` ORE function shown in an earlier section of this chapter.

The `rqRowEval` SQL API function has the following syntax:

```
rqRowEval (
     INP_CUR REF CURSOR IN
     PAR_CUR REF CURSOR IN
     OUT_QRY VARCHAR2 IN
     ROW_NUM NUMBER IN
     EXP_NAM VARCHAR2 IN)
```

Table 10-6 describes the parameters for the `rqRowEval` SQL API function.

Parameter Name	Description
INP_CUR	This is the cursor that defines the data to be passed to and used by the R code defined in the ORE script.
OUT_QRY	This specifies the format of the returned results. These formats and their values include the following: ■ **NULL**: This returns the data and any image objects. ■ **A SQL SELECT statement**: This will list the column names (and data types) of the table returned by the `rqRowEval` function. If an image has been created, it will be ignored and not returned in this particular scenario. The table format can be based on an existing table structure, or you can create a structure of the results based on using the DUAL table. ■ **XML**: Used to specify that the results will be returned in XML format for both table results and any images created. You will need to use the XML format if your query results contain a CLOB. ■ **PNG**: Can be used when the results contain a BLOG that contains an image created in the R script.
ROW_NUM	The number of rows to include in each invocation of the R script.
EXP_NAM	This is the name of the R script.

TABLE 10-6.   *Parameters for the* `rqRowEval` *SQL API Function*

In the section earlier in this chapter on how to use the `ore.rowApply` function, an example was given on how to apply a linear regression model to the `WHITE_WINE` data set. This data set was divided into chunks of records consisting of 500 records each. You can follow a similar approach when using the `rqRowEval` function. The following example uses the exact same example as the `ore.rowApply` function. The R code we want to use is contained in the R script `DEMO_LM_APPLY`. This R script was created in the section of this chapter that covered the `rqTableEval` function. The `DEMO_LM_APPLY` ORE script contains the code that loads a linear regression model from the ORE datastore called `MODELS_DS`. It then applies the `LMmodel` to the data set supplied to the R script. In the following example, this data will consist of chunks of the `WHITE_WINE` data set divided into 500 records each:

```
select *
from table(rqRowEval(cursor(select * from white_wine),
        cursor(select 1 as "ore.connect", 'DEMO_LM_DS' as "ds_name" from dual),
        'select 1 as "alcohol", 1 as "PRED" from dual',
        500,
        'DEMO_LM_APPLY') );
```

You can add a call to use the parallel processing feature of the Oracle Database. When using this feature, you need to test to find the optimal degree of parallel processing to use. When your data set is small, it might be better to process the data serially because the overhead in managing the parallel processes might be large. But when your data set is large, you can specify the optimal degree of parallelism. The following example illustrates how the degree of parallelism can be added to the previous example of using the `rqRowEval` function:

```
select *
from table(rqRowEval(cursor(select /*+ parallel(w,4) */ * from white_wine w),
        cursor(select 1 as "ore.connect", 'DEMO_LM_DS' as "ds_name" from dual),
        'select 1 as "alcohol", 1 as "PRED" from dual',
        500,
        'DEMO_LM_APPLY') );
```

Summary

Oracle R Enterprise has both an R and a SQL interface for using the embedded R execution features. Embedded R execution allows you to write R functions that can then be run against data that is defined in the Oracle Database. Some of these functions can allow for multiple R processes to be created on the Oracle Database server, and each of these parallel processes can be used to process a subset of the entire data set being processed. This allows you to analyze significantly larger volumes of data than you would typically be able to do using the traditional R programming environment, by using the computing resources of the database server.

For me, one of the major features of Oracle R Enterprise is the set of SQL API interfaces. These SQL interface functions allow you to call R scripts that have been defined in the Oracle Database. This can greatly expand the analytics available in the R language. In addition to the analytic capabilities of the R language, you can use some of the graphing capabilities of the R language. By using these ORE SQL API functions, you can easily include vast analytic and graphing capabilities within your traditional applications and your analytic dashboards produced by OBI, as well as build custom applications using APEX, ADF, and so on. Basically, any tool or language that can call SQL can now use the analytic and graphing features of the R language.

CHAPTER
11

Oracle R Advanced Analytics for Hadoop

Oracle R Advanced Analytics for Hadoop (ORAAH) is one of the components of the Oracle Big Data Connectors. ORAAH provides a set of R functions that allows you to connect to and manipulate data stored on HDFS using Hive transparency. ORAAH allows you to build map-reduce analytics and use the prepackaged algorithms exposed through an R interface. Additionally, you can integrate with Apache Spark and other tools and languages for greater performance for nine algorithms, including multilayer neural networks, logistic regression, and more.

This chapter provides examples of some of the typical tasks you will perform when using ORAAH, including how to connect and read data, process data, move data, create a map-reduce process, and use the Spark features of ORAAH.

NOTE
Not everyone will have access to a Hadoop environment to be able to test out and use Oracle R Advanced Analytics for Hadoop. Oracle provides us with a virtual machine that comes prebuilt and configured with Hadoop, Hive, an Oracle Database, ORAAH, and lots of other software. This virtual machine is called BigDataLite VM and can be downloaded from the Oracle VirtualBox Pre-Built Appliances website. This virtual machine also has a number of demonstration data sets and tutorials on how to use some of the products. This is a great virtual machine to have as part of your personal or work lab environment.

ORAAH allows you to use your R code to process data stored on HDFS, in Hive tables, and in your local R environment, by providing a set of functions, defined in the ORCH R packages, that makes it easy for you to process and analyze your data. This can give you the appearance of using the familiar R syntax to process your data on Hadoop. The ORCH package contains a Hadoop Abstraction Layer (HAL) that manages the similarities and differences across various Hadoop distributions. ORAAH allows you to manipulate Hive data using the same type of transparency provided by Oracle R Enterprise, but for use on top of Hive tables. So just as Oracle R Enterprise maps `data.frame` functions to Oracle SQL, Oracle R Advanced Analytics for Hadoop uses the same abstraction to map those `data.frame` functions to HiveQL. The Hadoop distribution you are using will be detected when the ORCH R packages are loaded.

HINT
*The Oracle R Advanced Analytics for Hadoop
(ORAAH) product is sometimes referred to or
called Oracle R Connector for Hadoop (ORCH).
Oracle R Connector for Hadoop is the earlier name
for the product, but the abbreviation (ORCH) is
still used for the set of R top-level packages for the
ORAAH product.*

When you are working in an environment that has ORAAH installed along with
the supporting R packages, you can start using ORAAH by loading ORCH into your
R environment. The following command loads the ORCH package and the supporting
packages required:

```
> library(ORCH)
Loading required package: OREstats
Loading required package: MASS
Loading required package: ORCHcore
Loading required package: rJava Oracle R Connector for Hadoop 2.5.1 (rev. 307)
Info: using native C base64 encoding implementation
Info: Hadoop distribution is Cloudera's CDH v5.4.7
Info: using auto-detected ORCH HAL v4.2
Info: HDFS workdir is set to "/user/oracle"
Warning: mapReduce checks are skipped due to "ORCH_MAPRED_CHECK"=FALSE
Warning: HDFS checks are skipped due to "ORCH_HDFS_CHECK"=FALSE
Info: Hadoop 2.6.0-cdh5.4.7 is up
Info: Sqoop 1.4.5-cdh5.4.7 is up
Info: OLH 3.5.0 is up
Info: loaded ORCH core Java library "orch-core-2.5.1-mr2.jar"
Loading required package: ORCHstats
```

A great way to check some of the capabilities of the ORCH R package is to view
the built-in demonstrations. In Chapter 5, I showed you how to look at the various
demonstrations provided with ORE. You can follow a similar approach for exploring
the ORCH demonstrations, as shown here:

```
> demo(package="ORCH")
Demos in package 'ORCH':

hdfs_cpmv               ORCH's copy and move APIs
hdfs_datatrans          ORCH's HDFS data transfer APIs
hdfs_dir                ORCH's HDFS directory manipulation APIs
hdfs_putget             ORCH's get and put API usage
hive_aggregate          Aggregation in HIVE
hive_analysis           Basic analysis & data processing operations
hive_basic              Basic connectivity to HIVE storage
hive_binning            Binning logic
hive_columnfns          Column function
hive_nulls              Handling of NULL in SQL vs. NA in R
hive_pushpull           HIVE <-> R data transfer
hive_sequencefile       Creating and using HIVE tables stored as sequencefile
mapred_basic            Basic mapreduce job execution in ORCH
mapred_modelbuild       Parallel model building and plotting in hadoop using ORCH
```

```
orch_cov_cor               ORCH's functions for computing Covariance and Correlation
                           Matrices
orch_hive_hdfs             ORCH's HIVE<->HDFS transformation functions
orch_kmeans                ORCH's kmeans clustering
orch_lm                    ORCH's lm algorithm
orch_lmf_jellyfish         ORCH's LMF algorithm
orch_lmf_mahout_als        Mahout's LMF algorithm from ORCH
orch_map_only
orch_model_matrix          Using ORCH to create a model matrix for HDFS input
orch_neural                ORCH's neural network algorithm
orch_part_biglm
orch_part_lm               ORCH's parallel partitioned model building
orch_princomp              ORCH's Principal Components Analysis (PCA)
orch_pristine
orch_reduce_only
orch_sample                ORCH's sampling function orch_task_timeout
```

The demonstrations for the ORCH package use some of the standard data sets
that come with the R language, so you do not have to install any additional data sets
for these to run.

To run one of the ORAAH demonstration scripts, you need to use the demo
function. This function accepts two parameters. The first parameter is the name
of the demonstration, and the second parameter is the name of the package.
For example, the following illustrates how to run the hive_basic and
hive_aggregrate demonstrations:

```
> demo(hive_basic , package="ORCH")
> demo(hive_aggregate , package="ORCH")
```

The outputs from running these are not shown here, as these demonstrations
have a lot of examples in them.

You can also list the functions available in the various ORCH packages. In
addition to the standard packages, most of the Hive and HDFS functions are located
in the ORCHcore and ORCHstats packages. Use the following commands in R to
list the contents of these packages:

```
> ls("package:ORCHcore")
> ls("package:ORCHstats")
```

Connecting to Apache Hive and Processing Data

To connect to Hive, you can use the ore.connect() function. You have seen
this function used in previous chapters to illustrate how to connect to an Oracle
Database. The format of the connection to Hive depends on what version of ORAAH
you are using. If you are using a version previous to 2.6, you can use the following:

```
> ore.connect(type="HIVE")
```

If you are using ORAAH 2.6 or higher, there is a different connection type that requires more details, including the Hive server, port, user, password, and database. The ore.connect() function for ORAAH 2.6 or higher establishes a JDBC/Thrift connection to the Hive database. The following is an example of the connecting to Hive:

```
> # Connect to HIVE. The following environment variables must be set:
> # HIVE_SERVER - hostname or IP of HiveServer2 to connect to;
> # HIVE_PORT - HiveServer2 port to connect to;
> # HIVE_USER - Hive user name to use;
> # HIVE_PASSWORD - Hive user password to use;
> # HIVE_DATABASE - Hive database name (i.e. schema) to use.
> ore.connect( host = Sys.getenv("HIVE_SERVER"),
               port = Sys.getenv("HIVE_PORT"),
               user = Sys.getenv("HIVE_USER"),
               password = Sys.getenv("HIVE_PASSWORD"),
               schema = Sys.getenv("HIVE_DATABASE"),
               type = "HIVE")
> ore.attach()
```

You can use the ore.connect() function to connect to the Hive database on a local as well as a remote Hadoop cluster.

Only one connection using ore.connect() can be open at a time. When working with your data and analytics, you need to be careful that you manage your connections to ensure you process your data in the way that you want.

When you are connected, you can read data from Hive and write data out to Hive using the ore.get() and ore.push() functions, respectively. Indeed, many of the ORE functions covered in the previous chapters have been overloaded to work with Hive, including many of the data frame and numeric functions.

The following example illustrates the loading of a data set using R, pushing this data set to Hive, and then performing some analytics on this data. The data set being used here has been used in other chapters and is based on the WhiteWine data set.

```
> # Connect to Hive
> ore.connect(type="HIVE")
> ore.attach()
> # Download the White Wine data set
> WhiteWine = read.table("http://archive.ics.uci.edu/ml/machine-learning-
databases/wine-quality/winequality-white.csv", sep=";", header=TRUE)
> # Get some of the details of the data set based on local R data frame
> dim(WhiteWine)
> names(WhiteWine)
> head(WhiteWine)
> table(WhiteWine$quality)

> # Push the R data frame to Hive.  wine_table now points to a Hive table.
> wine_table <- ore.push(WhiteWine)
> # Check that wine_table is and ORE data frame
> class(wine_table)
```

```
> # Performs some statistics on the data set in Hive
> nrow(wine_table)
> summary(wine_table)
```

There are some limitations with using Hive with ORAAH. Some of the data types you are used to using are not supported or are limited. ORAAH can access any Hive table that is using numeric or string data types. Similarly for when you want to write an R data frame to Hive, you need to be careful that the data frame does not contain any factors. The following illustrates two examples. The first example takes a data set that contains a factor data type. When we write this data set to Hive, we get an error. The second example takes the data set and converts it to a string data type before writing the data set to Hive.

```
> ore.connect(type="HIVE")
> IRIS_data <- iris
> # Inspect the structure of the iris data.
> #    You will see the Species has a Factor data type
> str(IRIS_data)
> # Try writing this data set to Hive and we get an error
> IRIS_hive <- ore.push(IRIS_data)
> # You will get an error
 Error: column type 'factor' not supported in HIVE
> # convert the factor data type to string
> factfilt <- sapply(IRIS_data, is.factor)
> IRIS_data[factfilt] <- data.frame(lapply(IRIS_data[factfilt], as.character),
                                    stringsAsFactors = FALSE)
> # Check that the Factor variable has been converted to string
> str(IRIS_data)
> # Try writing this data set to Hive again
> IRIS_hive <- ore.push(IRIS_data)
> # Success
> class(IRIS_hive)
 [1] "ore.frame"
 attr(,"package")
 [1] "OREbase"
```

NOTE
Depending on the version of ORAAH you have installed you may now be able to use data frames that contain factors.

The following code example illustrates using the `orch.lm()` function to generate a model for the WhiteWine data set we have used in several chapters. The WhiteWine data set exists as a data frame in our local R environment. This data set is written out to HDFS using the `hdfs.put()` function. The `orch.lm()` function is used to process the data set (on HDFS) and generate the model.

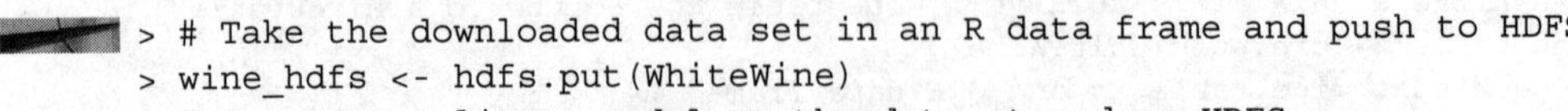

```
> # Take the downloaded data set in an R data frame and push to HDFS
> wine_hdfs <- hdfs.put(WhiteWine)
> # Generate a linear model on the data stored on HDFS
```

```
> LMmodel_hdfs <- orch.lm(alcohol  ~., wine_hdfs)
> # View the model details
> LMmodel_hdfs
> summary(LMmodel_hdfs)
> # Remove the data set from HDFS
> rm(wine_hdfs)
> # remove the model
> rm(LMmodel_hdfs)
```

ORAAH comes with a wide range of functions that allows you to work with Hive tables and HDFS files. Some of these functions allow you to perform a variety of analytics directly on the data in Hive or HDFS. ORAAH also comes with a number of data-mining algorithms that can be used on Hive and HDFS data. Table 11-1 lists commonly used statistical and machine learning algorithms that come with ORAAH. Table 11-1 is based on version ORAAH 2.6, which comes with

Function Name	Description
`orch.cor`	Generates a correlation matrix using Pearson correlation.
`orch.cov`	Generates a covariance matrix.
`orch.glm`	Generates a generalized linear model for your data.
`orch.glm2`	Generates a Spark-based generalized linear model.
`orch.kmeans`	Generates a *k*-Means clustering model for your data.
`orch.lm`	Generates a linear model using QR factorization and parallel distribution.
`orch.lmf`	Generates a low rank factorization model using the jellyfish algorithm or the Mahout alternating least squares algorithm.
`orch.neural`	Generates a Spark-based neural network model for your data.
`orch.ml.dt`	Generates a decision tree model using the Apache Spark MLlib implementation.
`orch.ml.kmeans`	Generates a *k*-Means model using the Apache Spark MLlib implementation.
`orch.ml.lassor`	Uses the least absolute shrinkage and selection operator (Lasso) with stochastic gradient descent, using the Apache Spark MLlib implementation.

TABLE 11-1.   *Commonly Used Statistical and Machine Learning Algorithms in ORAAH (Versions 2.6 and Above)*

Function Name	Description
`orch.ml.linear`	Generates a linear regression with stochastic gradient descent model using the Apache Spark MLlib implementation.
`orch.ml.logistic`	Generates a logistic regression model using the Apache Spark MLlib implementation.
`orch.ml.pca`	Performs principal component analysis (PCA) using the Apache Spark MLlib implementation.
`orch.ml.random.forest`	Generates a random forest ensemble model using the Apache Spark MLlib implementation.
`orch.ml.ridge`	Generates a ridge regression with stochastic gradient descent using the Apache Spark MLlib implementation.
`orch.ml.svm`	Generates a support vector machine (SVM) model using the Apache Spark MLlib implementation.
`orch.nmf`	Generates a non-negative matrix factorization model. Has been designed to scale for larger data sets than the traditional function in R.
`orch.model.matrix`	Creates a distributed model matrix. Machine learning and statistical algorithms require a distributed model matrix (DMM) for the training phase.
`orch.princomp`	Analyzes the performance of principal components.
`orch.sample`	Allows you to sample the data.
`orch.scale`	Performs scaling.
`hdfs.write`	Distributed model matrix (DMM) can be saved in Comma Separated Values (CSV) format on HDFS via a call to `hdfs.write()`.
`orch.save.model`	This function saves models created using Apache Spark MLlib in ORAAH to HDFS for scoring/prediction later on. It also enables model sharing among different users if the other users have access to the path where models are saved.
`orch.load.model`	This function loads models created using Apache Spark MLlib in ORAAH from HDFS for scoring/prediction. It also enables loading of models created by other users if access to the HDFS path where models are saved is provided.

TABLE 11-1. *Commonly Used Statistical and Machine Learning Algorithms in ORAAH (Versions 2.6 and Above) (Continued)*

over 11 machine learning algorithms that are based on using Apache Spark and some additional functions to help you manage the Spark-based models. You can check out the ORAAH statistical and machine learning algorithms in the ORAAH documentation.

Managing Map-Reduce Jobs Using ORCH

ORAAH comes with a number of functions that allows you to create and manage map-reduce jobs in Hadoop. A map-reduce process takes a data set that has been distributed over Hadoop, performs analysis on the distributed data set, and finally calculates and returns the results. Figure 11-1 gives an overview of the map-reduce process.

With ORAAH/ORCH, you can define your map-reduce job and submit it using the `hadoop.exec()` function. Table 11-2 lists the various functions in ORCH associated with map-reduce jobs. There are three main parts to defining a map-reduce job in ORCH. The first is to define the data set you are going to use. This data set can exist on Hadoop, in Hive, or as an R object. The second step is to define the mapper function. This allows you to define what data you want selected from the data set to be used in the later steps. The third step is to apply the reducer

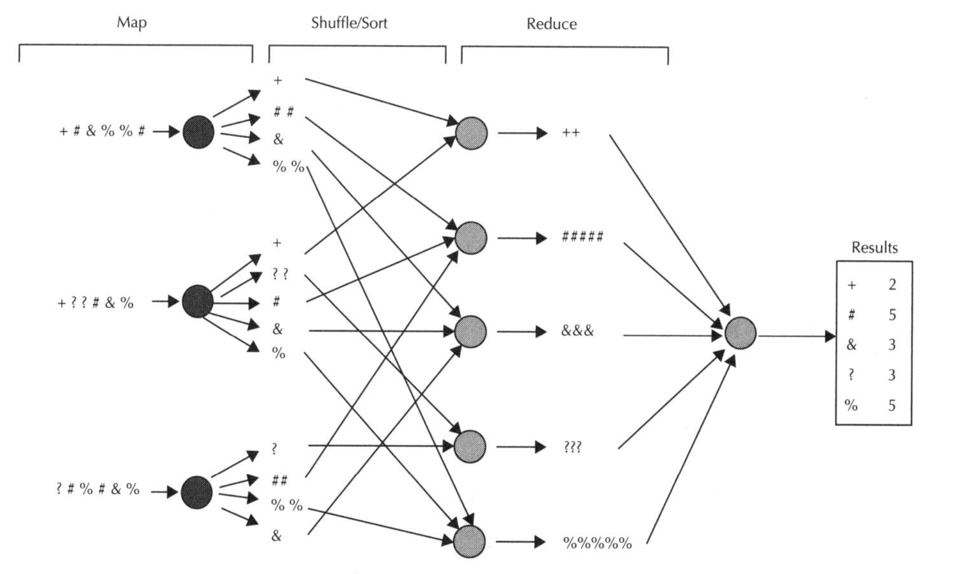

FIGURE 11-1.   *Overview of the map-reduce process*

Function Name	Description
`hadoop.exec`	This function starts the Hadoop engine and sends the mapper, reducer, and combiner R functions for execution. The data must exist in HDFS.
`hadoop.jobs`	Lists the running Hadoop jobs.
`hadoop.run`	This starts the Hadoop engine and sends the mapper, reducer, and combiner R functions for execution. This is very similar to `hadoop.exec`, except that if the data is not in Hadoop, it will copy the data to Hadoop before commencing the map-reduce job.
`orch.dryrun`	Changes the execution platform between the local host and the Hadoop cluster.
`orch.export`	Makes R objects in the local R session available in Hadoop so that they can be referenced in map-reduce jobs.
`orch.keyval`	Outputs the key-value pairs in a map-reduce job.
`orch.keyvals`	Outputs the sets of key-value pairs in a map-reduce job.
`orch.pack`	Compresses an R object that map-reduce will write as the values in key-value pairs.
`orch.tempPath`	Sets the path where temporary data is stored.
`orch.unpack`	Uncompresses an R object that was compressed using the `orch.pack` function.
`orch.create.parttab`	Enables partitioned Hive tables to be used with the ORCH map-reduce framework.

TABLE 11-2.   *Hadoop Map-Reduce Functions Available in ORCH*

function, which is the function to be applied to the selected data. The output from this function will be the result from applying the reducer function or calculation.

When using ORCH for your map-reduce jobs, you can also specify any additional parts for these jobs using the Configuration setting (config). This section allows you to fine-tune various aspects of your map-reduce jobs to achieve better performance or to change the behavior of the ORCH map-reduce driver.

To illustrate the creation of a map-reduce job, the following example uses the WhiteWine data set from earlier. Because the map-reduce job will work off key-value pairs, we need to define the attribute that's used to define the key. This value does not have to be unique because the attribute will be used to group the calculations defined in the reducer section. In our WhiteWine data set, we can set the key to the Quality attribute. We can define this key at the same time as writing the R data set out to HDFS.

```
> # Write the White Wine data set out to HDFS
> WhiteWine.dfs <- hdfs.put(WhiteWine, key='quality')
```

Next, we can construct the map-reduce job. The following example takes the WhiteWine data set that was written out to Hadoop, selects all the data from the data set in the mapper section, and then calculates the mean value for the residual sugars for each value contained in the Quality attribute. The results from these calculations are then stored in the variable mrRes.

```
> # Submit the hadoop job with mapper and reducer R scripts
> mrRes <- try(hadoop.run(
            WhiteWine.dfs,
            mapper = function(key, val) {
                      orch.keyvals(key, val)
                 },
            reducer = function(key, vals) {
                 X <- sum(vals$residual.sugar)/nrow(vals)
                 orch.keyval(key, X)
               },
            config = new("mapred.config",
                      map.tasks = 1,
                      reduce.tasks = 1 )
      ), silent = TRUE)
```

The mrRes variable points to the results from the executed map-reduce job. These results exist on HDFS because the original data used (WhiteWine.dfs) is located on HDFS. In this particular scenario, we can use the hdfs.get() function to copy the results data from HDFS into a data frame in our R environment and then display the results.

```
> hdfs.get(mrRes)
    val1        val2
1      3 6.392500
2      4 4.628221
3      5 7.334969
4      6 6.441606
5      7 5.186477
6      8 5.671429
7      9 4.120000
```

In the results displayed here, the values under val1 represent the unique values in the Quality attribute in the WhiteWine data set, and the values under val2 are the mean residual sugar results that were generated by the reducer function in our map-reduce job.

Using Spark with ORAAH

The ORCH R package for ORAAH comes with support for Spark to take advantage of an Apache Spark cluster on your server. This can give significant performance improvements over building and scoring models. Nine algorithms take advantage of the Spark cluster. These algorithms include logistic regression using `orch.glm2()`, multilayer perceptron neural networks using `orch.neural()`, and more, and are listed in Table 11-2.

When creating a Spark context, you can do so using Yarn or a stand-alone mode. Before you can use these functions, you need to load the ORCH library because these Spark algorithms are contained within it; plus, when you go to create a Spark connection, it will need the details of the configuration of the Hadoop cluster.

The first step you need to perform before using these Spark algorithms is to create a Spark connection. A Spark connection can be set up to use Yarn or a stand-alone mode. The following example illustrates the `spark.connect()` function. This function has four parameters. The first defines whether you are going to use Yarn or stand-alone mode. This parameter is called the master. The second parameter is a name variable (and is optional) that helps centralize logging in the session on the Spark master. By default, this is set to ORCH. The third parameter is used to define the amount of memory to allocate per Spark worker for this Spark context. The fourth parameter, `dfs.namenode`, points to the HDFS namenode server in order to exchange information with HDFS.

```
> # First you need to load the ORCG R package
> library(ORCH)
> # Create the Spark connection using Yarn
> spark.connect("yarn-client",
                memory="512m",
                dfs.namenode="bigdatalite.localdomain")
```

When your Spark connection is set up, you can then proceed to process the data and run the algorithm you need to use. The following example illustrates using the Spark algorithm `orch.glm2()` to fit a model for the kyphosis data set that is part of the `rpart` R package:

```
> # Write the data set to HDFS
> dfs.dat <- hdfs.put(kyphosis)
> # Call the orch.glm2 function to generate the model
>     sparkModel <- orch.glm2(Kyphosis ~ Age + Number + Start, dfs.dat = dfs.dat)
 ORCH GLM: processed 1 factor variables, 0.365 sec
 ORCH GLM: created model matrix, 2  partitions, 0.398 sec
 ORCH GLM: iter  1,  deviance   1.12289843250711020E+02,  elapsed time 0.216 sec
 ORCH GLM: iter  2,  deviance   6.64219993846240600E+01,  elapsed time 0.304 sec
 ORCH GLM: iter  3,  deviance   6.18628545282569460E+01,  elapsed time 0.277 sec
 ORCH GLM: iter  4,  deviance   6.13897990884807400E+01,  elapsed time 0.313 sec
 ORCH GLM: iter  5,  deviance   6.13799331446360300E+01,  elapsed time 0.460 sec
 ORCH GLM: iter  6,  deviance   6.13799272764552550E+01,  elapsed time 0.214 sec
```

A similar approach can be used for the neural network function `orch.neural()`.

When you are finished performing your analytics and are ready to close your Spark connection, use `spark.disconnect()`, like so:

```
> # Disconnect from Spark
> spark.disconnect()
```

Summary

ORAAH provides a set of R functions that allows you to connect to and manipulate data stored on HDFS using Hive transparency. ORAAH allows you to build map-reduce analytics and can use the prepackaged algorithms exposed through an R interface. ORAAH provides a range of functions that allows you to work with your data on Hadoop and build advanced analytics for your data, as well as build map-reduce jobs to utilize the processing capabilities of your Hadoop infrastructure. Additionally, ORAAH has some specific algorithms that work with Spark.

CHAPTER 12

Using ORE with Oracle Data Mining

Oracle R Enterprise and Oracle Data Mining combine to form the Oracle Advanced Analytics option. In Chapter 7, I covered how you can use the features of Oracle R Enterprise to take advantage of the in-database Oracle Data Mining algorithms. Oracle also provides a number of SQL functions and PL/SQL packages to enable you to use these same in-database algorithms. Additionally, Oracle has a workflow-based tool called Oracle Data Miner that comes as part of the Oracle SQL Developer tool. As an organization grows its analytics capabilities and analytic assets, the work that the data scientists have been performing using R and Oracle R Enterprise can be used within wider business applications such as Business Intelligence. To do so the data scientists will need to work with some of the many tools that the organization uses. Similarly, as the skills of the Oracle developers expand, they too will need to be able to work with or integrate the work of the data scientists. In this hybrid world, the data scientists and Oracle developers will be working side by side, or their work might even overlap. In this chapter and in the next, we will look at how you can use the analytics and scripts created by data scientists with other Oracle-based tools. For example, in this chapter we will look at how user-defined R scripts, stored in the ORE script repository, can be included with the Oracle Data Miner tool. In the next chapter, we will look at how you can use Oracle R Enterprise with APEX and OBIEE.

In this chapter, I give a quick overview of Oracle Data Mining, the Oracle Data Miner tool, and I show you how to use two features of the Oracle Data Miner tool that allow you to define and use ORE user-defined R scripts in your Oracle Data Miner workflow.

Oracle Data Mining

The Oracle Advanced Analytics option comprises Oracle Data Mining and Oracle R Enterprise. Oracle Advanced Analytics is a extra priced option for the Oracle Database Enterprise Edition. By combining the powerful in-database advanced data mining algorithms and the power and flexibility of R, Oracle has provided a set of tools that allows everyone—from the data scientist to the Oracle developer and the DBA—to perform advanced analytics on their data, thus gaining deeper insights into their data and giving them an advantage over their competitors.

Oracle Data Mining contains a suite of advanced data mining algorithms that are embedded into the Oracle Database that you can use to perform advanced analytics on your data. The data mining algorithms are integrated into the Oracle Database kernel and operate natively on data stored in tables in the database. This removes the need for extraction or transfer of data into stand-alone data mining/analytic servers, as is typical with most data mining applications. This can significantly reduce the timeframe of data mining projects by having near-zero data movement.

Table 12-1 lists the various data mining algorithms available in the Oracle Database as part of the Oracle Advanced Analytics option. In addition to these data

Data Mining Technique	Data Mining Algorithms
Anomaly Detection	One-class Support Vector Machine
Association Rule Analysis	Apriori
Attribute Importance	Minimum Description Length
Classification	Decision Tree
	Generalized Linear Model
	Naïve Bayes
	Support Vector Machine
Clustering	Expectation Maximization
	k-Means
	Orthogonal Partitioning Clustering
Feature Extraction	Non-Negative Matrix Factorization
	Singular Value Decomposition
	Principal Component Analysis
Regression	Generalized Linear Model
	Support Vector Machine

TABLE 12-1.   *Data Mining Algorithms Available in Oracle Data Mining (for Oracle Database version 12.1)*

mining algorithms, Oracle has a variety of interfaces to enable you to use the algorithms. These interfaces include PL/SQL packages that allow you to build and apply models to new data, a variety of SQL functions for real-time scoring of data, and the Oracle Data Miner tool, which provides a graphical workflow interface for creating your data mining projects. Chapter 7 showed how to use the ORE APIs to take advantage of these same in-database data mining algorithms.

By default, the Oracle Database Enterprise Edition comes with Oracle Data Mining already installed and configured, so there is no additional installation.

Oracle Data Mining comes with a number of data dictionary views, SQL functions, and PL/SQL packages to enable you to prepare data for data mining, build a data mining model, modify and tune the settings of a data mining algorithm, analyze and evaluate the models, and then apply these models to your data. Because Oracle Data Mining is an in-database data mining tool, all objects and models created will be stored in the Oracle Database, which allows you to use SQL as the main interface for performing your data mining tasks. This chapter provides examples on how you can use some of these ODM data dictionary views, the various SQL scoring functions, and the main PL/SQL packages.

The Oracle Data Mining models and other objects reside in the schema that they were created in. They can be shared, queried, and used by any schema in the database that has been given access to them. A number of Oracle Data Dictionary views exist that allow you to query the Oracle Data Mining models and their various properties. Table 12-2 lists the data dictionary views specific to Oracle Data Mining.

In this table, * represents either ALL, DBA, or USER, where

- ALL contains the ODM information that is accessible to the users.

- DBA contains the ODM information that is accessible to DBA users.

- USER contains the ODM information that is accessible to the current user.

Oracle Data Miner comes with some in-database PL/SQL packages. These packages allow you to perform all your data mining tasks. Three PL/SQL packages are associated with Oracle Data Miner:

- DBMS_DATA_MINING

- DBMS_DATA_MINING_TRANSFORM

- DBMS_PREDICTIVE_ANALYTICS

Dictionary View Name	Description
*_MINING_MODELS	This view contains the details of each of the Oracle Data Mining models that have been created. This information will contain the model name, the data mining type (or function), the algorithm used, and some other high-level information about the models.
*_MINING_MODEL_ATTRIBUTES	This view contains the details of the attributes that have been used to create the Oracle Data Mining model. If an attribute is used as a Target, this will be indicated by the Target column.
*_MINING_MODEL_SETTINGS	This view contains the algorithm settings that were used to generate the Oracle Data Mining model for a specific algorithm.
DBA_MINING_MODEL_TABLES	This view, which is only accessible by users with DBA privileges, lists all the tables that contain the metadata related to the data-mining models that exist in the database.

TABLE 12-2. *Oracle Data Mining Data Dictionary Views*

DBMS_DATA_MINING is the main PL/SQL package you will use to perform your data mining tasks, such as creating new models, evaluating and testing the models, and applying the models to new data. An overview of this package is given in the following sections, and examples of how to use the various procedures in this package to create a data mining model are given in the rest of this chapter.

The PL/SQL package DBMS_DATA_MINING_TRANSFORM allows you to define various data transformations that can be applied to your data sets to prepare them for input to the data mining algorithms.

The PL/SQL package DBMS_PREDICTIVE_ANALYTICS contains a number of procedures that allow you to perform an automated form of data mining. When you use this PL/SQL package, you allow the Oracle Data Mining engine to determine what algorithm and settings to use. The output from the procedures will be the prediction results, and any model produced will not exist after the procedure has completed. This PL/SQL package differs significantly from the DBMS_DATA_MINING package, as that package allows you to determine the algorithm, define the setting, investigate the model performance results, and so on.

The PL/SQL package DBMS_DATA_MINING contains the main procedures that allow you to create your data mining models, define all the necessary algorithm settings, investigate the results to determine the efficiency of the models, apply the data mining models to your data, and explore the details of the models that were produced.

Table 12-3 lists all the functions and procedures you will find in DBMS_DATA_MINING.

Functions and Procedures	Description
`ADD_COST_MATRIX`	Adds a cost matrix to a classification model
`ALTER_REVERSE_EXPRESSION`	Changes the reverse transformation expression to an expression you specify
`APPLY`	Applies a model to a data set (scores the data)
`COMPUTE_CONFUSION_MATRIX`	Computes the confusion matrix for a classification model
`COMPUTE_LIFT`	Computes a lift for a classification model
`COMPUTE_ROC`	Computes a receiver operating characteristic (ROC) for a classification model
`CREATE_MODEL`	Creates a model
`DROP_MODEL`	Drops a model
`EXPORT_MODEL`	Exports a model to a dump file
`GET_ASSOCIATION_RULES`	Returns the rules from an association model

TABLE 12-3.   *Procedures and Functions in DBMS_DATA_MINING*

Functions and Procedures	Description
GET_FREQUENT_ITEMSETS	Returns the frequent item sets for an association model
GET_MODEL_COST_MATRIX	Returns the cost matrix for a model
GET_MODEL_DETAILS_AI	Returns details about an Attribute Importance model
GET_MODEL_DETAILS_EM	Returns details about an Expectation Maximization model
GET_MODEL_DETAILS_EM_COMP	Returns details about the parameters of an Expectation Maximization model
GET_MODEL_DETAILS_EM_PROJ	Returns details about the projects of an Expectation Maximization model
GET_MODEL_DETAILS_GLM	Returns details about a Generalized Linear Model
GET_MODEL_DETAILS_GLOBAL	Returns high-level statistics about a model
GET_MODEL_DETAILS_KM	Returns details about a *k*-Means model
GET_MODEL_DETAILS_NB	Returns details about a Naive Bayes model
GET_MODEL_DETAILS_NMF	Returns details about a Non-Negative Matrix Factorization model
GET_MODEL_DETAILS_OC	Returns details about an O-Cluster model
GET_MODEL_DETAILS_SVD	Returns details about a Singular Value Decomposition model
GET_MODEL_DETAILS_SVM	Returns details about a Support Vector Machine model with a linear kernel
GET_MODEL_DETAILS_XML	Returns details about a Decision Tree model
GET_MODEL_TRANSFORMATIONS	Returns the transformations embedded in a model
GET_TRANSFORM_LIST	Converts between two different transformation specification formats
IMPORT_MODEL	Imports a model into a user schema
RANK_APPLY	Ranks the predictions from the APPLY results for a classification model
REMOVE_COST_MATRIX	Removes a cost matrix from a model
RENAME_MODEL	Renames a model

TABLE 12-3.   *Procedures and Functions in DBMS_DATA_MINING (Continued)*

Function Name	Description
PREDICTION	Returns the best prediction for the target.
PREDICTION_PROBABILITY	Returns the probability of the prediction.
PREDICTION_BOUNDS	Returns the upper and lower bounds of the interval wherein the predicted values (linear regression) or probabilities (logistic regression) lie. This function only applies for GLM models.
PREDICTION_COST	Returns a measure of the cost of incorrect predictions.
PREDICTION_DETAILS	Returns detailed information about the prediction.
PREDICTION_SET	Returns the results of a classification model, including the predictions and associated probabilities for each case.
CLUSTER_ID	Returns the ID of the predicted cluster.
CLUSTER_DETAILS	Returns detailed information about the predicted cluster.
CLUSTER_DISTANCE	Returns the distance from the centroid of the predicted cluster.
CLUSTER_PROBABILITY	Returns the probability of a case belonging to a given cluster.
CLUSTER_SET	Returns a list of all possible clusters to which a given case belongs, along with the associated probability of inclusion.
FEATURE_ID	Returns the ID of the feature with the highest coefficient value.
FEATURE_DETAILS	Returns detailed information about the predicted feature.
FEATURE_SET	Returns a list of objects containing all possible features along with the associated coefficients.
FEATURE_VALUE	Returns the value of the predicted feature.

TABLE 12-4. *Oracle Data Mining SQL Functions*

One of the most powerful features of Oracle Data Mining is the ability to use SQL to run and score your data using the data-mining models via SQL functions. These functions, listed in Table 12-4, can apply a mining model to your data or they can dynamically mine the data by executing an analytic clause. SQL functions are available for all the data mining algorithms that support the scoring operation. By using these SQL functions, you can easily embed data mining functionality into all parts of your Oracle environment (including Hadoop), including your batch processing tasks, your reporting tools, your analytical dashboards, and your front-end applications.

The following example illustrates how you can use a data mining model (DEMO_CLASS_DT_MODEL) that was created using Oracle Data Mining to make a prediction and to give the probability for the prediction:

```
SELECT cust_id,
       PREDICTION(DEMO_CLASS_DT_MODEL USING *) Predicted_Value,
       PREDICTION_PROBABILITY(DEMO_CLASS_DT_MODEL USING *) Prob
FROM   mining_data_apply_v
FETCH first 8 rows only;

   CUST_ID PREDICTED_VALUE        PROB
---------- --------------- ----------
    100001               0 .952191235
    100002               0 .952191235
    100003               0 .952191235
    100004               0 .952191235
    100005               1 .736625514
    100006               0 .952191235
    100007               0 .952191235
    100008               0 .952191235
```

Oracle Data Miner

The Oracle Data Miner tool is a component of SQL Developer. Oracle Data Miner is a GUI workflow-based tool that allows data scientists, data analysts, developers, and DBAs to quickly and simply build data mining workflows for their data and data mining business problems. The Oracle Data Miner workflow tool was first introduced in SQL Developer 3, and in all subsequent releases, additional functionality has been added.

The Oracle Data Miner tool, shown in Figure 12-1, allows you to build workflows by defining nodes so that you can perform the following tasks:

- Explore your data using statistics and various graphical methods.

- Build various data transformations that include sampling, use various data-reduction techniques, create new features, apply complex filtering techniques, and create custom transformations on your data.

- Build data mining models using the various in-database data mining algorithms.

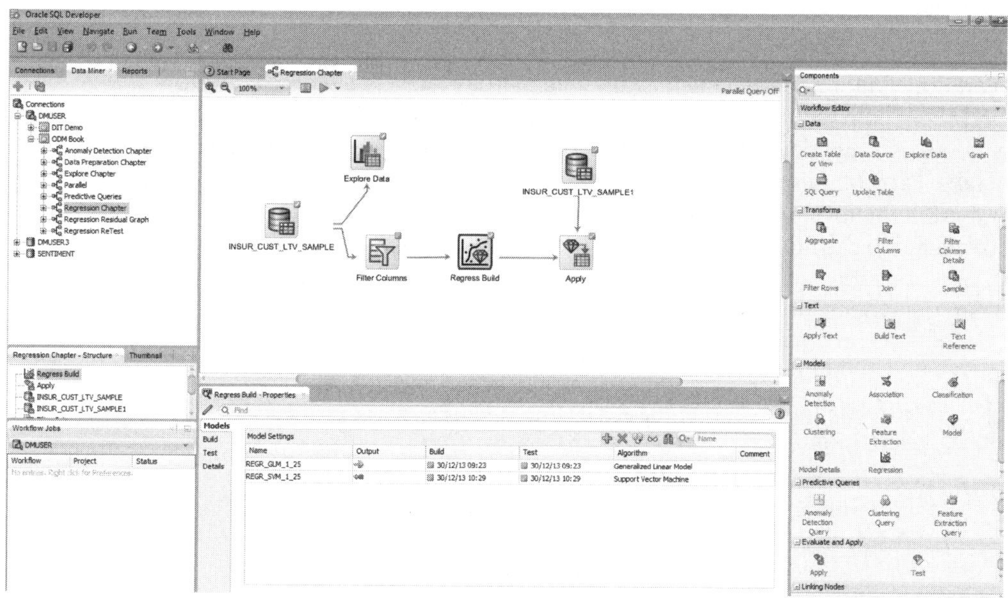

FIGURE 12-1.   *The Oracle Data Miner tool in SQL Developer*

- Apply your data mining models to new data to produce a scored data set that can be employed by your business users.

- Create and use transient data mining models using Predictive Queries.

- Create and apply complex Text Analytics models on your semi-structured and unstructured data.

When the time comes to productionize your workflows, full support is provided by the generation of all the required SQL scripts needed to run the workflow. These can be easily scheduled in the Oracle Database to run on a regular basis.

Including R Scripts Using the SQL Node

The SQL Query node allows you to write your own SQL statements that you want executed on the data in your schema. When creating the SQL Query node, you have two options. The first option is to create the SQL Query node with no inputs. With this option, you can write a query (using SQL, PL/SQL, and embedded R execution of user-defined R scripts in the ORE script repository) against any data that exists in your schema or that you have access to. The second option is to attach a SQL Query node to a data source or model build nodes. With this option, the code you specify in the SQL Query node will only be for the data source(s) that the node is attached to.

To create a SQL Query node, select it from the Data category in the Component Workflow Editor and then click again when your mouse is over the workflow worksheet. Next, double-click the node to open the SQL Query Node Editor window. This window has two main areas. The first of these areas contains a number of tabs. Each of these tabs will assist you in creating your SQL code or formatting the SQL API functions for embedded R execution. These tabs include the data sources connected to the SQL Query node, snippets that contain in-database functions, PL/SQL functions and procedures that are stored in your schema, and the R scripts defined in your schema or the R scripts you have access to.

TIP
The R scripts tab will only appear in the SQL Query Node editor if you have Oracle R Enterprise (ORE) versions 1.3 or higher installed on your Oracle Database server. Oracle Database needs to be 11.2.0.3 or higher for ORE.

The second area, on the right side of the SQL Query Node Editor window, is where you can write your SQL code with embedded R execution. Figure 12-2 shows the list of R scripts that have been created in various chapters throughout this book. To create a template for your R script, you first need to select the SQL API function from the drop-down list. Then double-click the R script you want to use. The template will then appear on the right side of the SQL node window. You can then edit this template to include the additional elements and parameters needed for it to run. Figure 12-2 illustrates the code for running the R script HelloBrendan.

After you have edited your SQL query to include the type of ORE SQL API function and parameters, you can test the code to see whether it runs and to explore some of the data returned by the query. The query results are displayed in the bottom-right corner of the SQL node window.

When you are finished editing the SQL node to include calls to your user-defined R scripts, you can proceed with building up the remainder of your workflow. For example, you might want to join the outputs from the R script (produced when the SQL node is run) onto some other data node or to feed the data into another node in your workflow.

You can generate the SQL and PL/SQL code for the work, which will include the ORE SQL API code defined in the SQL node. This code can be scheduled to run in the database by your DBA, or you can use the scheduling feature available in the Oracle Data Miner tool.

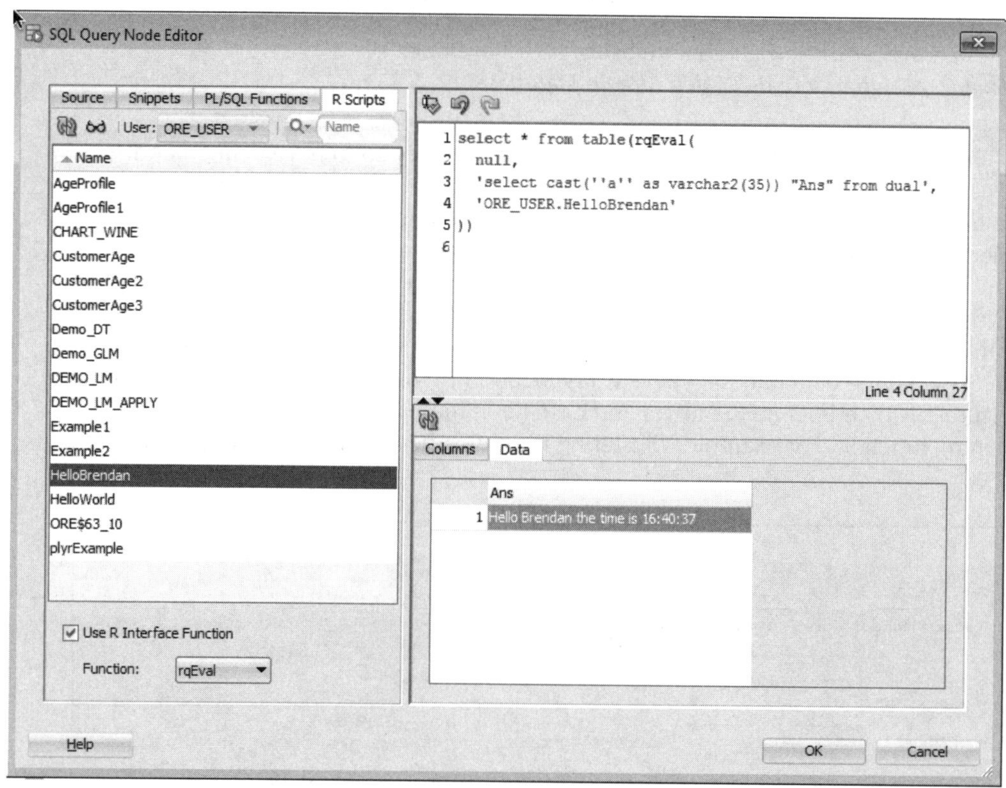

FIGURE 12-2.   *Using the SQL Query node to run an in-database R script*

Using the R Node

Oracle Data Miner provides a number of nodes for each of the data mining types available in the Oracle Database. When you use one of these nodes (for example, the classification node), it provides a framework for defining all the components needed to build and test a data mining model and to examine the various elements of the model, such as the settings, attributes used, and performance matrix. With SQL Developer 4.2 and greater, a new R node is available in the Models section of the Components palette. This R node allows you to use user-defined R scripts that build, test, and apply data mining models, stored in the R scripts repository, to be used within the Oracle Data Miner framework for data mining. This allows you to expand the number and type of data mining algorithms already available in the Oracle Database.

IMPORTANT
*The R node will only become visible in the Oracle
Data Miner tool when you are using SQL Developer
4.2 or higher and also using Oracle Database 12.2.*

Before you can commence using the R node, you need to have defined and
created the user-defined R scripts that perform all the necessary steps for building,
testing, and scoring, and for producing any of the other information about the
models, such as model details, performance matrices, and so on.

To create an R node, select the node from the Models section of the Components
window and then click your workflow worksheet. When the node is created, you
can connect your data source node to it. When you open the node, you can then
select what the data mining type is (Classification in the example shown in
Figure 12-3) and define the target and case ID, if these are relevant for your data
mining function. For example, Clustering is an unsupervised data mining technique,

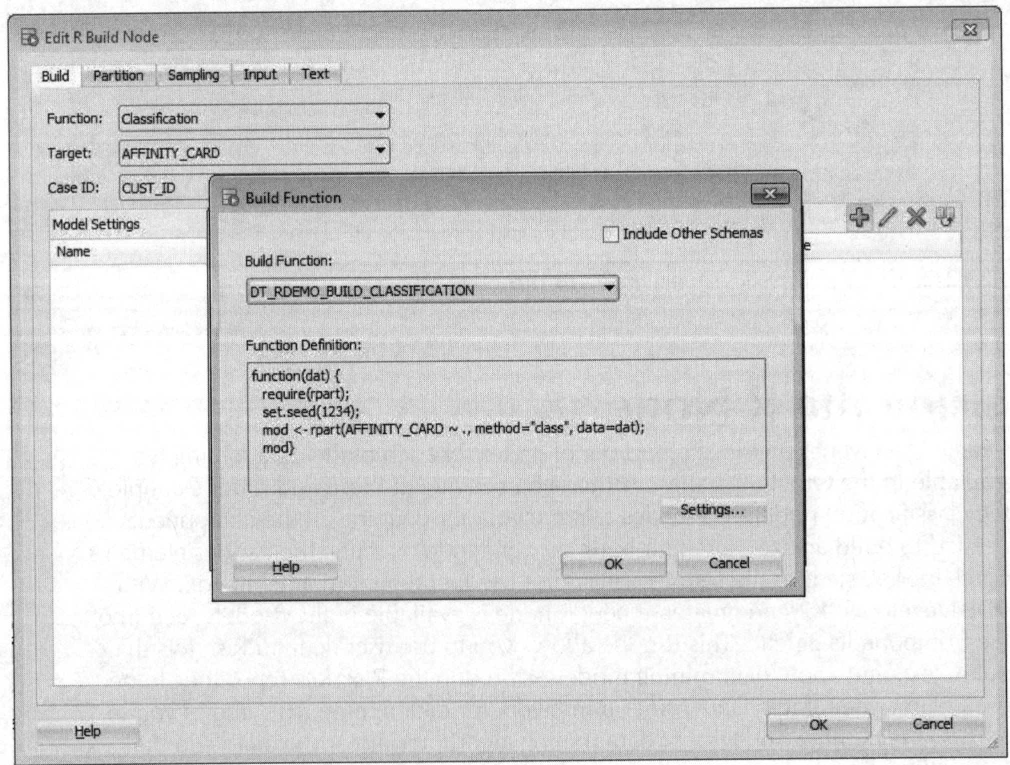

FIGURE 12-3. *Defining an R node for Classification*

so the Target field will be disabled. After defining these initial properties for the
R node, you can then select the user-defined R script in your database that contains
the R code that will generate the model, as shown in Figure 12-3.

Each of the data mining model nodes follows the same framework for building
and testing models. Therefore, for our R node, we need to define some additional
R scripts that support this framework. These will include the R script that will be used
to score the data. We can also define a user-defined R script that defines the weight
function, as well as an R script to retrieve the model details, as shown in Figure 12-4.

When you are finished defining your R node, you can run it. This will take the
data set that was defined in your Data node, input this data into the R node, sample
the data to create the build and test data sets, and then apply the R scripts you
defined in the R node to each of these sampled data sets. You can view the results
from building and testing the R node in a similar way to how you view other Oracle
Data Miner data mining nodes.

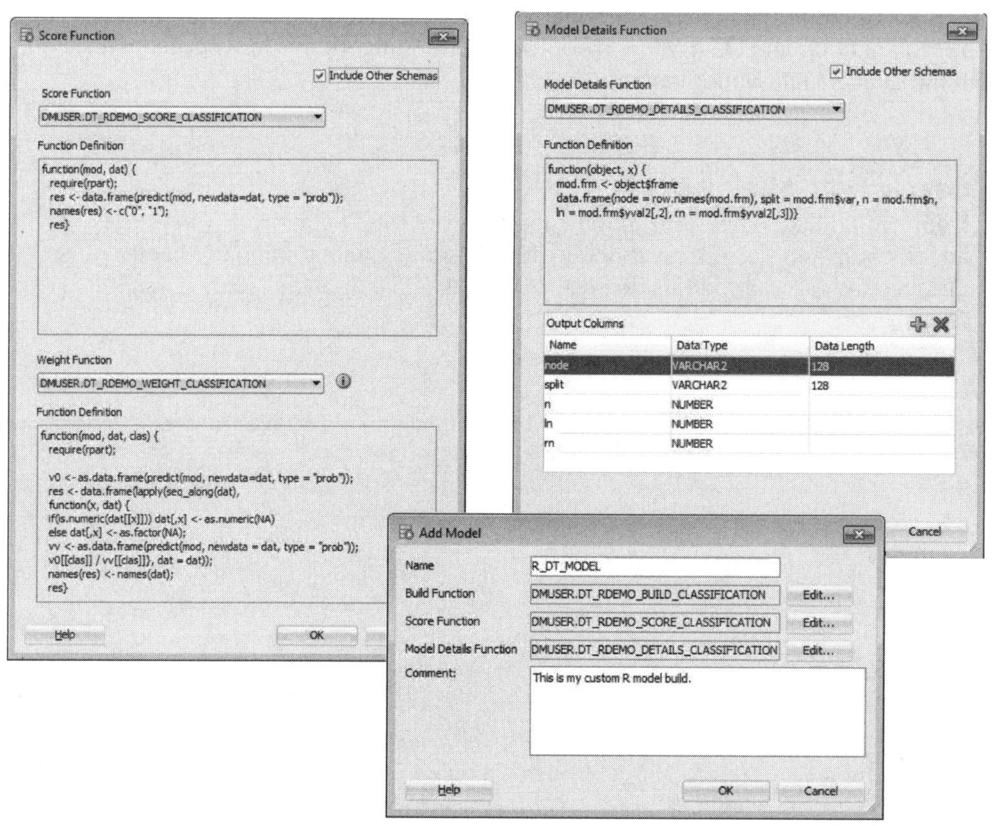

FIGURE 12.4.   *Defining the R scripts for each stage of the R node*

Summary

This chapter provided an overview of Oracle Data Mining. Oracle Data Mining and Oracle R Enterprise combine to form the Oracle Advanced Analytics option. You saw in Chapters 9 and 10 how to create user-defined R scripts that contain the R code to process the data in your Oracle Database. You can easily include this R code in your SQL queries by creating R scripts that contain your R code. For Oracle Data Mining, you have two ways of accessing and using the in-database features. The first is to use the SQL and PL/SQL functions and procedures. The second is to use the Oracle Data Miner tool that is built into the SQL Developer tool. Oracle Data Miner allows the data analyst to quickly and easily build up a workflow that processes data and performs data mining using the in-database data mining algorithms. When creating a workflow, you can include one or more of the R scripts you have created. An example was given showing how to do this using the SQL node. A new feature with the Oracle Data Miner tool is the R node. This is only available when using Oracle Database 12.2c and SQL Developer 4.2 (or higher). The R node allows you to define the R scripts to use for the building and testing phases as well as for examining other parts of the data mining models within the framework that Oracle Data Miner uses. This allows R algorithms to work seamlessly with the Oracle Data Miner framework.

Oracle Data Mining Book

If you would like to explore the full capabilities of the Oracle Data Miner tool and the SQL and PL/SQL functionality for performing data mining in Oracle Database, check out the Oracle Press book *Predictive Analytics Using Oracle Data Miner*.

CHAPTER
13

Using ORE in
APEX and OBIEE

One of the core advantages of using Oracle R Enterprise is the ability to use the analytics and graphing capabilities of the R language in your applications. Basically, any application or application development language that can issue SQL statements on an Oracle Database can now have its analytics and graphics generated using the R language. The embedded R execution SQL API functions can be used to generate the results from our in-database R scripts.

In this chapter, I show you how to easily add and use your in-database R functions, defined as an R script, in APEX and OBIEE. These examples will not teach you how to use APEX and OBIEE, but they will show you the specific elements of these tools needed to display results returned from your in-database user-defined R functions and how to display a basic R graphic in these applications. Using a similar approach, you can include R functions in any application that can use SQL to query the Oracle Database.

Oracle APEX

Oracle Application Express (APEX) is an application development framework that allows you to develop feature-rich web-based applications for desktop and mobile devices. The Oracle Database comes with APEX already installed and configured for you to start using. Because APEX is an in-database tool, the main languages you will be using to develop your application are SQL and PL/SQL. When you log into APEX using a web browser, you are provided with a complete application development tool that allows you to create your applications. APEX also comes with a wide range of reporting and charting capabilities, and these allow you to create advanced reporting and analytics dashboards, as shown in Figure 13-1.

APEX is a zero-cost option for the Oracle Database and can be used with all versions of the Oracle Database, from the Oracle Express Edition right up to the Oracle Enterprise Edition. Because APEX is SQL and PL/SQL based, it is easy for a wide range of users—DBAs, developers, analysts, and so on—to get up and running with APEX. Because APEX is an in-database development tool, your applications will automatically use all the performance and scalability features of the Oracle Database. Additionally, the data in your Oracle Database will remain secured, using the various in-database security features.

APEX comes with the ability to detect what type of browser and device are being used to call the APEX application. APEX will dynamically adjust the application layout to choose the best layout for your device. This does not require any additional coding by the developer, so the developer can concentrate on the business logic of the application.

ORE and the embedded R execution feature of Oracle R Enterprise share some of the characteristics of APEX. Both products utilize the performance and scalability features of the Oracle Database and server, both tools use the Oracle Database and server as a compute engine, and most importantly both tools are based on SQL and

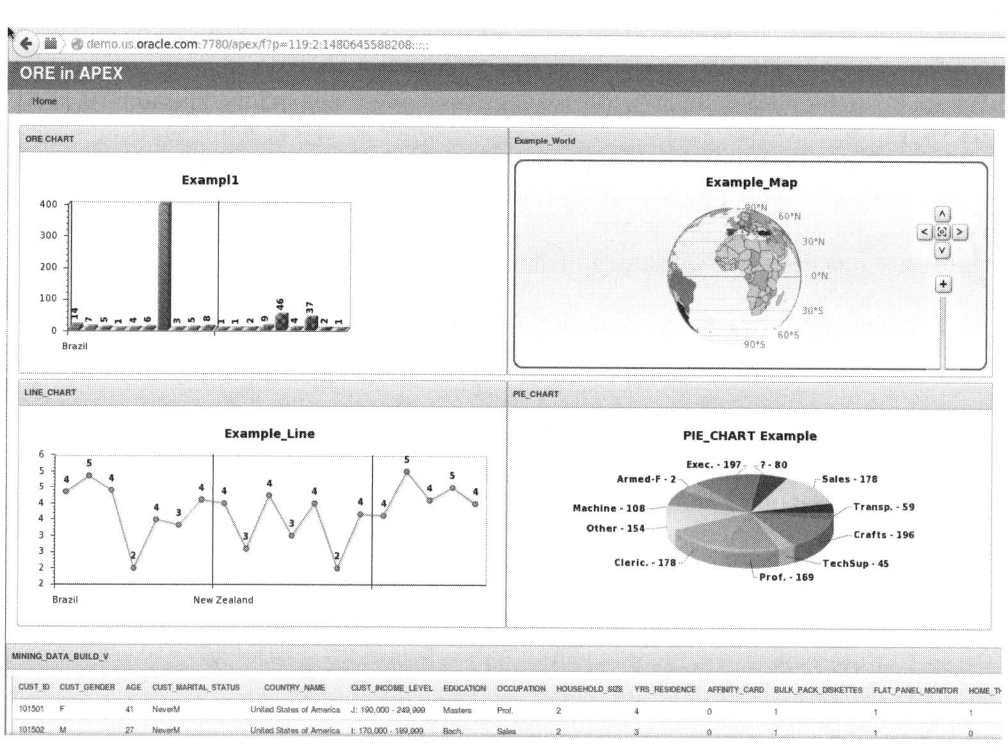

FIGURE 13-1.   *Example of a reporting dashboard in APEX*

PL/SQL. This last common feature means that you can very easily include Oracle R Enterprise into your APEX application, just like any application that can run SQL in the Oracle Database.

Oracle APEX is also available on the various DBaaS cloud solutions offered by Oracle, and in some cases APEX is the main tool you will have to interface with the database. If you don't have access to APEX in your own environment, you can download one of the pre-built virtual machine appliances available on the VirtualBox website. A very popular virtual machine image is the Developer Day VM. If you use this virtual machine, you will need to install R and Oracle R Enterprise. Alternatively, you could use the OBIEE Sample App virtual machine or the Big Data Lite virtual machine, as these come with R, ORE, an Oracle Database, and APEX already installed.

In the following sections I show you how to include R functions within an APEX application, using the embedded R execution feature of ORE. These R functions perform some analytics on the data in our database and then display the results generated by R in our APEX application. The R language comes with a wide range of graphics. I show how you can quickly and easily include a simple graphic created using R in your APEX application. You can follow the same process to include more complex R graphics available in the R language or in one of the many thousands of R packages.

The examples shown in these sections are the user-defined R functions created in Chapter 9 and used in Chapter 10. The examples are based on the data set contained in the `MINING_DATA_BUILD_V` view in the `DMUSER` schema, and the user-defined functions to aggregate this data set and to display an R chart of the aggregated results.

It is assumed that you are set up to use APEX and have some experience using the tool to create various elements and objects.

Including an ORE Script in Your APEX Application

The first example I show you is how to add results from using embedded R execution to call to a user-defined R function. The example used for this is the `AgeProfile1` function. This function, created back in Chapter 9, is shown here:

```
-- Create ORE script to aggregate on the AGE attribute
BEGIN
    --sys.rqScriptDrop('AgeProfile1');
    sys.rqScriptCreate('AgeProfile1',
        'function(dat) {
            aggdata <- aggregate(dat$AFFINITY_CARD,
                                  by = list(Age = dat$AGE),
                                  FUN = length)
        } ');
END;
```

The `AgeProfile1` function accepts one parameter and the data set that will be used within this function. The `aggregate` function within our script aggregates this data set based on the `AGE` variable. The final aggregated results are then returned to the query that called this function.

When you are using SQL to call this `AgeProfile1` function, you can use a `SELECT` statement. Chapter 10 covered all the various options available for running this function using a `SELECT` statement. The simplest way is to use the `rqTableEval()` function within your `SELECT` statement, as shown here:

```
-- Call the AgeProfile1 script passing in the data from MINING_DATA_BUILD_V
select *
from table (rqTableEval(cursor(select* from MINING_DATA_BUILD_V),
                NULL,
                'select 1 AGE, 1 AGE_NUM, from dual',
                'AgeProfile1'));
```

It is this SELECT statement that we will use within APEX to call our R function (AgeProfile1), and we will use APEX to display the results.

In your APEX application, you can create a new APEX report (within a new region, if this is needed). This can be an interactive report or a classic report. You will then need to fill in the various properties for the APEX Report region. When you get to the stage of entering the SELECT statement for the APEX report, you can enter the SELECT query shown previously and illustrated in Figure 13-2.

You just need to complete the APEX Report properties, and the easiest way to do this is to accept the defaults. When you run your APEX application, the results are displayed as shown in Figure 13-3.

At this point, you have a simple APEX application that is running ORE using the embedded R execution feature. That was all very simple, right? In the next section, I show you how to include a graph produced using R and how to display this in your APEX application.

Enter SQL Query or PL/SQL function returning a SQL Query:

```
select *
from table(rqTableEval(cursor(select * from MINING_DATA_BUILD_V),
              NULL,
              'select 1 AGE, 1 AGE_NUM from dual',
              'AgeProfile1') )|
```

Query Builder

Page Items to Submit

Columns Headings: ⦿ Derived from query columns   ○ Generic columns

Max.Columns   60

> Items

> SQL Query Example

FIGURE 13-2.   *Entering the embedded R execution SQL query for the APEX report*

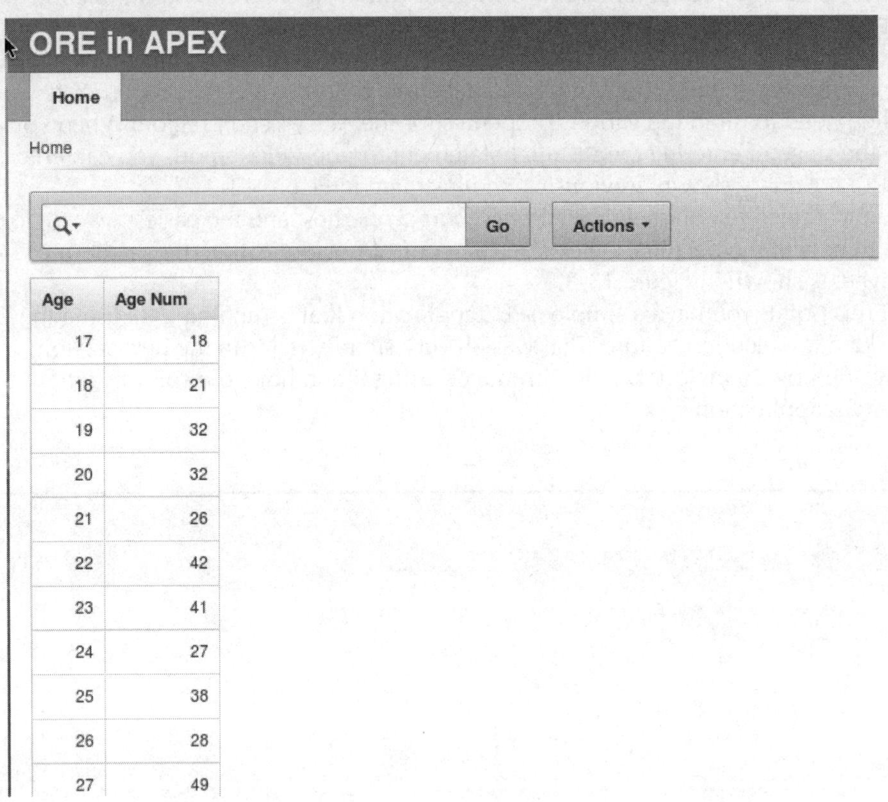

FIGURE 13-3. *Results from calling an embedded R execution function displayed in APEX*

Adding an R Graph to Your APEX Application

Oracle APEX has a wide range of charting functions built into it. These charting functions will work for most of the charts you will want to include in your APEX application. But the R language and the many thousands of supporting R packages come with a vast array of charting and graphics capabilities.

The following example shows you how to include a very simple chart, created by R, within your APEX application. If you would like to include a more sophisticated R chart or graphic, you can follow the same set of steps.

This example was created and demonstrated in Chapters 9 and 10. The following code illustrates the R code that will create a line chart based on the aggregated data demonstrated in the previous section:

```
BEGIN
    --sys.rqScriptDrop('AgeProfile2');
    sys.rqScriptCreate('AgeProfile2',
        'function(dat) {
            aggdata <- aggregate(dat$AFFINITY_CARD,
                                 by = list(Age = dat$AGE),
                                 FUN = length)
            res <- plot(aggdata$Age, aggdata$x, type = "l")
        } ');
END;
```

This example is an extended version of the `AgeProfile1` R function, and
`AgeProfile2` returns a line chart for the aggregated data. When you use the
following `SELECT` statement to call the `AgeProfile` R function, one of the
attributes returned by the query will be a BLOB object. You saw in Chapter 10 how
to view this BLOB object image using SQL Developer.

To display this R-generated chart using embedded R execution, the first step is to
create a new object in the same region in the APEX tool that you created and used
in the previous section. Create a new page item, and from the list of options select
the Display Image option. You can use most of the default settings, but for the Based
On drop-down select "Blob Column returned by SQL statement." You can then enter
the following query in the SQL Statement box, as shown in Figure 13-4, and accept
the defaults for the remaining settings:

```
select image
from table(rqTableEval(cursor(select * from MINING_DATA_BUILD_V),
                NULL,
                'PNG',
                'AgeProfile2') )
```

Based On	BLOB Column returned by SQL statement ↕

```
select image
from table(rqTableEval(cursor(select * from MINING_DATA_BUILD_V),
                NULL,
                'PNG',
                'AgeProfile2') )
```

*SQL Statement

FIGURE 13-4.   *Query to generate the R chart using ORE embedded R execution*

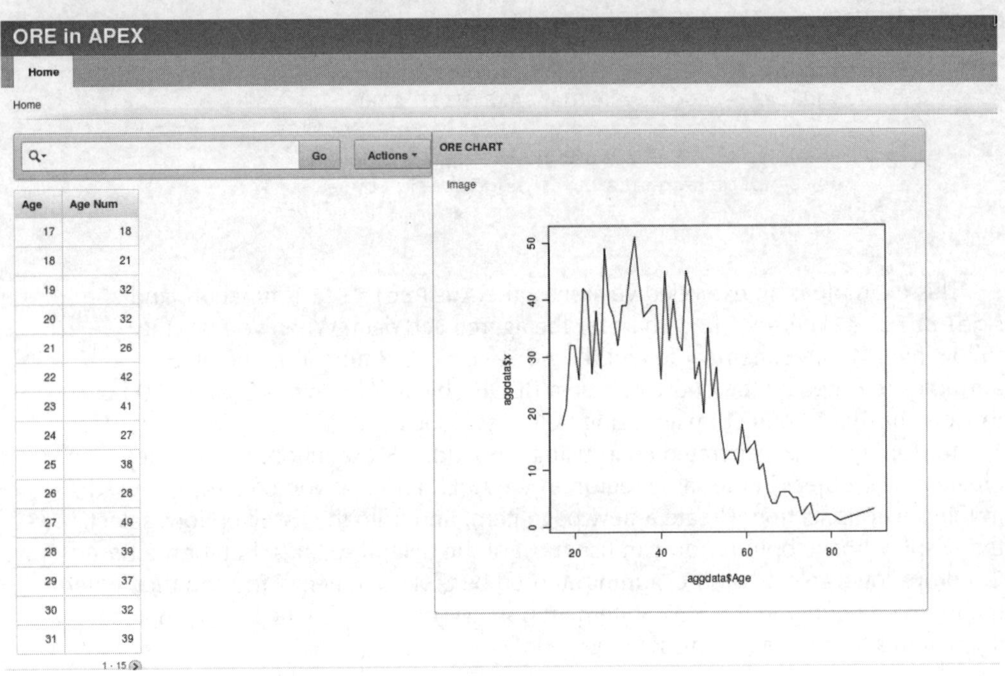

FIGURE 13-5. *APEX application with its data and chart generated by Oracle R Enterprise*

When you run your APEX application (see Figure 13-5), you will now have two areas in your application, and the data and chart displayed in these areas are generated by R using embedded R execution in the Oracle Database.

As your analytics capabilities grow, your ability to use some of the more sophisticated R functionality and the advanced charting and graphics features of the R language and supporting packages will grow as well. You can update the R code contained in your in-database, user-defined R functions with these new advanced features. For example, if we updated the `AgeProfile2` R user-defined function to use the R ggplot package, we could alter the charting produced to create something more informative, like what is shown in Figure 13-6.

Hopefully these sections have shown you how quickly and easily including Oracle R Enterprise in your APEX application can be done. I've used two very simple examples. The embedded R execution feature of ORE allows you to deploy your R analytics within your business applications. Although APEX was used in this section, you can see that any application that has the ability to run SQL on the Oracle Database can now also run R code.

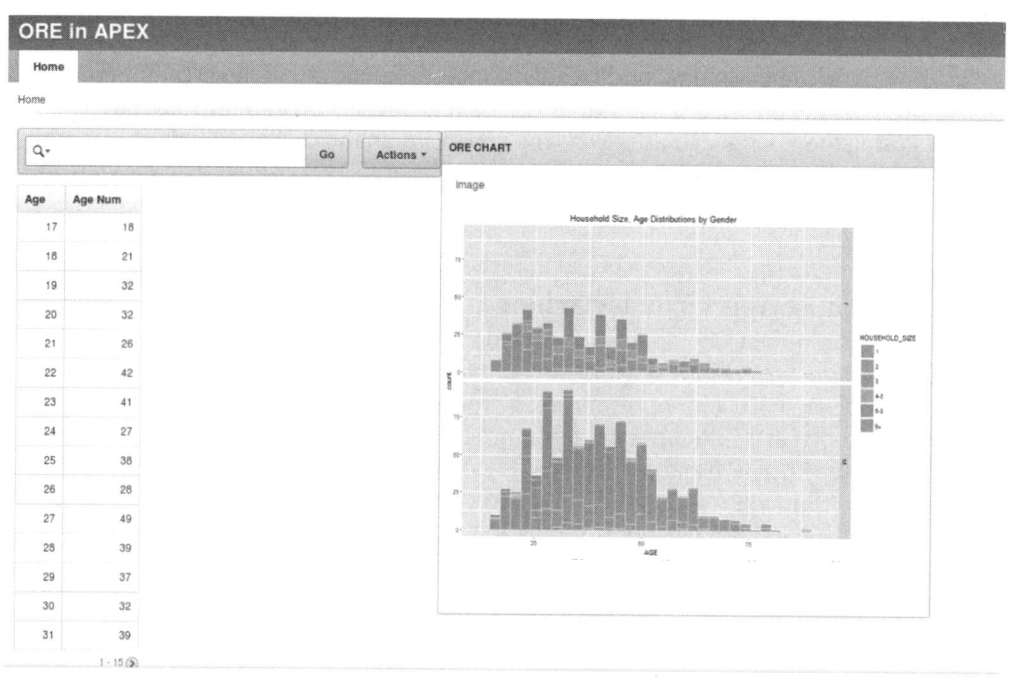

FIGURE 13-6.   *Adding new R results without changing the APEX application*

Oracle Business Intelligence

Oracle Business Intelligence Enterprise Edition (also commonly referred to as Oracle Business Intelligence) is a enterprise-level analytics and reporting tool that allows you to collect data from a variety of data sources. It provides this data using various reporting techniques and dashboards, and allows you to work interactively with the provided analytics to gain a better understanding of your organizational data. Oracle Business Intelligence is a very commonly used tool for cloud-based solutions and on-premises.

Traditionally, Oracle Business Intelligence has been used to provide a structured environment and tool for the integration and presentation of your organizational data. This can be done using a range of different reporting and charting techniques. These can be grouped in separate dashboards that give an integrated reporting and analysis view of the data based around different business functions or roles within the organization.

With the more recent releases of Oracle Business Intelligence, more functionality has been built into the tool, giving the end user greater control to create and manage their own reporting and analytics requirements based on the integrated data presented by Oracle Business Intelligence. The end user now has Visual Analyzer as part of the on-premises implementation, which is also part of the cloud offerings from Oracle (BICS and DVCS).

In addition to the traditional and more advanced analytic capabilities built into Oracle Business Intelligence since the release of version 12, you can now include analytics using the R language as well as the advanced analytics capabilities of Oracle R Enterprise. Figure 13-7 shows some of the examples provided by Oracle in the OBIEE Sample App virtual machine.

OBIEE Sample App Virtual Machine

A great way to try out OBIEE is to download and run the OBIEE Sample App virtual machine image. This is available on the VirtualBox website. This virtual machine does require a lot of resources. It is recommended that you allocate 8GB of memory, at a minimum, and four processors. This virtual machine comes with an Oracle Database as well as R, ORE, APEX, and OBIEE, among lots of other OBI tools, already installed and configured for you to use.

The OBIEE and ORE examples shown in this chapter were created on the OBIEE Sample App virtual machine.

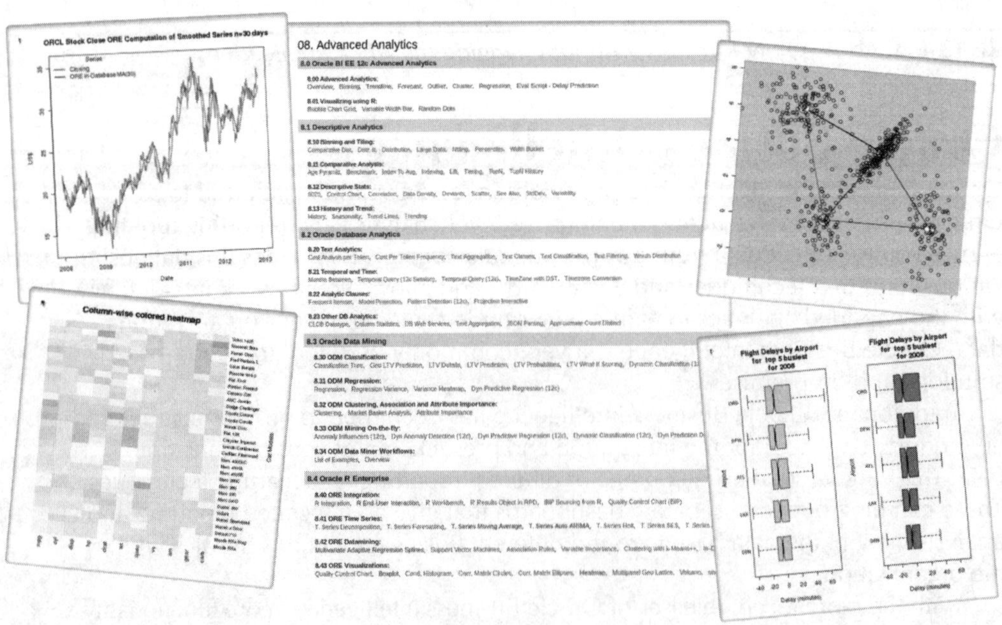

FIGURE 13-7.   *Examples of Oracle R Enterprise on an OBIEE Sample App virtual machine*

Before you can use Oracle Business Intelligence, you need to create a repository, also known as the RPD. Using the Oracle BI Administration tool, you can define what data will be incorporated into the RPD. You can define how each of the data items is related to the others, transformed through the Business Model layer and Presentation layer, and made available to the reporting/dashboard developer or end user for analysis. The Oracle Business Intelligence repository has the following three layers:

- **Physical layer**   This is where the metadata of the data sources is defined. These data sources provide the data that will end up in the OBIEE dashboards.

- **Business Model layer**   This contains the logical dimensional models for the business and are based on the data sources defined in the Physical layer.

- **Presentation layer**   This is where various subsets of the Business Model layer are defined and each subset is created to meet the reporting and analytics requirements of each of the end users from each of the business functional areas.

Oracle Business Intelligence Enterprise Edition comes with R installed. This allows you to use the analytics and graphing capabilities of the R language and include these in your dashboards. OBIEE comes with a number of interfaces to allow you to include R. As with most of the typical installations of R, the data needs to be extracted from the Oracle Database and loaded into an R environment. The analytics or graphing is then applied to the data, and finally the results are loaded back into OBIEE and displayed on the dashboards. These can work really well in scenarios where the data volumes are small. But as your data volumes increase (even to just a few thousand records), there can be a large time lag with displaying the dashboard.

With Oracle R Enterprise, the time lags are significantly reduced. This is because the R code is being run on the Oracle Database server, which will typically have significantly greater computing resources than the server that is hosting OBIEE. In the following sections we walk through the typical steps required to set up and include R scripts that are called using Oracle R Enterprise API functions, just like in Chapter 10 and earlier in this chapter.

Setting Up OBIEE to Use ORE

The first step you will need to perform to get ORE working with OBIEE is to install ORE on your Oracle Database server, where the data you are going to use within your OBIEE tools and dashboards resides. Chapter 2 walks you through how to install ORE on your Oracle Database server.

As your analytics capabilities with the R language grow, you will commence using many of the packages available for the R language. If you are using any additional R language packages for your analytics or charting, you will also need to ensure that these R packages are installed on the Oracle Database server where the data resides. Chapter 14 has a section that shows you how to install R packages into your R and ORE installation on the Oracle Database server.

You will be using the R scripts stored in the R Script Repository in your Oracle Database, and the schema you will be using to connect OBIEE to the Oracle Database will need to have the R scripts created in it, or it will need to have been granted the privileges on the R scripts (see Chapter 9 for more details on granting privileges on R scripts). Additionally, the schema used by OBIEE to connect to the Oracle Database will need to have the system privilege RQADMIN granted to it by the Oracle DBA. After completing these steps, you should have the Oracle Database configured and ready for OBIEE to use the data and the in-database R scripts.

Before you can start using the data in OBIEE, you also need to configure the OBIEE environment to use Oracle R Enterprise. To do this, you need to change a configuration setting to tell OBIEE to use ORE instead of R by changing the TARGET setting from R to ORE. You also need to define the connection pool that will be used.

You can configure both of these settings in the NQSConfig.INI file on the OBIEE server. Figure 13-8 shows an example of the NQSConfig.INI file with the

```
oracle@demo:~
File  Edit  View  Search  Terminal  Help
#########################################################################
#
#  Advance Analytics Script Section
#
#########################################################################

[ ADVANCE_ANALYTICS_SCRIPT ]

# R EXECUTABLE PATH
# Specify the script executable binary path.
R_EXECUTABLE_PATH = "/usr/bin/R";

# R COMMAND ARGS
# Specify the script executable command line arguments.
R_COMMAND_ARGS = "--no-restore --no-save --no-timing";

# Max Time to wait for R Process to complete gracefully.
# The R Process would be terminated beyond this max time
R_PROCESS_TIMEOUT = 3600;       # in seconds.

# Max Number of R Process that can be active at any given point in time
R_MAX_PROCESS = 20;

# EXECUTION TARGET WHERE SCRIPT GETS EXECUTED
# Defaults to Mid Tier R. The other targets are ORE, etc
TARGET = "ORE";

# THE CONNECTION POOL HAS TO BE SET IF Advanced Analytics NEED TO RUN ON THE DATABASE (eg: ORE)
 CONNECTION_POOL = "Y10 - Movies Demo (ORCL)"."MovieDemo Connection Pool";
```

FIGURE 13-8. *ORE configuration changes in the NQSConfig.INI file for OBIEE*

changes made. This example is based on the NQSConfig.INI file on the OBIEE Sample App VM provided by Oracle. The NQSConfig.INI file can be found in the following location:

```
/app/oracle/biee/user_projects/domains/bi/config/fmwconfig/biconfig/OBIS
/NQSConfig.INI
```

After you have made the change to the TARGET (changed it to ORE) and the Connection Pool Name setting, you will need to restart the BI Server so that the changes to the NQSConfig.INI file can take effect.

HINT
Something you will see and hear when working with OBI and ORE is that you need to register your R script with the Oracle Database. What this really means is the R script needs to be created in the R Script Repository in the Oracle Database. Chapter 9 provides an example of how you can create your user-defined R scripts using the ORE R API functions and the SQL API functions. Therefore, registering your R script is the same as creating your R script in the Oracle Database.

Using an R Script in the OBIEE RPD

You have two main approaches to using ORE in OBIEE. The first is to use the built-in functionality that allows you to "register" an R script. This approach requires you to construct an XML document that contains all the necessary information and R code to register the R script.

Alternatively, if you have been creating your user-defined R scripts in your Oracle Database, you can incorporate these into the Physical layer of the RPD (Figure 13-9). There are two ways to do this. The first is to define a view in your schema that contains the attributes you want to expose to OBIEE. As part of this view definition, you can also define what attributes are returned by an R Script, executed using a `SELECT` statement, to include in the view definition. The second way to include the outputs of an R script is to define, in the Physical layer, a Physical Table object, with Table Type set to Select, and then to provide the `SELECT` statement that returns the data you want to expose in your OBIEE dashboards and tools like Visual Analyzer. The `SELECT` statement would then use one of the ORE SQL API functions that executes the in-database R script.

After you have created the new table object in the Physical layer, you can then migrate the object through the Business Model and Presentation layers. In the

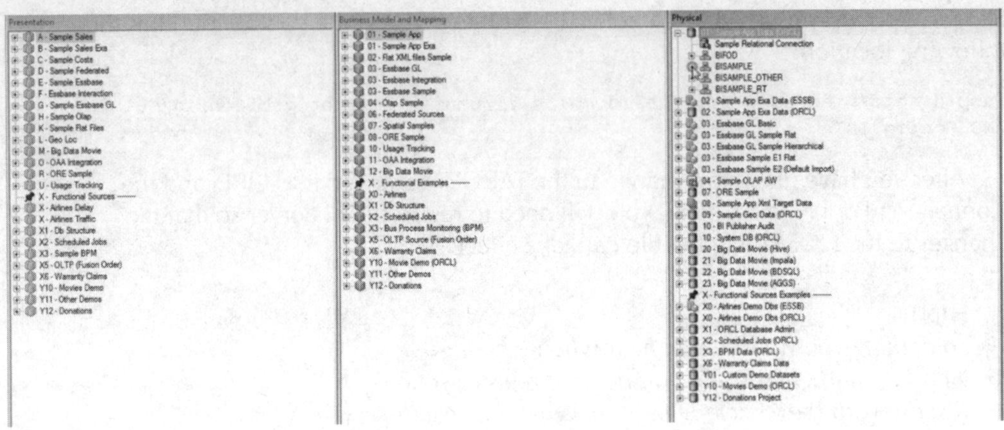

FIGURE 13-9. *OBIEE RPD for the OBIEE Sample App*

Business Model layer, you can combine the data generated by ORE with other data from other parts of your data sources and defined in the Physical layer. A similar approach can also be used to incorporate the images produced by your in-database R scripts by using lookups to join onto related data. The Presentation layer then allows you to define how the data will finally be presented to the various business functions and end users.

When you have finished updating the OBIEE repository (RPD), you can update the OBIEE server to contain the newly updated RPD. This will then expose the newly defined ORE-generated data to the data analysts who can then create dashboards in OBIEE and/or use other tools like Visual Analyzer to create some new analytics for their end users.

Presenting Results from an R Script on Your Dashboard

After you have defined the data and how it is modeled with the other data in the RPD, you can use OBIEE and the tools within it to analyze the data and create your dashboards and reports for publishing. A number of options are available for analyzing and processing your data within OBIEE, and a subset of them is shown in Figure 13-10.

You create a new analysis and dashboard as private or make them available to some or all. This is determined by where you save your analysis and dashboard. If you save these as part of the shared folders, they will be public, and additional permissions are needed to restrict access to certain users.

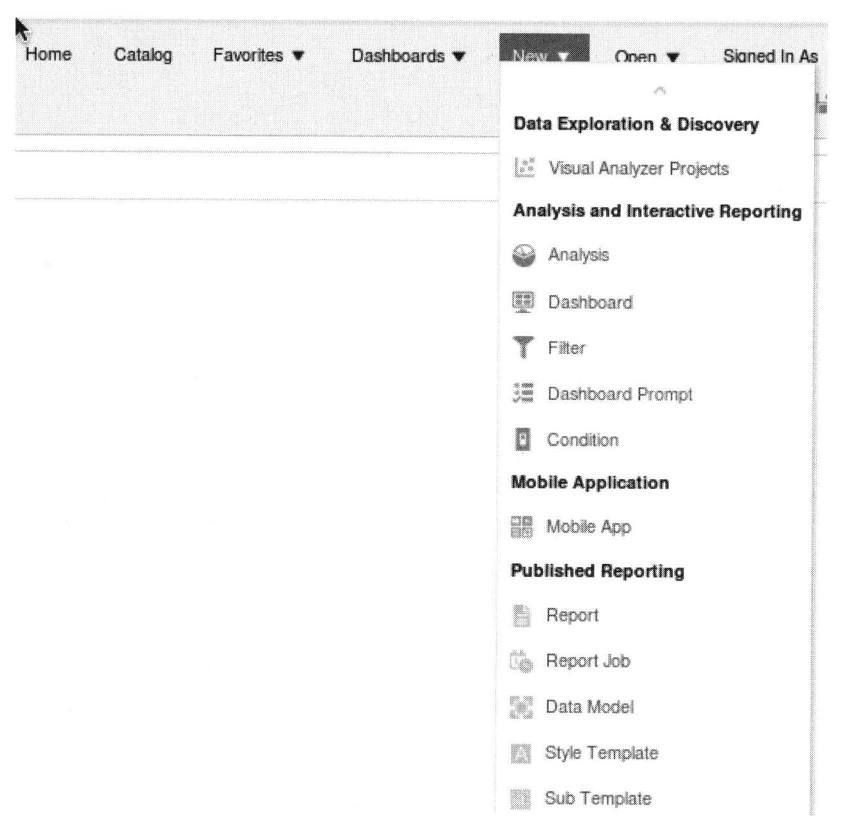

FIGURE 13-10.   *Different analytics options available in OBIEE*

When creating a new dashboard, you can drag and drop data columns on your
workspace, adding different groupings and laying out your dashboard in a way that
suits you. After creating the various data areas on your dashboard, you can save and
run it. When the dashboard is run, OBIEE will take the data defined for the
dashboard and perform the necessary queries back on the data sources and
databases. When using the embedded R execution, you will have defined the
SQL query that uses the SQL API functions. These in turn run the in-database
R script, returning the results to the SQL query, which will then be displayed on
the dashboard. This also applies to any of the graphics generated using embedded
R execution, as these graphics are returned to the SQL query as a BLOB data type
and then displayed on your dashboard, as shown in Figure 13-11.

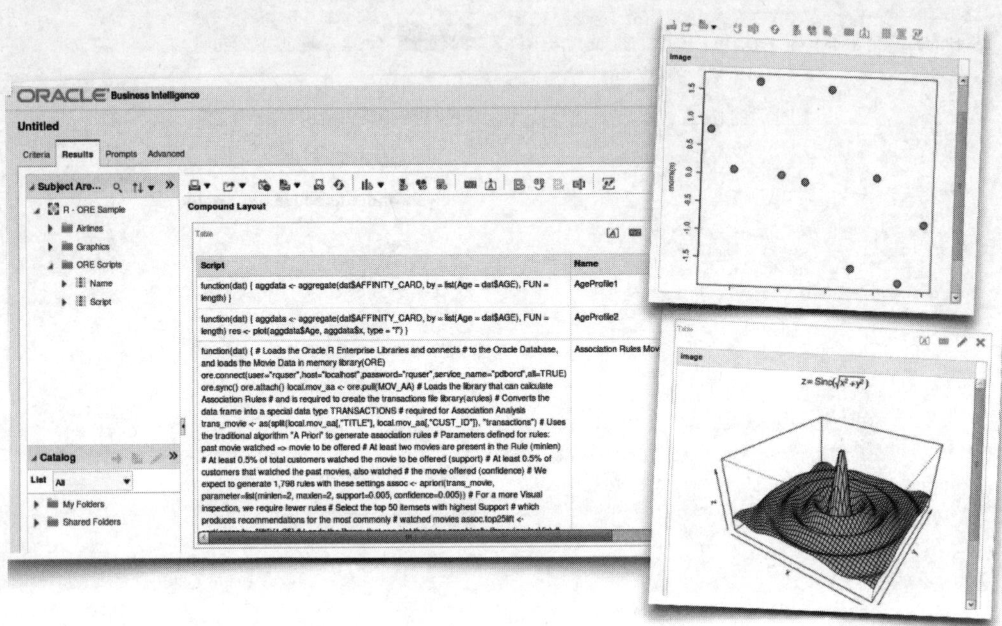

FIGURE 13-11. *Building your analytics using OBIEE dashboards and Visual Analyzer*

The various analyses and dashboards can be further enhanced by adding parameters. This will involve changes to the RPD to detail the definition of the parameters and how these should be used in the SQL that is used to generate the results from the in-database R script.

Summary

Using the embedded R execution feature of Oracle R Enterprise opens up the possibility of including the advanced analytics and graphing features available as part of the R language and ecosystem in your applications. Examples were given of how you can include Oracle R Enterprise in your APEX applications and in your OBIEE dashboards. The examples shown in this chapter illustrate how easy it is to incorporate and deploy R via Oracle R Enterprise within your applications. These examples can be extended into many other environments and programming languages. As long as you can execute SQL, you can incorporate R using Oracle R Enterprise in your applications.

CHAPTER 14

ORE for the Oracle DBA

Throughout this book you've seen various ways of using Oracle R Enterprise. All of these examples have been aimed at helping the data analyst/scientist work with Oracle R Enterprise to utilize the in-database and embedded R execution performance features. In addition, there are a number of common tasks that are applicable for the database administrator or a similar type of person who is responsible for administrating and supporting the Oracle R Enterprise environment on the Oracle Database server.

In this chapter, we discuss a number of the common topics and tasks an administrator will be looking after. These include setting up new Oracle schemas for the data analysts to use for their analytics; enabling these users to perform embedded R execution, installing, setting up, and configuring new R packages on the Oracle Database server and client; managing or being aware of the ORE global environment variables; managing the parallel settings for embedded R execution; and, finally, how to go about uninstalling Oracle R Enterprise from the Oracle Database server and client machines.

Creating a New ORE Schema in the Database

In Chapter 2, which covered installing and setting up Oracle R Enterprise, an Oracle schema called ORE_USER was created during the installation process. During the installation of Oracle R Enterprise, we were able to define a Oracle schema to create. As your data science team grows, you are going to need to create additional Oracle schemas that the data scientists can use to create, store, and process their data and ORE objects in the Oracle Database.

For each new Oracle schema, you will need your Oracle DBA to create a schema in the Oracle Database. You then need to grant the new Oracle schema the necessary database privileges so that users can connect to the database and run their R code in the Oracle Database. The following SQL code shows the database privileges needed, at a minimum, for an ORE schema:

```
GRANT create session,
      create table,
      create view,
      create procedure,
      create mining model
TO  ORE_USER2;
```

These privileges will be granted to a schema called ORE_USER2. You need to be connected to one of the Oracle DBA schemas (for example, SYS schema) to run the preceding code statement.

This same set of privileges can be granted to any other Oracle schemas used by the developers, and they will then be able to run ORE commands on the objects in their schemas. An additional privilege is required to run embedded R execution: RQADMIN.

Privilege Required to Run Embedded R

To be able to run the embedded capabilities of ORE and create, drop, and use scripts for embedded R execution, you will need to grant an additional Database system privilege (RQADMIN) to the schemas that require it.

When you run the ORE installation script and create your first ORE schema using that installation script, the necessary database privileges are granted as part of the process. For all subsequent schemas, you or your Oracle DBA will need to grant the RQADMIN database privilege.

The following example illustrates granting this database privilege to the ORE_USER2 schema:

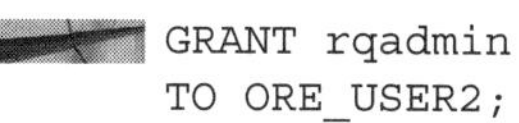

```
GRANT rqadmin
TO ORE_USER2;
```

This database privilege has some powerful features because it allows the data scientist to create and drop R scripts in the Oracle Database. Care needs to be taken that this database privilege is only given to those schemas that require it, and it should not be given by default to all schemas that will be used by people using Oracle R Enterprise. The granting of the RQADMIN privilege allows the user to run R scripts on the Oracle Database server.

Installing a New R Package into Oracle R Enterprise

The Oracle R Distribution (or the main R Distribution) comes with a wide range of R packages. As your analytics skills grow, a time will come when you want to use one (or more) of the many thousands of additional R packages available. With the embedded R execution capability of Oracle R Enterprise, you are able to install these packages and use them within your Oracle R Enterprise environment. This means you can run any R package on the Oracle Database server, as long as it is compatible with the version of R you have installed on your Oracle Database server.

Before you can use a new R package within your Oracle R Enterprise analytics environment, you will need to install the R package on the Oracle Database server and also install the same version of the R package on the client machines that are being used by your data analysts.

The following sections step you through the process of installing a new package for these two parts of the installation, and Chapter 8 illustrates how you can use some of the available R packages for building data mining models.

Installing a New R Package on the Database Server

To install a new R package into the Oracle R Enterprise environment on your Oracle Database server, you need to complete a number of steps. These steps are outlined as follows:

Step 1: Identify the R package that is required.

Step 2: Verify the version of the R package that is compatible with the version of R installed on your Oracle Database server.

Step 3: Download the package from the R CRAN site or from one of the mirrored sites available from around the world.

Step 4: Install the R package into the same location as the other Oracle R Enterprise packages. An example of doing this follows. R packages can be installed in other locations, but these locations need to be defined within your R environment using `libPaths()`.

Step 5: Verify that the new R package has been installed correctly by using one of the functions available in the package or by using the `ore.doEval()` function to make use of a function in the new R package.

To illustrate the installation of a new R package into our Oracle R Enterprise environment, we'll install the e1071 package, which is a popular R package that provides a range of different machine learning algorithms, such as support vector machines, Naïve Bayes, clustering, and so on.

When it comes to installing the e1071 package, you have two options. The first method is to use the built-in R functionality to automatically install the new package. This method uses the `install.packages()` function:

```
> install.packages("e1071")
```

As part of the installation, the R language will examine the new package and all dependent packages (that is, other R packages required by the R package you are installing). These other, dependent R packages will be downloaded and installed automatically when you use the `install.packages()` function. Using this approach requires that you have access to the Internet at the time of package installation.

The second method is to use the operating system command-line option. This requires you to download the correct version of the R package to the Oracle Database server. Then, to install the new R package, you can use the `ORE CMD INSTALL` command. This command ensures that the new R package is installed in the same location as the Oracle R Enterprise packages, which is `$ORACLE_HOME/R/Library`:

```
ORE CMD INSTALL e1071_1.6-6.tar.gz
```

You can check that the package has been added to the Oracle R Enterprise packages by examining the directory `$ORACLE_HOME/R/Library`. In that directory you will see a new subdirectory for each of the new packages you installed alongside the other Oracle R Enterprise packages.

To verify that the installation was completed correctly on the Oracle Database server, you need to start up R and use one of the functions that comes with the package. The following example illustrates how you can test to see if the installed package is installed on the Oracle Database server:

```
> # Using Embedded R Execution check that package is installed on Database server
> ore.doEval(function() packageVersion("e1071"))
> # List all the packages installed on the Database server
> ore.doEval(function() row.names(installed.packages()))
```

After verifying that the package has been installed and is visible, you can then use one of the functions to test to make sure that it works correctly. The following example assumes that you have already connected to your Oracle Database schema using `ore.connect`. The new package is loaded into your R environment, an existing table is used, and a Naïve Bayes model is created.

```
# Load the e1071 package and test
#   the following assumes that you are already connected to your ORE schema
#     and a table or view exists called ANALYTIC_RECORD (see Chapter 7)
library(e1071)
df<-ore.pull(ANALYTIC_RECORD)
naiveBayes(AFFINITY_CARD ~., df)
```

An additional test you can perform is to make sure you can use this newly installed package using the embedded R execution method. The following example is very similar to the one given earlier. It uses the `tableApply()` function to pass in the iris data set and to create a Naïve Bayes model for this data.

```
# Test the embedded execution of the e1071 package
nbmod <- ore.tableApply (
    ore.push(iris),
    function(dat) {
       library(e1071)
       dat$Species <- as.factor(dat$Species)
       naiveBayes(Species ~ ., dat)
    }
)
```

After completing all these steps, you are now ready to complete the install of the package on the client machine.

> When you are installing an R package that has dependencies on other R packages, you need to ensure that all these additional packages are also installed in the ORE Server library directory, which is located at `$ORACLE_HOME/R/Library`. You should verify the correct version the R packages use because this may not be the current version. Inspect this directory to verify that it contains all the additional R packages. If it does not, you will need to download and install these R packages using the ORE `CMD INSTALL` command.

Installing a New Package on the Client Machine

The installation of a new R package is a two-step process. In the previous section, I covered what you need to do when you want to install a new R package as part of the Oracle R Enterprise installation on the database server. The second step is to install this same package on the client machine of the data analyst/scientist. This step is only required if the data scientist wants to use the R package locally. Alternatively, they can use the R package installed on the Oracle Database server by using R scripts or the SQL APIs.

This is a relatively simple process where the data analyst can install the package from an R CRAN repository from within their R environment or download the R package and then install it using that file.

To install a new R package, you can use the `install.packages` function in R. For example, the following command will install the e1071 R package on the client machine:

```
> install.packages("e1071")
```

If you are using a tool such as RStudio, you can use the built-in feature to automatically install the R package for you. Alternatively, you can go to the CRAN Repository for the R website (cran.r-project.org or www.r-project.org), locate the R package you are looking for, and download the compressed file for your operating system. When you have downloaded the package file, you can then load it into your local R environment using the `install.packages` function, like so:

```
> install.packages("C:/app/ORE_Install/new/e1071_1.6-7.zip")
```

ORE Global Variables and Options

When working with the R language, you have a large number of environment variables available to you. It would be impossible to go through them all here, and I'll leave these for you to explore in more detail. Generally, the R language environment variables allow you to define certain default values to be used; these can be grouped into variables for your local R session, variables for certain packages, and variables for how your R sessions and environment will interact with the operating system. The following example illustrates how you can collect all the current settings for the environment variables and display them. In the version of R that is being used (Oracle R Distribution version 3.2), there are 68 environment variables.

```
# Get the current environment variable settings
> s <- options()
> s
```

You can change the value of an environment variable to match your requirements. This can be done when you have an open R session and use the options function to define the new value for a variable. In the following examples, I show you how to change the display width for your R session and the number of digits to display after a decimal point.

```
# Changing environment variable settings
> options("width")
> options(width = 100)
> options("digits")
> options(digits = 5)
```

Oracle R Enterprise has a number of global options that can be set in the same way as the R environment variables because they are global to your ORE connection. These are outlined in Table 14-1.

You can inspect the default or current value of each of these ORE global variables in the same way as the other R environment variables. The following example lists the current or default setting for each of the ORE global variables:

```
# Checking the current settings of the ORE environment variables.
> options("ore.envAsEmptyenv")
> options("ore.na.extract")
> options("ore.parallel")
> options("ore.sep")
> options("ore.trace")
> options("ore.warn.order")
```

ORE Global Environment Variable	Description
`ore.envAsEmptyenv`	A logical value that specifies whether an environment referenced in an object should be replaced with an empty environment during serialization to an Oracle Database. When TRUE, the referenced environment in the object is replaced with an empty environment whose parent is `.GlobalEnv`, and the objects in the original referenced environment are not serialized. In some cases, this can significantly reduce the size of serialized objects. When FALSE, all of the objects in the referenced environment are serialized, and they can be unserialized and loaded into memory. The default value for this option is FALSE.
`ore.na.extract`	The default value is FALSE. When FALSE, the NA value will result in the removal of the corresponding row or element. When TRUE, rows or elements with an NA will produce rows or elements with NA values. This is similar to how R treats missing values in data frames and vector objects.
`ore.parallel`	Allows you to specify the degree of parallelism to use for your Oracle R Enterprise session for the subsequent commands. The default value is NULL. The degree of parallelism can be set using the following options: N This is the degree of parallelism. N should be a number greater than or equal to 2. TRUE This will use the default degree of parallelism for the database session or object. NULL This will use the database default for the operation. FALSE This is where no parallelism is to be used. Defaults to 1.

TABLE 14-1.   *Oracle R Enterprise Global Environment Variables*

ORE Global Environment Variable	Description
`ore.sep`	This is the character to be used as a separator between multiple column row names of an `ore.frame`. The default character is |.
`ore.trace`	If set to TRUE, this indicates that Oracle R Enterprise functions should print output at each iteration of the function, where available. The default value is FALSE.
`ore.warn.order`	The default value is TRUE. This determines if Oracle R Enterprise should display warning messages when ORE objects lack certain information such as row names, objects that do not have a defined ordering, and so on. When set to FALSE, these warning messages are not displayed.

TABLE 14-1.   *Oracle R Enterprise Global Environment Variables*

To change the value of one of these ORE global variables, you can use the `options()` function and assign what the new value is. For example, the following illustrates how to inspect the current value, how to change the value, and then how to change it back to the default value:

```
> # Changing the ORE environment variable values.
> # Change the column separator
> options("ore.sep")
> options("ore.sep" = ":")
> options("ore.sep")
> options("ore.sep" = "|")
> # Change the ORE warning messages level
> options("ore.warn.order")
> options("ore.warn.order" = FALSE)
> options("ore.warn.order")
> options("ore.warn.order" = TRUE)
```

Using the `ore.parallel` Feature

In the previous section, I showed you how to access the R environment variables and the ORE global variables. One of these ORE global variables is `ore.parallel`, which allows you to see the degree of parallelism to use when you are performing embedded R execution. In particular, the `ore.groupApply`, `ore.rowApply`, and `ore.indexApply` functions support parallel data execution when called from your R environment. For the SQL functions `rqGroupEval` and `rqRowEval`, you can specify a value for the parallel variable in the function call.

When you use the `ore.groupApply`, `ore.rowApply`, and `ore.indexApply`, one of the parameters in the call to these functions is `parallel`. By default, this parameter is determined by the value of the `ore.parallel` global variable.

The following example illustrates how you can view and set the ORE global variable `ore.parallel`:

```
> # Check the current value for ore.parallel. The default is Null or no parallel
> options("ore.parallel")
> # set the ore.parallel variable to 4
> options("ore.parallel" = 4)
> # set the ore.parallel variable to the database default
> options("ore.parallel" = NULL)
```

When using `ore.groupApply`, `ore.rowApply`, and `ore.indexApply`, you can set the `parallel` parameter to TRUE, FALSE, or to the degree of parallel to use. When the value is TRUE, the function looks to see what the current setting is for the `ore.parallel` global variable. It will then use this value for the degree of parallelism. If a number is used for the parameter, this value will be used for the degree of parallelism and the value of `ore.parallel` will be ignored. This number should, at a minimum, be 2 or higher. If the value of the parameter is set to FALSE or 1, the function will be performed serially and no parallelism will be used.

When `ore.groupApply` and `rqGroupApply` are used, Oracle R Enterprise will initiate one or more R engines that perform the required task on different partitions of the data. Whereas when `ore.rowApply` and `rqRowEval` are used, Oracle R Enterprise will initiate one or more R engines to perform the required task on different chunks of the data.

The Oracle Database and Oracle R Enterprise manage all the data requirements for these parallel requests and multiple R engines. Oracle R Enterprise also acts as the coordinator for all the partitions and R engines, monitoring them during execution and for when they complete. If any errors occur during the parallel execution, these will be returned and reported to the user.

Uninstalling Oracle R Enterprise

There may be occasions when you are required to uninstall and remove Oracle R Enterprise from your Oracle Database server and from the client machines. The installation of Oracle R Enterprise was shown in detail in Chapter 2. The installation process consists of two steps. The first step involves installing Oracle R Distribution and Oracle R Enterprise on the Oracle Database server. The second step involves the installation of Oracle R Distribution and the client and supporting packages for Oracle R Enterprise.

When it comes to uninstalling Oracle R Enterprise, you have a similar set of two steps. The first is the removal of Oracle R Enterprise from the Oracle Database server. The second step is the removal of the Oracle R Enterprise client and supporting packages from the client machines.

In both steps, for the Oracle Database server and for the client machines, you may want to remove the installed version of the R language. In Chapter 2, the Oracle R Distribution was installed. If required, you may also want to uninstall the Oracle R Distribution from the Oracle Database server. However, if it is needed for other processes or analytical methods, the R engine can remain. It is unlikely that the Oracle R Distribution (or the latest version of R) will be removed from the client machines because the data scientists will still want to use the R language for their analytics.

Uninstalling Oracle R Enterprise from the Oracle Database Server

To uninstall or remove Oracle R Enterprise from the Oracle Database server, you have two options: you can perform a partial or a full uninstall.

With a partial uninstall, Oracle R Enterprise removes the `rqsys` metadata and supporting PL/SQL packages from the Oracle Database server. Only the Oracle R Enterprise elements that are installed in the Oracle Database are removed. The libraries and R packages that support Oracle R Enterprise will remain untouched. A partial uninstall is the default uninstall method when you use the `server` script. This is the same script used to install the Oracle R Enterprise packages and to set up the Oracle Database for Oracle R Enterprise. When you use the `server` script, the default uninstall method used is a partial uninstall. The following commands all perform a partial uninstall, and you can choose which of these you would prefer to use:

```
./server.sh --uninstall
./server.sh -u
./server.sh -u --keep
./server.sh --uninstall --keep
```

If you would prefer to perform a full uninstall of Oracle R Enterprise, then in addition to what is uninstalled during the partial uninstall, all the supporting R packages that support Oracle R Enterprise are also uninstalled. These will be removed from the Oracle home directories. The following commands each perform a full uninstall of Oracle R Enterprise. You can choose which one to use.

```
./server.sh --uninstall --full
./server.sh -u --full
```

WARNING
The uninstall process just outlined does not remove any schemas created during the installation process (for example, the ORE_USER schema that was created in Chapter 2 during the installation process). This preserves the data and objects that were created. Also, the uninstall does not remove the ORE schema (ORE_USER) that was created during the installation of Oracle R Enterprise.

You will need to examine all schemas that have been given the privileges to run Oracle R Enterprise to determine what needs to be done with the data and ORE objects that might be contained in them.

After uninstalling Oracle R Enterprise from your Oracle Database server, the next thing you need to consider is whether you need to remove the installed Oracle R Distribution or the corresponding open-source version of the R language. When working in a CDB/PDB environment, you need to be aware of whether any of the other pluggable databases are using ORE. If there are, you will need to leave the installed version of Oracle R Distribution on your server. If no other pluggable databases are using Oracle R Distribution, you can go ahead and uninstall it.

After removing Oracle R Distribution, you may need to look at removing any references to the directory where Oracle R Distribution was installed from the PATH environment variable, and also remove any other associated environment variables created during the installation.

Uninstalling Oracle R Enterprise from the Client

After Oracle R Enterprise has been removed from the Oracle Database server, any attempts to connect to and run your ORE code will result in errors. It is important to keep the installation of Oracle R Enterprise consistent on the Oracle Database server and on all clients using Oracle R Enterprise. To update the client software and uninstall Oracle R Enterprise, you need to work with your data scientist team to ensure that all affected people will have the Oracle R Enterprise packages removed from their R environment.

In Chapter 2, it was shown how to install the Oracle R Enterprise client software, and the various client ORE Core and Supporting packages were listed. The following code gives the R commands necessary to remove Oracle R Enterprise from your client install of R:

```
> # Uninstall the ORE Client packages
> #
> # Uninstall the ORE core packages r
> remove.packages("ORE")
```

```
> remove.packages("OREbase")
> remove.packages("OREcommon")
> remove.packages("OREdm")
> remove.packages("OREeda")
> remove.packages("OREembed")
> remove.packages("OREgraphics")
> remove.packages("OREmodels")
> remove.packages("OREpredict")
> remove.packages("OREstats")
> remove.packages("ORExml")
> # Uninstall the ORE supporting packages
> remove.packages("arules")
> remove.packages("Cairo")
> remove.packages("DBI")
> remove.packages("png")
> remove.packages("randomForest")
> remove.packages("ROracle")
> remove.packages("statmod")
```

After you have run these commands to remove the ORE Core and Supporting packages, you will have completed the removal of Oracle R Enterprise from your client R environment.

NOTE
The installation process detailed in Chapter 2 includes the installation of the Oracle R Distribution. The uninstall process does not remove this from the client machine. The data scientists can still use the Oracle R Distribution as their main version of R.

Summary

In this chapter, we looked at a variety of topics the Oracle Database administrator or the data analyst/scientist might need to manage for their Oracle R Enterprise environment. Because Oracle R Enterprise mainly resides on the Oracle Database server, there are a number of setup and configuration steps that the administrator needs to be aware of. Throughout this chapter we looked at the most common topics, including setting up new users and their associated privileges, installing new R packages, managing the Oracle R Enterprise global environment variables, setting the degree of parallelism for embedded execution, and how to go about uninstalling Oracle R Enterprise and cleaning up your environment.

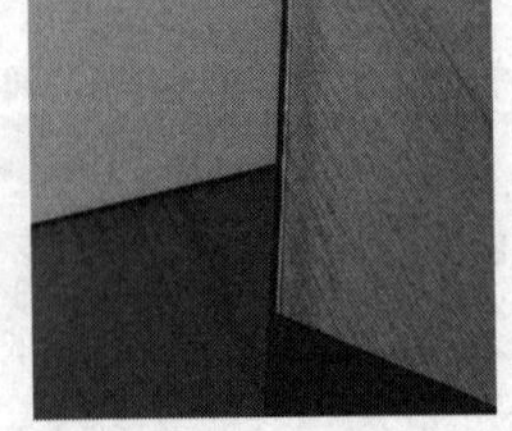

Index

Symbols

? (help)
    accessing package help, 73
    getting help with tasks or command, 78–79

A

ADP (Automatic Data Preparation)
    `ore.odmAI` and, 111
    preparing data for Oracle Data Mining,
        108–109, 131
Advanced Analytics. See Oracle Advanced Analytics
`aggregate()`, 98–99
aggregation
    data aggregation techniques, 98–100
    example of benefits of transparency layer, 61
    statistical functions built into Oracle Database, 7
algorithms
    available in OREmodels package, 130
    clustering algorithms, 124–126
    for data mining. See data mining algorithms
    interfaces for using data mining algorithms, 5–6
    preparing data for Oracle Data Mining,
        108–109
`ALL_RQ_SCRIPTS`, data dictionary view for
   user-defined R scripts, 157
An Post, examples of use of ORE, 15
analytics
    advantages of ORE, 11–12
    building using OBIEE dashboard and Visual
        Analyzer, 228
    categories of, 2–3
    OBIEE options, 227
    options for advanced, 5–7
    Oracle Database functions, 8

    Oracle R Advanced Analytics for Hadoop, 14
    predictive, 70–71
anomaly detection
    data mining algorithms, 201
    SVM applied to, 120–121
Apache Spark cluster, ORAAH support for, 196–197
APEX (Oracle Application Express)
    adding R graph to APEX application, 218–221
    including ORE script in APEX application,
        216–217
    overview of, 214–216
applications, using pre-built, 34–37
`apropos` function, searching available functions,
   72–73
architecture, ORE, 9
Association Rule Analysis
    data mining algorithms, 201
    `ore.odmAssocRules` algorithm, 108
    overview of, 111–114
attribute importance
    data mining algorithms, 201
    determining, 110–111
    overview of, 108
attributes
    binning attributes, 102
    derived attributes, 101–102
    `ore.summary` applied to one numeric
        attribute, 88
Automatic Data Preparation. See ADP (Automatic
   Data Preparation)

B

Bayes' Theorem, 121–122
Big Data, advanced analytics and, 2
binning attributes, 102

S

Join the Largest Tech Community in the World

 **Download the latest software, tools, and developer templates**

 **Get exclusive access to hands-on trainings and workshops**

 **Grow your professional network through the Oracle ACE Program**

 **Publish your technical articles – and get paid to share your expertise**

**Join the Oracle Technology Network
Membership is free. Visit community.oracle.com**

@OracleOTN facebook.com/OracleTechnologyNetwork

Climb the Career Ladder

Think about it—97 percent of the Fortune 500 companies run Oracle solutions. Why wouldn't you choose Oracle certification to secure your future? With certification through Oracle, your resume gets noticed, your chances of landing your dream job improve, you become more marketable, and you earn more money. It's simple. Oracle certification helps you get hired and get paid for your skills.

93% Hiring managers who say IT certifications are beneficial and provide value to the company[1]

7% Salary growth for Oracle Certified professionals[5]

70% Believe that Oracle certification improved their earning power[2]

90% Say that Oracle certification gives them credibility when looking for a new job[2]

68% Think that certification has made them more in demand[3]

6x Increased LinkedIn profile views for people with certifications, boosting their visibility and career opportunities[4]

Take the next step
http://education.oracle.com/certification/press

ORACLE®

Push a Button
Move Your Java Apps to the Oracle Cloud

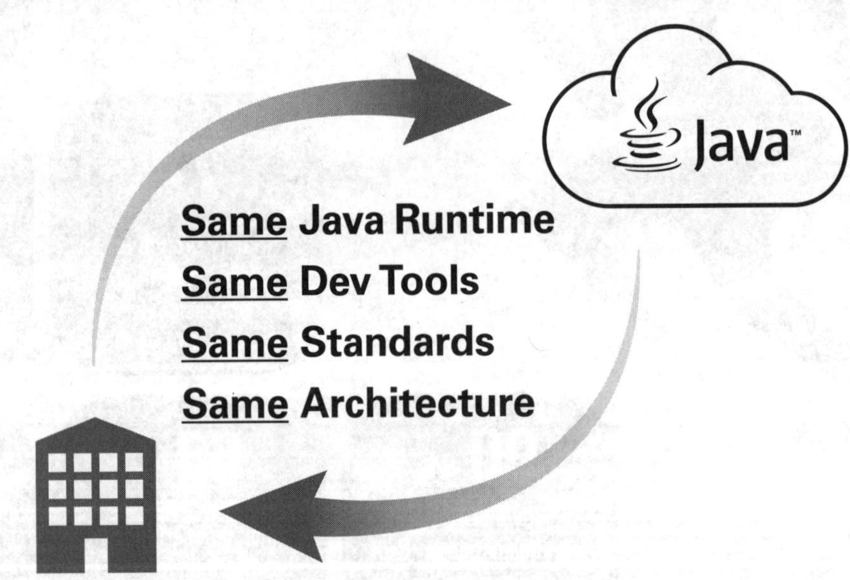

... or Back to Your Data Center

cloud.oracle.com/java

Reach More than 640,000 Oracle Customers with Oracle Publishing Group

Connect with the Audience that Matters Most to Your Business

Oracle Magazine
The Largest IT Publication in the World
Circulation: 325,000
Audience: IT Managers, DBAs, Programmers, and Developers

Profit
Business Insight for Enterprise-Class Business Leaders to Help Them Build a Better Business Using Oracle Technology

Circulation: 90,000
Audience: Top Executives and Line of Business Managers

Java Magazine
The Essential Source on Java Technology, the Java Programming Language, and Java-Based Applications

Circulation: 225,00 and Growing Steady
Audience: Corporate and Independent Java Developers, Programmers, and Architects

For more information or to sign up for a FREE subscription: Scan the QR code to visit Oracle Publishing online.

Beta Test Oracle Software

Get a first look at our newest products—and help perfect them. You must meet the following criteria:

- ✓ Licensed Oracle customer or Oracle PartnerNetwork member
- ✓ Oracle software expert
- ✓ Early adopter of Oracle products

Please apply at: pdpm.oracle.com/BPO/userprofile

If your interests match upcoming activities, we'll contact you. Profiles are kept on file for 12 months.